Interviewing and Investigation
for Paralegals

Interviewing and Investigation for Paralegals

A Practical Approach

First Edition

Ann M. Dobmeyer
Associate Professor of Law
Bay Path College
Adjunct Professor of Law
Western New England College

ASPEN LAW & BUSINESS
A Division of Aspen Publishers, Inc.

Permissions
Aspen Law & Business
1185 Avenue of the Americas
New York, NY 10036

Printed in the United States of America

ISBN 1-56706-640-2

Library of Congress Cataloging-in-Publication Data

Dobmeyer, Ann M., 1946-
    Interviewing and investigation for paralegals : a practical
approach / Ann M. Dobmeyer.
        p.   cm.
    Includes bibliographical references and index.
    ISBN 1-56706-640-2 (casebound : alk. paper)
    1. Interviewing in law practice—United States.
2. Investigations.   3. Legal assistants—United States—Handbooks,
manuals, etc.   I. Title.
KF311.Z9D63   1998
340'.023'73—dc21   97-43295
                                                                CIP

About Aspen Law & Business, Law School Division

In 1996, Aspen Law & Business welcomed the Law School Division of Little, Brown and Company into its growing business—already established as a leading provider of practical information to legal practitioners.

Acquiring much more than a prestigious collection of educational publications by the country's foremost authors, Aspen Law & Business inherited the long-standing Little, Brown tradition of excellence—born over 150 years ago. As one of America's oldest and most venerable publishing houses, Little, Brown and Company commenced in a world of change and challenge, innovation and growth. Sharing that same spirit, Aspen Law & Business has dedicated itself to continuing and strengthening the integrity begun so many years ago.

ASPEN LAW & BUSINESS
A Division of Aspen Publishers, Inc.
A Wolters Kluwer Company

To Emily, Hannah, and John

Summary of Contents

Table of Contents	*xi*
About the Author	*xxi*
Acknowledgments	*xxiii*
Preface	*xxv*
Foreword	*xxvii*
1. Introduction	1
2. Preparing for the Interview	29
3. Interviewing Skills	49
4. The Client Interview	75
5. The Witness Interview	99
6. Preserving Information	111
7. The Investigation Process	145
8. Investigation Skills	171
Appendices	203
Appendix A: Case Investigation File of Hannah West	205
Appendix B: Sample Client Letter	219
Appendix C: Intake Sheet	223
Appendix D: Privacy Act of 1974	225
Appendix E: Freedom of Information Act	243
Appendix F: Sample Letters (FOIA)	251
Appendix G: Federal Rules of Civil Procedure (Selected Rules)	253
Appendix H: Federal Rules of Evidence (Selected Rules)	259
Appendix I: California Notice Statute	269
Appendix J: Massachusetts Lawyers Diary and Manual	271
Glossary	*273*
Bibliography	*281*
Index	*283*

Table of Contents

About the Author	*xxi*
Acknowledgments	*xxiii*
Preface	*xxv*
Foreword	*xxvii*

1. Introduction ... 1
  A. Interviewing and Investigation ... 1
    1. Litigation Overview ... 4
    2. Procedural and Substantive Law ... 5
    3. Nonlitigation ... 5
  B. The Paralegal's Role ... 6
  C. Ethics ... 6
  D. Clients ... 7
  E. Case Facts and Client Facts ... 8
    1. Case Facts ... 8
    2. Client Facts ... 8
    3. Both Case Facts and Client Facts ... 9
  F. The Effect of Discovery on the Interview and Investigation Process ... 9
    1. Informal Discovery ... 9
    2. Formal Discovery ... 9
    3. Nondiscoverable Information ... 12
      a. Attorney-Client Privilege ... 12
      b. Work Product Doctrine ... 15
      c. Other Privileged Communications ... 16
  G. Evidence ... 17
    1. Introduction ... 17
    2. Relevant Evidence ... 17
    3. Direct and Circumstantial Evidence ... 18
    4. Evidence of Character ... 19
    5. Special Considerations ... 19
      a. Subsequent Repair ... 19
      b. Offer to Compromise ... 20
      c. Offer to Pay Expenses ... 20
      d. Insurance Coverage ... 20

      6. Hearsay   20
        a. Admission of a Party Opponent   21
        b. Records   21
        c. Present Sense Impression and Excited Utterance   21
        d. Dying Declaration and Statements Against Interest   22
      7. Impeachment   22
        a. Prior Conviction   22
        b. Bias of a Witness   24
        c. Interest   24
        d. Prior Inconsistent Statement   24
        e. Reputation for Truthfulness   24
        f. Contradiction   24

Summary   25
Key Terms   25
Review Questions   25
Chapter Exercises   26

2. Preparing for the Interview   29
  A. Introduction   29
  B. Purpose of Interviewing   31
  C. Interviewing and Ethics   32
    1. Role of the Paralegal   32
    2. Paralegal-Attorney Relationship   32
  D. Finding the Relevant Law   34
    1. Legal Theory   34
    2. Legal Sources   34
    3. Citators   35
    4. Computer Assisted Legal Research   37
      a. LEXIS and Westlaw   37
      b. CD-ROM   37
      c. Internet   38
  E. Organizing the Law for the Interview   39
    1. Preparing for the Litigation Interview   39
    2. Preparing for the Transaction Interview   43

Summary   45
Key Terms   46
Review Questions   46
Chapter Exercises   46

3. Interviewing Skills   49
  A. Structuring the Interview   49
  B. Asking Questions   50
    1. Introduction   50

2. Types of Questions   51
   a. Nonleading Questions   51
      i. Open   51
      ii. Closed   52
      iii. Direct   52
   b. Leading Questions   53
3. Silence   57
4. Follow-up Questions   57
5. Obtaining the Chronology   58
C. Keeping It Simple   59
D. Listening to Your Client   60
   1. Listening Effectively   60
   2. Active Listening   60
   3. Passive Listening   61
E. Controlling the Interview   62
F. Telephone Interviews   62
   1. Preparation   62
   2. Disadvantages   63
   3. Advantages   63
   4. Caveats   63
   5. Considerations   64
G. Dynamics of Communication   64
   1. Assumptions   64
   2. Nonverbal Communication   65
   3. Cultural Differences   66
   4. Gender   67
H. Special Situations   67
   1. Elderly   67
   2. Competency   68
   3. Inability to Read   68
   4. Children   68
I. Flexible Thinking   70
J. Ethical Considerations   71

Summary   71
Key Terms   71
Review Questions   72
Chapter Exercises   72

4. The Client Interview   75
   A. Introduction   75
   B. The Paralegal-Client Relationship   76
      1. Introduction   76
      2. Ethics   76
         a. Scope of Paralegal Responsibility   76
         b. Confidentiality   77
         c. Conflicts of Interest   78

        3. Client Rapport   79
           a. Attorney-Client Relationship   79
           b. Establishing Rapport   80
           c. Dress   80
     C. Preparing the Client for the Interview   81
        1. Initial Contact   81
        2. Greeting the Client   81
        3. Physical Setting   82
        4. Setting the Tone   84
     D. Maintaining Rapport   86
        1. Correspondence   86
        2. Telephone Calls   86
        3. Electronic Mail   87
     E. Motivators   87
        1. Empathy   87
        2. Doing the Right Thing   88
        3. Winning the Prize   88
        4. Praise   88
     F. Inhibitors   88
        1. Threat to Self-Esteem   89
        2. Jeopardy to the Case   89
        3. Authoritative Client   90
        4. Subservient Client   90
        5. Embarrassment   90
        6. Inability to Focus   90
        7. Unaware of Importance of Information   91
     G. Clients Accused of Crimes   92
     H. Difficult Clients   93
        1. The Client Who Lies   93
        2. The Angry Client   94
     I. Helping Theories   94
        1. Psychoanalysis   94
        2. Person-Centered Theory   95
        3. Behaviorism   95
        4. Rational-Emotive Therapy   95
        5. Transactional Analysis   95

Summary   96
Key Terms   96
Review Questions   96
Chapter Exercises   97

5. The Witness Interview   99
     A. Introduction   99
        1. Relationship   100
        2. Purpose   100
        3. Level of Interest   100

    B. Ethical Considerations   100
       1. Overview   100
       2. Guidelines and Rules   101
          a. Truthfulness   101
          b. Contact with Unrepresented Persons   101
          c. Respect for Rights of Third Persons   102
       3. Payments to Witnesses   102
    C. Arranging the Interview   102
    D. Witness Evaluation   103
    E. Strategy   103
       1. Dress   103
       2. Manner   103
       3. First-Hand Knowledge   104
       4. The Reluctant Witness   106
    F. Writing about the Interview   106
    G. Expert Witnesses   107
       1. When Used   107
       2. Yours   107
       3. Theirs   108
       4. Finding Experts   108

Summary   108
Key Terms   109
Review Questions   109
Chapter Exercises   109

6. Preserving Information   111
    A. Introduction   111
    B. The Importance of Preserving Information   112
       1. Accurate Record   112
       2. Reliance on Information in Another Forum   113
       3. Malpractice Action   113
    C. Preserving Client Information   114
       1. Preliminary Information   114
       2. Taking Notes   116
       3. Writing the Summary   116
       4. Follow-Up Interview   118
       5. Interoffice Memorandum   118
       6. Gladys Winston File   118
          a. Pre-Interview   118
          b. Interview   120
          c. Post-Interview   123
          d. Interoffice Memorandum   125
    D. Preserving Witness Information   127
       1. Should You Preserve the Information?   127
       2. Written Statement   127
       3. Memorandum to the File   129
    E. Diagrams   130

    F. Other Methods of Preserving Information   131
       1. Audio Recording   131
       2. Video Recording   132
       3. Photographs   132
    G. Evidentiary Considerations   134
       1. Real and Demonstrative Evidence   134
       2. Other Evidence   134
    H. Preserving the Files   136
       1. Status/Notes File   137
       2. Correspondence File   138
       3. Court Documents File/Pleadings   139
       4. Research File   139
       5. Documents File   139
       6. Deposition File   140
       7. Witness File   140
       8. Miscellaneous File   140
       9. Other Files   140
    I. Case Management/Calendaring   140

Summary   142
Key Terms   142
Review Questions   142
Chapter Exercises   143

7. The Investigation Process   145
    A. Introduction   145
    B. The Unexpected   146
    C. Paralegal-Attorney Relationship   147
       1. Getting Good Instructions   147
       2. Understanding Limitations   147
    D. Legal Identities   148
       1. Individuals   148
       2. Organizations   149
          a. Partnership   149
          b. Corporation   149
          c. Closed Corporation   149
          d. Nonprofit Corporation   149
          e. Limited Liability Company   149
       3. Government Unit   150
    E. Defining the Scope of the Investigation   150
       1. Who?   151
       2. What?   151
       3. Why?   151
       4. When?   152
       5. Where?   152
       6. How?   152
    F. The Investigation Plan   152

G. Supporting Statements 158
H. Special Topics 159
  1. Real Property 160
    a. Sole Tenancy 160
    b. Tenancy in Common 161
    c. Joint Tenancy 161
    d. Tenancy by the Entirety 161
    e. Community Property 161
    f. Fee Simple Absolute 161
    g. Life Estate 162
    h. Grantor/Grantee Indices 162
    i. Homestead Exemption 162
    j. Title Search 162
  2. Business Organizations 164
    a. Licenses 164
    b. Annual Reports 164
    c. Articles of Incorporation 164
  3. Family 165
    a. Marriage 165
    b. Divorce 165
    c. Separation 165
    d. Custody 166
H. Paralegal as Witness 166
  1. Circumstances 166
  2. Procedure 166
I. The Power of Observation 167

Summary 167
Key Terms 168
Review Questions 168
Chapter Exercises 168

8. Investigation Skills 171
A. Introduction 171
B. Federal and State Laws 171
  1. The Privacy Act 171
  2. The Freedom of Information Act 172
  3. Open Meeting Laws 173
C. Documents 173
  1. Public 173
  2. Private 173
  3. Authorizations 174
    a. Scope of Authorization 174
    b. Obtaining an Authorization 174
  4. Organization 179
D. Finding People 180
E. Finding Information 181
  1. Sources 181

a. Department of Motor Vehicles   181
b. Courthouse   182
   i. Plaintiff and Defendant Tables   183
   ii. Criminal Records   183
   iii. Sealed Records   183
   iv. Divorce Records   183
   v. Probate   184
c. Registry of Deeds   184
d. Registry of Vital Statistics   184
   i. Birth   184
   ii. Death   185
   iii. Marriage   186
   iv. Divorce   186
e. Real Property Tax Rolls   186
f. Voters' Lists   186
g. Census   186
h. Religious Records/Cemetery Records   187
i. Military/Department of Defense Records   187
j. VFW and Veterans Organizations   187
k. United States Postal Service   187
l. State Offices   187
m. Other Records   188
   i. Pet Licenses   188
   ii. Sporting Licenses   189
   iii. Town Permits   189
n. Martindale-Hubbell Directory and Bar Associations   189
o. Newspapers   190
p. Libraries   190
q. Federal Government/FOIA   190
r. Cross-Reference Directory   191
s. Medical Records   191
t. Coroner   191
2. Computer Assisted   192
a. Internet   192
   i. Access and Terminology   192
   ii. General Sites   194
   iii. Individuals and Businesses   194
   iv. Medical   194
   v. Corporate   196
   vi. Miscellaneous   196
b. LEXIS   196
c. Westlaw   196
d. Other Databases   197
3. Obtaining Copies   197
a. Certified   197
b. Noncertified   198
F. Ethical Considerations   199

Summary   199
Key Terms   199
Review Questions   200
Chapter Exercises   200

Appendices   203

Appendix A   Case Investigation File of Hannah West   205
Appendix B   Sample Client Letters   219
Appendix C   Intake Sheet   223
Appendix D   Privacy Act of 1974   225
Appendix E   Freedom of Information Act   243
Appendix F   Sample Letters (FOIA)   251
Appendix G   Federal Rules of Civil Procedure (Selected Rules)   253
Appendix H   Federal Rules of Evidence (Selected Rules)   259
Appendix I   California Notice Statute   269
Appendix J   Massachusetts Lawyers Diary and Manual   271

Glossary   *273*
Bibliography   *281*
Index   *283*

About the Author

Ann Dobmeyer has nearly twenty years of legal experience. She worked at the Carter White House in the Office of Counsel to the President and spent ten years as a civil litigation attorney working with paralegals in a Washington, D.C., law firm. For the past eight years she has taught paralegals and law students about interviewing and investigation and was honored by her students for inclusion in *Who's Who Among America's Teachers.* She is a graduate of Ohio State University, Antioch University School of Law, and the Harvard Law School Negotiation Workshop. She is an Associate Professor of Law at Bay Path College and an Adjunct Professor of Law at Western New England College School of Law.

Acknowledgments

I did not intend to write this book. Faced with teaching a course in interviewing and investigation, I reviewed the books available for paralegals and came up dissatisfied. I had taught interviewing to law students for a number of years and was surprised at the lack of materials for paralegals. My call to Little, Brown was answered by Carolyn O'Sullivan who said they did not have such a book and challenged me to write one. And so I did. I thank Carolyn for believing in the project long before I did and never losing sight of the product. I also thank Betsy Kenny, the book's developmental editor, for being so helpful, supportive, and accommodating throughout the process; her ability to "review the reviewers" and separate the wheat from the chaff in record time was extraordinary.

I want to express gratitude to Bay Path College for supporting my endeavor, and to my students—those past and those yet to come—for allowing me the privilege of teaching them. I owe a debt to Carol Rolf for sharing her information on using the Internet, and special recognition is due H. Gregory "E.B." Williams for his thoughtful suggestions about style and content, and his sustaining wit.

And special thanks to my parents for years of love and support, to my children for giving up so many days and nights to "mom's book," and to my husband for his insightful comments, unending assistance, counsel, and love.

Preface

Eighteen years ago, I was asked to interview a woman for a newly developed paralegal position in a small general-practice law firm in which I was an associate. She was a bright, articulate person with a remarkably pleasant disposition. On behalf of the firm I made her an offer, and fortunately for us, and especially for me, she accepted. When we hired her, I was not exactly sure how she would fit—what exactly could a paralegal do? I did not know what kind of tasks we could assign her and what impact she would have on our practice. She changed my legal life. I relied on her to research, write, interview, and investigate a variety of matters, both transaction and litigation, involving federal and state laws. On one occasion, when I was trying a civil case, and the defendant denied having been arrested (before his attorney could object), she obtained a certified copy of his arrest record during the lunch break to use for impeachment in the afternoon.

We worked together as the firm grew, hired another paralegal, moved (twice) to new quarters, and hired more paralegals. By the time the firm disbanded some years later, she had finished law school and was beginning a different journey.

Since that time 18 years ago, I have been involved continually with paralegals in some manner, supervising, mentoring, and, for the past seven years, teaching. As for my first paralegal, she is a partner in a major law firm.

It is to her and to paralegals everywhere, I dedicate this book.

Foreword

In this book you will meet a variety of clients who have enlisted the help of your law firm to resolve legal matters. They include:

Raymond Jamison
Harold Wizzen, M.D.
Phillip and Mary Lou Williams
Hannah West
The Town of Windale
Harold Madden
Morgan and Rita Downey
Maggie Winchon
Gladys Winston

Through their characters and their cases, you will see the practical side of interviewing and investigation. The book begins with an overview of the litigation process because, whether we are involved in litigation or not, it always looms as a possibility in any legal interaction. Rules of procedure, evidence, and ethics are discussed as a framework for the interviewing and investigation process.

Against the backdrop of law, evidence, and procedure, the book considers how to ask questions, and how to listen to determine whether questions are answered. You will learn how to diffuse the angry or hostile person and how the way you dress, sit, and talk influences the interview. The book reviews issues involved in interviewing children and individuals from different cultures. It also examines what motivates a person to provide information and what inhibits one from doing so.

Having learned how to acquire information from interviews and other sources, you will learn how to preserve information and make it accessible for later use. Finally, the book discusses the planning and organization of an investigation, complete with sources for finding people and finding information.

1

Introduction

CHAPTER OBJECTIVES

This chapter discusses interviewing and investigation within the framework of

- litigation and transaction;
- the rules of discovery;
- the rules of evidence;
- the paralegal's role;
- ethical considerations.

A. Interviewing and Investigation

Interviewing is the controlled exchange of information between an interviewer and a subject; this book focuses on the interviewing of witnesses and clients by a paralegal. Investigation is the gathering of information pertinent to a given matter; this book addresses the investigation typically conducted by a paralegal.

Although interviewing is part of the investigation process, we treat it separately because of its remarkable importance to the process and because it involves issues of relationship that are inapplicable to other aspects and forms of investigation.

Many cases result in litigation; for many others the possibility or threat of litigation is a constant shadow. The nature of interviewing and investigation requires an understanding of the litigation process. Consider the following scenarios:

First Scenario

Raymond Jamison has been a client of the firm for several years. This morning, he called an attorney in your office, Maxine Greene, to help him with a problem he is having with his uncle who is the trustee of his trust fund. Because Ms. Greene has a scheduled court appearance, she asked you to conduct the interview of Mr. Jamison.

Ms. Green told you that Mr. Jamison is the beneficiary of a trust fund managed by his uncle, Jack Burnson, a well-respected attorney in town who was just honored by the bar association for 50 years of service to the local bar. Mr. Burnson has managed the account for the past 25 years, since Mr. Jamison was 12. Although the trust fund increased in size for many years, within the past six months Mr. Jamison has lost over 25 percent of the fund because of stock trades made by Mr. Burnson. In fact, according to Jamison, the account lost 10 percent yesterday. He is furious. He called the brokerage house that handles the account, but was told by the broker that under the terms of the trust document, Mr. Burnson has absolute authority over the account, and the house could not restrict trade without judicial intervention. Before Mr. Jamison arrives for the interview, you begin writing down questions to ask him.

Second Scenario

At the weekly firm meeting, the list of new clients includes Harold Wizzen, M.D., who has been sued by Mary Stockton, a 35-year-old mother of two, for performing a complete hysterectomy during the cesarean-section birth of her second child. Wizzen has been practicing medicine for over 40 years and has never been sued before. In his phone call to your supervising attorney, Dr. Wizzen intimated that not only was his medical judgment correct, he actually did Ms. Stockton a favor by performing the hysterectomy. In his view no one should have more than two children, and because of the operation Ms. Stockton will not have to concern herself with birth control or menstrual cycles. You have been asked to prepare questions for Dr. Wizzen and sit in on the initial interview.

Third Scenario

Phillip and Mary Lou Williams have been clients of the firm for ten years. They have three children: Mitchell, an accountant with three children; Miriam, a psychiatrist without children; and Morgan, a teacher with two children. They want to do some estate planning.

Specifically, they said on the phone that they had read about irrevocable trusts and wanted to set up some trust accounts to pay for college for their five grandchildren. Mr. Williams also wants to be certain that Mitchell inherits the diamond broach that has been in the family for years. You have been asked to do the initial interview.

Fourth Scenario

Hannah West called your firm this morning after the father of her three children, Jeffrey West, failed to return them to her after the weekend. She was referred by another attorney, Brian Schubert, who does not practice family law. Ms. West is panicked. She does not know where the children are and is concerned that the father has removed them from the country. Because this case may require immediate action by your supervising attorney who is in court this morning on another matter, you have been asked to prepare questions and sit in on the initial interview.

The four scenarios provide insight as to the types of cases that come into law firms for resolution.

- Raymond Jamison needs legal help to stem the tide of losses from his trust fund.
- Harold Wizzen, M.D., wants to practice medicine, not spend precious time defending a medical malpractice action.
- Phillip and Mary Lou Williams want to provide for their grandchildren but do not know how to do it.
- Hannah West fears her children may have been removed from the country.

Mr. Jamison may need immediate judicial intervention in the form of a temporary restraining order to address the problem with his uncle. For Dr. Wizzen the legal process started when Ms. Stockton filed her lawsuit against him. Mr. and Mrs. Williams need careful legal planning to achieve their goals. And Ms. West needs immediate help to find her children.

The initial interviews of these five people involve different legal principles and applications. These interviews, like most interviews, take place within two contexts: litigation, as in Dr. Wizzen's case, and transaction, as in Mr. and Mrs. Williams's case. Sometimes interviewing concerns both litigation and transaction as in Mr. Jamison's case. It is important to distinguish between the two in the context of interviewing and investigation because litigation is an adversarial process resulting in a winner and a loser. Statutes and procedural rules control the process in terms of substance and time. Regardless of how a legal matter begins, it can result in litigation. What follows is an overview of the litigation process, including basic principles and terminology.

1.   Litigation Overview

Litigation resolves cases through the court system. People also frequently resolve issues between themselves and official and business entities through administrative processes. The practice of administrative law involves procedural and evidentiary rules different from civil or criminal rules of procedure and evidence. The principles of investigation and interviewing, however, involved in each of these areas of law are essentially the same.

In the second scenario, Mary Stockton is suing Dr. Wizzen for medical malpractice. She believes the doctor was at fault for her injuries. Stockton wants to recover some amount of money to compensate her for, among other things, the loss she has suffered—that of not being able to bear another child. Although she has tried to settle this matter without going to court, Dr. Wizzen refuses to compensate her for any of her losses and in fact has just sent her a rather large bill. Ms. Stockton has the right to try to prove Dr. Wizzen committed malpractice and obtain compensation from him. The process of the lawsuit—from beginning to end—is called litigation.

An outline of the general process is as follows. Ms. Stockton, or "plaintiff," files a complaint against Harold Wizzen, M.D., the "defendant." The defendant responds to the complaint by filing an answer in which he admits or denies the statements or allegations made in the complaint. The complaint and the answer are called pleadings.

In some jurisdictions, the aggrieved party must file a demand letter before beginning the lawsuit. This letter puts the defendant on notice that a lawsuit is imminent and provides the parties an opportunity to discuss settlement before a complaint is filed.

In all jurisdictions, a person suing a public entity may not commence a lawsuit against the entity unless the person has presented a claim to that entity within a given time period (for example, six months) after the plaintiff has been harmed. Claims not timely presented are forfeited and no lawsuit can be filed thereafter. A section of the California Code dealing with notice to public entities is in the Appendix.

After the pleadings are filed, the parties file additional documents to learn about the other side's case. This process is called discovery. Discovery reveals facts and legal theories relied on by the parties; it also exposes strengths and weaknesses of each party's case. For example, the parties can file written questions, called interrogatories, to be answered under oath by the other side, they can request relevant documents, and they can ask questions under oath or depose the other party or nonparty witnesses.

The discovery process is controlled by a special set of rules written by courts or legislatures. Other rules control the entire litigation process, including evidentiary matters. Evidence consists of a single piece of information or a collection of documents and testimony used at trial to prove a case. Evidence that is relevant to the case and from a reliable source can be admitted by the judge at trial to prove or disprove a fact in issue.

In the medical malpractice case, evidence might include bills from the hospital indicating the cost of Ms. Stockton's stay, interrogatory answers from Dr. Wizzen, deposition testimony from other doctors supporting or criticizing Dr. Wizzen's care of Ms. Stockton, and bills from nurses and other professionals who were involved in Ms. Stockton's care.

2. Procedural and Substantive Law

Throughout the case, there are two sets of laws that apply: procedural law and substantive law. Although these are complex concepts to master, they may be generally defined as follows. Procedural law is the law that controls the process. For example, if a party fails to file an answer to the complaint in the required time, usually 20 days, the court can enter a default judgment against that party denying him or her the opportunity to defend the case.

Substantive law, on the other hand, controls the legal aspects of the case. For example, in the medical malpractice case, if the evidence showed that Ms. Stockton contributed to her own injuries by failing to keep her prenatal appointments, the judge might find her comparatively negligent. That decision is a substantive legal decision because it determines the legal rights of the parties.

Some legal concepts like statutes of limitations, which determine the amount of time a plaintiff has to bring a lawsuit, are procedural in application but substantive in nature. If the statute requires that a medical malpractice complaint be filed within three years from the date of the injury and Ms. Stockton waits ten years to sue, the case will be dismissed by the court because it was not filed within the time the statute required. Even though the filing time is procedural, the substantive legal right the party once had is extinguished.

3. Nonlitigation

Interviewing and investigation also take place outside the litigation process in the transactional process where the focus is the preventative aspect of law, such as drafting the will to withstand the scrutiny of the heirs, or drafting the contract to ensure its enforceability. Transactions include, among others, estate planning, research and counseling for corporate clients, real estate, and other contracts. Each area has its own specialized terminology and substantive law. Although transactions are nonadversarial, in our litigious society even the most routine transactions or interactions are fraught with potential legal consequences and therefore carry with them the possibility of litigation.

B.   The Paralegal's Role

Whether litigation or transaction, the paralegal has a critical role to play in the interviewing and investigation process. Working under the attorney's supervision, you will interview clients and witnesses alone or with the attorney. You will investigate a variety of cases, civil and criminal, from real estate to fraud to medical malpractice to murder. Your relationship with the client is confidential; the obligation to keep things confidential extends to everyone in the office.

Consider the scenarios at the beginning of the chapter. In the first, what questions will you ask Mr. Jamison, who complains that his uncle is mishandling his trust fund? What legal issues are involved? What nonlegal issues are involved? How do you handle his anger? What documents are important to the case? With whom will you talk?

In the second scenario, what preliminary research will you do before Dr. Wizzen's arrival? What if his "medical talk" is unfamiliar to you? How can you best prepare yourself? How do you investigate this case?

In the third scenario, Mr. and Mrs. Williams's needs appear to be straightforward enough. But will they need a trustee, and, if so, should it be a family member, a bank, or other entity? What about tax consequences?

Ms. West needs immediate help to find her children. Can the father remove them from the country without her knowledge? Could he have obtained passports for them? What are the custody laws of the jurisdiction? Does he live in this jurisdiction? If not, what laws apply to the children?

C.   Ethics

Paralegals must maintain high standards of ethics. Unlike attorneys for whom sanctions are available for a violation of the Code of Professional Responsibility, paralegals are not currently governed by any code; therefore no sanctions apply. There are compelling reasons, however, to maintain high standards of behavior. First, under a principle-of-agency law, called *respondeat superior*, the attorney for whom the paralegal works is responsible for the paralegal's behavior. Thus, to advance in employment within the firm or to transfer to new employment, the paralegal's ethical record must be without blemish. Second, a client may sue a paralegal in tort for any injuries suffered as a result of the paralegal's intentional or negligent misconduct. To be a defendant in a legal malpractice action is highly undesirable. And third, acting ethically is simply the right thing to do. Maintain the highest ethical standards. You will reap rewards of continued employment, advancement, and job satisfaction if you do so.

Two professional associations, the National Association of Legal Assistants (NALA) and the National Federation of Paralegal Associations (NFPA), have codes of ethics to help guide paralegals in their profession. These codes, however, are not mandatory provisions as is the Code of Professional Responsibility that governs the conduct of lawyers.

D.   Clients

Clients are rich, poor, old, young, pleasant, and ill-tempered. Some are sophisticated about the law, others are not. Clients seek legal help for a variety of reasons, including

- redressing a wrong;
- resolving a crisis;
- planning for business;
- or planning for personal needs.

As discussed earlier in the chapter, on some occasions the purpose of the lawyer-client relationship is litigation, that is, initiating or defending a lawsuit. On other occasions the purpose of the relationship is a transaction, or legal planning to meet the client's goals as well as to prevent litigation. For example, preparing real estate documents, drafting or probating wills, incorporating businesses, negotiating and drafting contracts, applying for patents or business licenses, and anticipating financial and tax consequences are all matters in which careful planning ensures the desired result and avoids litigation. Although many of the "routine" services provided by attorneys to clients may become the focus of litigation, perhaps a business contract gone awry, these services more frequently result in a satisfying transaction between the client and the lawyer.

In litigation the attorney and paralegal prepare together with the client to represent the client's interests in an adversarial confrontation that may result in a trial. In a transaction, the attorney and paralegal represent the client's interests, without the focus of litigation. Nevertheless, the possibility of future litigation should always be considered and, to the extent possible, avoided by careful planning based on a thorough understanding of the client's needs, goals, and circumstances.

E.   Case Facts and Client Facts

An interview with a client will yield facts that can be separated into case facts (legal concerns) and client facts (nonlegal concerns) depending on the nature and primary purpose of the attorney-client interaction. In some instances a fact may be both a case fact and a client fact.

1.   Case Facts

Case facts address the client's legal concerns; in an adversarial context (litigation), they tend to prove or disprove a theory of law. Proof of a legal theory, like a breach of contract or negligence, allows a party to recover damages. In the nonadversarial context (transactional), case facts help form the basis of a transaction or arrangement. For example, in medical malpractice litigation based on the theory of negligence, the fact that Dr. Wizzen left Ms. Stockton in the delivery room unattended while he went to the cafeteria to have a cup of coffee is one case fact that helps to establish his negligence. In the transaction context, the fact that Mr. and Mrs. Williams have five grandchildren is a case fact that helps to form the basis of the transaction, the will, and trust.

Case facts differ from and are critical to each case. Case facts determine which legal theories are suitable and which are not, which legal precedents are applicable and which are not. Although legal professionals spend a great deal of time reviewing case law and studying theory, it is generally not the law but the facts of a case that make it unique. In the end, it is the application of the facts to the law that determines who wins and who loses.

Whether in the litigation or transaction context, case facts evolve during the process. As one moves from the interview to the investigation stage of a case, facts are supplemented, clarified, and verified. The factual landscape is painted with information.

2.   Client Facts

By comparison, client facts are those facts that address the client's nonlegal concerns; they give an understanding of the client's goals, interests, and limitations. Using the above examples, a client fact in the malpractice example is that Ms. Stockton is apprehensive about the lawsuit because she has a full-time job as a chemical engineer and has two small children. The fact that Raymond Jamison wants to buy a house with the income from his trust fund is a client fact.

Client facts state or affect the client's position or goals. For example, a client who has been convicted of perjury may not make a credible witness in a later case even though the conviction has nothing to do with the current case. The client fact affects his or her position and may hinder, or render impossible, attainment of goals. Similarly, a client with limited resources may be unable to take advantage of expensive discovery mechanisms or a private investigator.

3.   Both Case Facts and Client Facts

Frequently, a fact may be both a case fact and a client fact. For example, the injury, a hysterectomy, suffered by Ms. Stockton in the medical malpractice example is a case fact because it demonstrates the damage suffered by the client. At the same time it is a client fact because it represents or affects the client's goals in the litigation.

F.   The Effect of Discovery on the Interview and Investigation Process

Discovery is the process of learning about the other party's case before trial. Discoverable information includes a person's written or oral statement, police or medical reports, photographs, business reports, or any information of any kind that is relevant to the case and not excluded by reason of privilege. Discovery is accomplished two ways: informally through investigation and formally through use of court rules. Regardless of the way it is accomplished, the paralegal plays an important role in discovery.

1.   Informal Discovery

Informal discovery is gathering information in a casual manner and usually takes place before a lawsuit has been initiated. It is part of the investigation process. For example, if your firm represents Mr. Jamison in an action against his uncle, a request by telephone to his uncle or his attorney for a copy of the account activity from the brokerage house is informal discovery. Paralegals commonly gather factual information informally by making telephone calls, by retrieving information from a government office, such as the recorder of deeds (real property information), the bureau of vital statistics (birth, death, and marriage records), or the office of the secretary of state (corporate information).

2.   Formal Discovery

Formal discovery occurs after a complaint has been filed but before trial begins. This is called pretrial discovery. A party relies on state or federal rules of procedure to obtain information about the other side's case. Rules of civil and criminal procedure are guidelines issued by every state and the federal government to manage cases in the court system. The rules control what information may be discovered, how it may be discovered, and when it may be discovered. Once a lawsuit has been commenced with the court, the rules issued by that court control the discovery process. Using the example in the preceding paragraph, if Mr. Jamison's uncle refused to make the brokerage documents available through informal discovery, the documents could be obtained by making a formal discovery request under the court rules. Paralegals draft formal discovery requests with great frequency.

Formal discovery involves complex litigation procedural rules that require one party to provide case information that is relevant but not privileged to the adverse party before trial. Relevant means "relating to the case," "important to," or "of consequence" to the case. Privileged means protected by a statute from discovery by an adverse party. For example, suppose that Mr. Billings is being tried for the murder of his neighbor, Mr. Seltzer. The fact that Mr. Billings told his psychiatrist that he killed Seltzer is relevant because it is related to the case; however, the information is privileged because communication between patient and psychiatrist is often protected by statute and therefore not open to discovery by the other side. "Privileges" are covered later in this chapter.

There are two general categories of discovery, civil and criminal. Not all information that is not privileged is discoverable. The constitutions of the United States and the individual states guarantee us certain rights as citizens. In civil cases, procedural law concerning discovery is broad and there are few constitutional restrictions. In criminal cases the opposite is true; a defendant's right to an attorney and his or her privilege against self-incrimination are grave constitutional considerations that restrict or even prohibit some aspects of discovery. For example, in a civil case, a party has no constitutional right to refuse to be questioned under oath about non-incriminating matters. In a criminal case, however, the defendant has a Fifth Amendment right not to be deposed by the prosecution.

Discovery in civil cases is very broad and occurs long before trial. People new to the legal field are often surprised to learn that discovery of the opposing side's position is not only sanctioned, it is required by law under the Federal Rules of Civil Procedure and similar state rules. Trial judges and lawyers, generally speaking, do not want surprise; they want all parties to be aware of all facts, claims, and defenses. The extent to which this disclosure is mandated is reflected by the 1993 Amendment to the Federal Rules of Civil Procedure, Rule 26, General Provisions Governing Discovery; Duty of Disclosure, which imposes a duty on a party to disclose information that is needed to prepare for trial or settlement without waiting for a formal discovery request. This information includes the name, address, and phone number of any person likely to have discoverable information, copies or location of all documents, information and tangible things relevant to the allegations in the pleadings, computation of damages, and copies of insurance agreements. Rule 26 of the Federal Rules of Civil

Procedure also mandates disclosing the names of witnesses, including expert witnesses, who might be called at trial and copies of documents that might be used at trial. *See* Appendix for a full text of Federal Rule of Civil Procedure, Rule 26.

Discovery is also governed by ethical rules. ABA Model Rules of Professional Conduct, Rule 3.4(a), mandates that an attorney shall not "unlawfully obstruct another party's access to evidence." Subsection (d) of that section prohibits the filing of frivolous discovery requests and requires a "reasonably diligent effort to comply with a legally proper discovery request. . . ."

In addition to FED. R. CIV. P. 26, other federal court rules address discovery. The most frequently used are Federal Rules of Civil Procedure 30, 33, 34, 35, and 36. In addition to the Federal Rules of Civil Procedure, each federal district court has its own local rules that further refine court approved discovery.

PRACTICE TIP: The Bluebook: A Uniform System of Citation dictates how we refer to, or "cite," court rules and other legal materials. For example, Rule 26 of the Federal Rules of Civil Procedure, which regulates discovery, is cited as FED. R. CIV. P. 26.

Federal Rule of Civil Procedure, Rule 30, Depositions Upon Oral Examination, allows a party to take the oral testimony under oath of any person, not only a party. Generally, permission of the court is not required. Oral testimony is taken to gain information about an opponent's case or to preserve information—to lock a witness into his or her story. In our representation of Dr. Wizzen, we would seek to depose any physician Ms. Stockton intended to call as an expert witness.

Federal Rule of Civil Procedure, Rule 33, Interrogatories to Parties, lets a party ask questions, in writing, to another party. Under the federal rules the questions are limited to 25 in number, including subparts. Other court systems issue their own rules, but most state rules similarly restrict the number. Each question must be answered or objected to individually. Generally, interrogatories are served and answered before taking a deposition since the answers to interrogatories can provide basic information useful during the deposition. If we filed a complaint on Mr. Jamison's behalf against his uncle, we would send his uncle a set of interrogatories seeking information about his management of the trust.

Federal Rule of Civil Procedure, Rule 34, Production of Documents and Things and Entry Upon Land for Inspection and Other Purposes, restricts discovery to parties and compels a party to make available relevant documents, such as pictures and telephone records, medical and business records, and other data. Ms. Stockton might file a request for production of documents to review Dr. Wizzen's records. A nonparty may be compelled to produce documents pursuant to FED. R. CIV. P. 45.

Under Federal Rule of Civil Procedure, Rule 35, Physical and Mental Examinations of Persons, a party, for good cause shown, may ask the court to order the mental or physical examination of another party. For instance, in our family example, if custody becomes an issue, Ms. West may seek to have the father examined by an independent psychiatrist.

Finally, under Federal Rule of Civil Procedure, Rule 36, Requests for Admission, a party may serve on another party requests for the admission or denial of certain information. This helps to clarify issues for trial and avoids the time-consuming task of proving matters as to which the opposition neither disagrees nor objects. For example, if the action is one for breach of contract, one party may ask the other to admit that a signature on the contract is legitimate. Once admitted, that fact need not be proven at trial.

A chart summarizing the main discovery devices is shown in Exhibit 1.1.

In addition to factual information, claims, and defenses, parties may discover opinions of expert witnesses whom the opposition intends to produce at trial. Witnesses must be identified so that they may be deposed by the opposition before trial. Documents such as hospital records and medical bills must be provided as evidence of injury or financial loss.

Discovery promotes a clear assessment by both sides of a case and encourages settlement. Information requested in the discovery process must be relevant to the case. Simply because information is relevant, however, does not render it automatically discoverable; it might be privileged by law. Moreover, not all discoverable information is admissible evidence. Some discoverable evidence, for example, the existence and extent of insurance coverage, is critical to obtain in pretrial discovery but inadmissible at trial for public policy reasons.

Discovery requests made before trial remain alive throughout the trial and parties are obligated to amend their answers to discovery requests as circumstances change. In addition, if a judgment for damages is entered, a party may proceed with post-trial discovery in order to learn about the judgment debtor's assets so as to satisfy the judgment. Although the focus is narrow, the process is generally the same.

3.   Nondiscoverable Information

Certain kinds of information are not discoverable. Information that is the result of the working relationship between a client and attorney, for example, is not discoverable by another party.

a.   Attorney-Client Privilege

The relationship between a client and attorney (and the paralegal as the attorney's representative) is a privileged one. Rule 1.6 of the American Bar Association Model Rules of Professional Conduct states:

DEVICE	PURPOSE	LIMITATIONS	TIMETABLE
INTERROGATORIES (FED. R. CIV. P. 33)	Clarify claims and defenses; identify witnesses, experts, and documents; usually first step in discovery process; party must answer or object under oath.	PARTIES ONLY Limited to 25 in number, including subparts (more with court order); party under continuing duty to supply/correct requested information; party may object if irrelevant, privileged, or burdensome.	Responses due within 30 days of service unless served with complaint, then due within 45 days.
REQUEST TO PRODUCE (FED. R. CIV. P. 34)	Allows party to obtain documents and tangible things; allows party to enter land to inspect.	PARTIES ONLY No limit; party receiving request under continuing duty to supply; party may object if irrelevant, privileged, or burdensome.	Response due within 30 days of service.
REQUEST FOR ADMISSIONS (FED. R. CIV. P. 36)	Clarify issues for trial; admission of fact eliminates necessity to prove.	PARTIES ONLY No limit; party can admit, deny, or object to each request.	Response due within 30 days of service.
ORAL DEPOSITION (FED. R. CIV. P. 30)	Allows party to uncover facts about case through sworn testimony of deponent.	ANYBODY with information relevant to case (or information that may lead to relevant information) may be deposed.	May be taken any time with notice to court; plaintiff must wait 30 days from service to take defendant's oral deposition, unless defendant had already noticed a deposition of plaintiff.
MEDICAL EXAM (FED. R. CIV. P. 35)	Allows mental and physical exams of a party by a physician; report sets forth findings, results, and conclusions and reports of earlier exams for same condition.	PARTIES ONLY Court order required unless agreed to by stipulation.	Unless stipulation by party to be examined, court must issue order.

Exhibit 1.1 **Discovery Devices**

(a) A lawyer shall not reveal information relating to representation of a client unless the client consents after consultation, except for disclosures that are impliedly authorized in order to carry out the representation. . . .

Most jurisdictions allow an attorney to acknowledge that an attorney-client relationship exists; in some jurisdictions, however, even the existence of the attorney-client relationship is privileged. It is important to remember that the client, not the attorney or paralegal, holds the privilege. Therefore, it is the client, not the attorney or paralegal, who can waive the privilege and allow the information relating to representation to be released.

The confidential relationship between the attorney or paralegal and the client does not extend to a third party who is not necessary for the delivery of legal services, regardless of who is paying the attorney. Thus, if Mom and Dad pay Attorney Smart to get their son out of a jam, the confidential relationship is between Attorney Smart and the son. Sometimes when third parties pay, they feel they have the right to consult with the attorney or paralegal separately to learn about the case. They must be told that the ethical rules prevent them from discussing the case with anyone other than the client. As a matter of course, it is generally advisable to caution the client not to discuss the case with anyone because that third party can jeopardize the client's claim to privilege. For example, if your client chooses to confide in a friend, that friend could be subpoenaed to testify about the conversation; your client cannot prevent it. Note, however, that conversations between spouses are subject to different rules that usually allow one spouse to prevent the other from testifying about communications between them.

PRACTICE TIP: Warn your client not to discuss his or her case with anyone since that person could be subpoenaed by the adverse party and be forced to testify as to any conversation he or she had with your client.

The term "client" includes corporate clients and government clients. If Kansas City, Kansas, retains legal counsel to advise it on regulatory or eminent domain matters, an attorney-client relationship exists. If the Securities and Exchange Commission seeks legal advice from attorneys, the attorney-client relationship exists. There are, however, exceptions to this privilege. As a matter of public policy, the law will not shield information pertaining to the attorney-client relationship if there is a broader claim to be addressed. For example, assume that Ajax Corporation retains legal counsel to advise it in its business dealings. If the shareholders of Ajax Corporation bring a suit against the officers of the corporation alleging that the officers violated its corporate charter and defrauded the shareholders, and the shareholders can make a showing to the court of the fraudulent activity, Ajax Corporation cannot use the attorney-client privilege to prevent its attorneys from disclosing their conversations with the corporate officers.

Communication between an attorney or paralegal and an incompetent or underage person is privileged. The privilege includes the underage or incompetent client as well as the client's representative. If the client has more than one lawyer, all lawyers are bound by the privilege. If the attorney retains outside experts, such as a doctor, an accountant, or appraiser, those experts are bound by the privilege because they were retained to help the attorney provide competent legal services to the client.

Under Rule 1.6 of the American Bar Association Model of Professional Conduct, any communication, whether oral or written, between the client and the attorney is confidential. In other words, once the attorney-client relationship is established the attorney cannot generally be made to disclose any information the client has told the lawyer in confidence; the opposition cannot "discover" the information. The privilege is held by the client, not the attorney. The law supports this confidentiality because by guaranteeing to a client that the information provided to the attorney by the client is "secret," the client is encouraged to be forthright and truthful with the attorney.

Although the privilege protects the communication between the attorney and the client, it does not necessarily protect the information in the communication. For example, in a child custody case, if a witness is asked whether he told his lawyer he had a child from a previous marriage, the witness, through his attorney, will object to the question because his conversation with his lawyer is privileged. If the attorney simply asks the witness whether he has a child from a previous marriage, the witness may not assert the privilege and, if the question is relevant, must answer.

A third party present during the interview may destroy the privilege. The general test is whether or not the third party is necessary for the delivery of legal services: An interpreter is; the window cleaner is not. Because a paralegal is part of the legal staff, he or she will not defeat the privilege. Privacy becomes an issue when, for example, the client is incarcerated and the jail has no facilities where the communication with the attorney can be truly confidential. Presence of other inmates as third parties may jeopardize the privilege.

Finally, the privilege does not apply to circumstances in which the client informs the attorney of his or her intent to commit a crime, or retains the attorney to perpetrate or further a crime.

> **PRACTICE TIP:** Correspondence between attorney and client is privileged and should be labeled accordingly. Note the "Privileged and Confidential" designation on the sample letters in the Appendix.

b. Work Product Doctrine

The work product doctrine protects from discovery, except in very limited circumstances, all working documents, papers, and notes prepared by an attorney or staff in anticipation of litigation. The doctrine was first declared by the U.S. Supreme Court in *Hickman v. Taylor*, 329 U.S. 495 (1947). So long as the documents contain the attorney's or staff's mental impressions, legal theories, or opinions, they are generally not discoverable. Federal Rule of Civil Procedure, Rule 26(b)(3), however, allows a party access to the adversary's "documents and tangible things" prepared for litigation

> upon a showing that the party seeking discovery has substantial need of the materials in the preparation of the party's case and that party is unable without undue hardship to obtain the substantial equivalent of the materials by other means.

Notice the rule does not affect intangibles such as information not recorded—oral statements—which remain absolutely protected by the doctrine.

PRACTICE TIP: As a general rule, documents protected by the work product rule should not leave the office. If you want to take work home, copy a few cases to read and brief. In the event you must take the documents out of the office (for example, to do research), copy the necessary documents and leave the originals at the office. Further, if the client has no secure place to keep documents, have her review them at the office at her convenience, but discourage her from taking them home.

---

c. Other Privileged Communications

In addition to the attorney-client privilege, state statutes and common law recognize other privileges that guarantee privacy of communication. The theory is the same. By protecting the privacy of the communication, the law encourages open and candid discussion between a client and professional and between a client and her spouse. Even when information is clearly relevant to the case, this information is not discoverable. Examples of privileges held by the client include priest-penitent, doctor-patient, marital, and the privilege against self-incrimination. Note that the therapy records of a person who alleges a sexual assault may sometimes be discovered in cases in which the defense can show a need for the records consistent with a defendant's constitutional rights. *See Commonwealth v. Bishop*, 416 Mass. 169, 617 N.E.2d 990 (1993), in which the court held that if the accused shows a likelihood that counseling records otherwise privileged by statute contain important relevant evidence, the records may be available for judicial review and possible use at trial.

The existence of certain privileges may affect whether a given communication can be introduced into evidence or obtained in discovery. Consequently, when a potentially privileged communication is unearthed in a

---

**Examples of Privileged
Communications**

1. Attorney-client
2. Husband-wife
3. Priest-penitent
4. Doctor-patient
5. Therapist-patient
6. Against self-incrimination

Exhibit 1.2 **Examples of Privileged
Communications**

interview or during discovery, particular attention should be paid to the relationship between the parties to the communication, its purpose, and the circumstances surrounding its making.

G. Evidence

1. Introduction

In the previous section we looked at how state and federal rules of civil procedure control the process of litigation including discovery. We now consider how the information discovered is used in litigation.

Evidence is information offered by a party and accepted by the court to prove or disprove some aspect of a case. Information that is discoverable under the Federal Rules of Civil Procedure or state rules will not automatically be admitted into evidence at trial. Once discovered, information is judged by a different set of standards—federal or state rules of evidence—to determine whether the trier of fact (judge or jury) may consider it in making a decision. Although this text is not an evidence text, the following section addresses some of the evidence provisions pertinent to interviewing and investigation.

Over two thirds of the states have rules of evidence similar to the Federal Rules of Evidence; those states that do not, have many similar provisions. Although the paralegal must be knowledgeable about obtaining evidence and aware of potential evidentiary problems, the attorney will make the final decision about evidence.

2. Relevant Evidence

In order to be admissible, evidence must first be relevant. Under Federal Rule of Evidence, Rule 401:

"Relevant evidence" means evidence having any tendency to make the existence of any fact that is of consequence to the determination of the action more probable or less probable than it would be without the evidence.

Relevant evidence is evidence that tends to make a fact more probable or less probable than it would be without the evidence. Put another way, the proposition of fact the evidence is offered to prove or disprove must be material to the claim or defense. The fact that Dr. Wizzen left a sponge in Ms. Stockton's abdominal cavity after surgery is evidence relevant to the patient's claim of negligence/medical malpractice. The fact that he went to a movie the day following the surgery is probably not relevant evidence to her claim.

> **PRACTICE TIP:** The Bluebook citation form for these rules is FED. R. EVID. [rule number].

Under FED. R. EVID. 402, "[a]ll relevant evidence is admissible . . . [and evidence that] is not relevant is not admissible." Even if evidence is relevant, however, it may be excluded under FED. R. EVID. 403 if it tends to mislead the jury, unfairly prejudice a party, or waste time. For example, cumulative color photographs of the deceased may serve only to enflame the jury. Thus FED. R. EVID. 403 allows the judge to balance admissible evidence within the constraints of unfair prejudice, delay, or confusion.

> **PRACTICE TIP:** Simply because a piece of evidence can be obtained through the discovery process does not mean it is admissible in court to prove or disprove a fact. Getting the evidence is the first half of the battle; having it admitted is the second half.

3. Direct and Circumstantial Evidence

There are two types of evidence a judge or jury may use to determine the facts of a case: direct evidence and indirect evidence. Direct evidence does not require the judge or jury to draw any inferences from other facts. Examples of direct evidence include:

- testimony that the witness saw the accused pull a silver revolver from his pocket and shoot the victim; and
- testimony that the witness saw the plaintiff slip and fall in the icy parking lot.

Circumstantial or indirect evidence requires the judge or jury to draw a reasonable inference from other facts that have been proven. Examples of circumstantial evidence include

- testimony that the witness saw the accused at the gun store purchasing a silver revolver; and
- testimony that the witness saw the plaintiff leave the store and walk towards the parking lot.

4. Evidence of Character

Under FED. R. EVID. 404, evidence of a person's character is not admissible to prove that the person conformed to that character at the time the cause of action arose. Evidence of a person's character is generally unimportant at trial unless character is an element of the cause of action. For example, in a libel or slander case in which the plaintiff's character has been defamed and "truth" is a defense, evidence of the plaintiff's character is essential to the case. In a criminal case (for example, a murder trial), the defendant may present evidence of the deceased victim's violent nature/character if the defendant pleads the murder was committed in self-defense. Those cases are limited, however, and general evidence of character is not admissible.

Evidence of other crimes is not admissible to prove the character of the person in question to show he or she conformed to that character. Just because Harry was convicted of the May 24 robbery does not mean he committed the June 17 robbery. The evidence may be admissible, however, to prove motive, intent, common scheme or plan, identity, or absence of mistake. For example, at the trial of Jerome Waters for the rape of Susan Larson, Larson testified that the perpetrator, Waters, had an unusual tattoo of a giraffe on his upper leg. Waters did in fact have the unusual tattoo on his upper leg and was convicted of the rape. In a subsequent trial of Waters for the rape of Alice Zanyo, evidence that Waters raped Larson could not be admitted to prove that Waters raped Zanyo. Evidence of Waters's unusual tattoo, however, might be admissible to show that the identity of Zanyo's rapist is the same as Larson's.

5. Special Considerations

Four Federal Rules of Evidence important in interviewing are Subsequent Remedial Measures (FED. R. EVID. 407), Offers to Compromise (FED. R. EVID. 408), Payment of Medical and Similar Expenses (FED. R. EVID. 409), and Proof of Liability Insurance (FED. R. EVID. 411).

a. Subsequent Repair

Under FED. R. EVID. 407, evidence that a repair was made to remedy a dangerous situation after someone was injured by the danger is not admissible to prove liability. This rule is designed to encourage remedial measures to ensure safety. For example, if the plaintiff falls down defendant's stairs because of a missing step, evidence that the defendant fixed the step after plaintiff's fall cannot be used as evidence to prove defendant's negligence. Public policy considerations dictate that it is more important to fix the stair than to leave it broken for another to injure himself. Federal Rule of Evidence, Rule 407, encourages repair by shielding the owner from liability based on evidence of the repair. The evidence can, however, be used to show that defendant owned or had control over the premises.

b. Offer to Compromise

An offer to compromise under FED. R. EVID. 408 is also exempt from evidence, again for public policy reasons. Parties are encouraged to settle their disputes privately to avoid litigation, so much so that any information about settlement discussions or negotiations is not admissible at trial to show what a party may be willing to accept to settle the case. This includes conduct as well as statements. Again, there are circumstances under which the evidence may be admitted, such as to show bias or prejudice of a witness or obstruction of a criminal prosecution. If Dr. Wizzen offered to pay Ms. Stockton $250,000 to settle the medical malpractice case, then she could not use that information as evidence at trial to show that the doctor was liable or that he has the ability to pay the money.

c. Offer to Pay Expenses

Third, under FED. R. EVID. 409, evidence that a person offered to pay medical or other expenses is not admissible to prove the offeror was liable for the injury because our society does not want to discourage people from offering help for fear their offer of help will be held against them.

d. Insurance Coverage

Finally, under FED. R. EVID. 411, evidence that a person did or did not carry insurance at the time of the injury is not admissible to prove liability. Exclusion of this evidence prevents the jury from disposing of cases based on who can pay rather than focusing on the facts and merits of the case. Similar to "subsequent repairs," evidence of insurance may be used to show ownership or control, bias, prejudice, or agency.

6. Hearsay

Hearsay is any statement, including oral, written, and demonstrative, made out of court, and offered in court to prove what the statement says. The person who makes the statement is called the declarant. Hearsay is generally not admissible as reliable evidence because it is not believable. An interviewer must always keep the question "How do I prove this?" in the back of her or his mind, and if the person being interviewed is talking about what "Bob said that Mary said that Harold said," a red flag signals "credibility problems."

If you've ever played "telephone" you know why hearsay is usually not admissible—it is seldom reliable. Consider a medical malpractice example in which the surgeon left the sponge in the patient's abdomen. Testimony by a nurse that another nurse said that "the Doctor left the sponge in the patient's abdomen—he's done that before," is hearsay. It is a statement made out of court and offered at trial to prove the doctor left the sponge in the patient's abdomen.

As with many things in the law, there are exceptions to the hearsay rule. In other words, there are instances in which hearsay is deemed to be reliable for a variety of reasons. The exceptions are listed in FED. R. EVID. 801, 802, 803, and 804. All these rules have one thing in common: The statements they control were made under circumstances that tend to make them more reliable than other hearsay statements.

a. Admission of a Party Opponent

Statements made by a party, if relevant, are admissible against that party as an "admission of a party opponent." For example, a physician's statement that he "made an error in not checking the patient's record for drug allergies" would be admissible against him in a suit brought by the patient. Under FED. R. EVID. 801, statements of a party opponent are technically not hearsay because they are exempted from the rule. Under common law the statements are exceptions. The effect is the same.

b. Records

There are three exceptions to FED. R. EVID. 802 that allow records, which are hearsay, to be admitted into evidence: recorded recollection, business records, and public records. The recorded recollection exception to hearsay rule allows a statement that was made by a person who had personal knowledge of an incident at the time the statement was made, but no longer recalls the incident to be admitted as evidence. The business record exception allow records made in the ordinary course of business by a person who normally makes the record to be admitted as evidence. The public records exception allows documents that have been made and maintained by a government office to be admitted as evidence.

c. Present Sense Impression and Excited Utterance

Hearsay uttered by the declarant while observing an incident ("That driver's all over the road.") or reacting to an incident ("Oh no! He ran the light!") are exceptions to the hearsay rule and may be accepted as evidence under FED R. EVID. 803. The first is "present sense impression"; the second is "excited utterance." They are exceptions to the hearsay rule because a person observing or reacting to an incident presumably has little reason to make, or opportunity to fabricate, a false statement. Both rules generally require that the statement be made without the opportunity to reflect on the effect of the statement on a case, and that it be made by someone actually experiencing or viewing a startling or exciting event.

Statements made in furtherance of medical treatment and statements about the declarant's "state of mind" ("Joan told me she intended to stop at her brother's on her way home from work.") are also exceptions under FED. R. EVID. 803 and may be admitted.

d.   Dying Declaration and Statements Against Interest

Another exception to the general rule that hearsay is not admissible is FED. R. EVID. 804. This rule addresses the "dying declaration," a statement made by the declarant when death is imminent, based on the theory that a person about to die is unlikely to make false statements in his or her last breath. Note that in some states, the person has to die for the statement to be admitted, while in other states, the person need not actually die so long as he or she believed death was imminent.

Also under FED. R. EVID. 804, a statement made by a witness is admissible as a "statement against interest," if it was against the witness's financial, property, or criminal interests when made.

Some of the hearsay exceptions listed are only available if the declarant is unavailable because of death, infirmity, incompetency, or because the declarant is beyond the subpoena power of the court.

The chart in Exhibit 1.3 describes the more common hearsay exceptions.

7.   Impeachment

Impeachment is the discrediting of a witness at trial. During an interview, you must be alert to the potential of the person before you being impeached at trial. The rules of evidence allow a witness to be impeached under certain circumstances. The Federal Rules of Evidence provide six general justifications for impeachment: 1) prior conviction of a crime (FED. R. EVID. 609); 2) bias (FED. R. EVID. 607); 3) interest (FED R. EVID. 607); 4) prior inconsistent statement (FED. R. EVID. 613); 5) reputation for truthfulness (FED. R. EVID. 608); and 6) contradiction (FED. R. EVID. 607).

a.   Prior Conviction

If a person has been convicted of a crime punishable by death, or imprisonment of more than a year, or if the crime relates to "truthfulness," the witness may be impeached. For example, if a person were convicted of first-degree murder (punishable by death, or by a prison term in excess of a year), or if a person were convicted of tax fraud, the conviction can be used to impeach her or him at trial.

EXCEPTION	DEFINITION	DOES DECLARANT HAVE TO BE UNAVAILABLE?
Admission of a Party Opponent (FED. R. EVID. 801)	Anything a party has said/written introduced against him at trial.	No
Present Sense Impression (FED. R. EVID. 803)	Declarant describes event while or immediately after experiencing it.	No
Excited Utterance (FED. R. EVID. 803)	Declarant makes statement re startling event as a result of the stress the event caused.	No
Dying Declaration (FED. R. EVID. 804)	Declarant makes statement believing death is imminent.	Yes
Former Testimony (FED. R. EVID. 804)	Declarant's earlier testimony is admissible if party against whom testimony is later offered had opportunity and motive to cross-examine at time of statement.	Yes
Mental, Emotional, or Physical Condition (FED. R. EVID. 803)	Declarant makes statement concerning her state of mind, physical condition, intent, plan, or motive.	No
Statement for Medical Treatment (FED. R. EVID. 803)	Statement made for purpose of medical diagnosis or treatment.	No
Statement Against Interest (FED. R. EVID. 804)	Declarant makes statement that was against interest at time statement was made.	Yes
Records of Regularly Conducted Activity (FED. R. EVID. 802)	Record of any description made in the normal course of business.	No
Recorded Recollection (FED. R. EVID. 802)	Declarant made a record while memory was fresh about a matter once known but since forgotten.	No

Exhibit 1.3 **Chart of Common Exceptions to Hearsay Rules**

b. Bias of a Witness

A witness may be impeached on the grounds of bias. One who is biased is inclined to lie. For example, a brother may lie to protect his sister from conviction or liability.

c. Interest

A witness may also lie to protect his or her own interests. For example, if Joe stands to collect insurance money if Mary's death is not a suicide, he may lie in court as to the cause of her death. His testimony can be discredited.

d. Prior Inconsistent Statement

If a witness testifies in court and has made an earlier statement that is inconsistent with the statement made on the stand, the witness may be impeached using the former statement. The prior statement is usually introduced only to show that the witness has said something inconsistent with his or her testimony in court. The prior statement is not evidence.

e. Reputation for Truthfulness

After a witness testifies, evidence of the witness's character for telling the truth can be introduced by another witness who can describe the first witness's reputation for honesty or offer an opinion about the witness's truthfulness. Evidence that a witness is truthful is admissible only after the witness's character has been attacked by another witness.

f. Contradiction

The credibility of a witness is always in issue. As finders of fact, judges and juries continually assess witness credibility. Federal Rule of Evidence, Rule 607, states simply that "[t]he credibility of a witness may be attacked by any party, including the party calling the witness."

Grounds for Impeachment

1. Prior conviction of a crime (FED. R. EVID. 609)
2. Bias (FED. R. EVID. 607)
3. Interest (FED R. EVID. 607)
4. Prior inconsistent statement (FED R. EVID. 613)
5. Reputation for truthfulness (FED. R. EVID. 608)
6. Contradiction (FED. R. EVID. 607)

Exhibit 1.4 **Grounds for Impeachment**

SUMMARY

Interviewing and investigation should be viewed in the context of litigation. Case facts address the client's legal concerns while client facts address the client's personal concerns. Rules of discovery allow each party access to other parties' information. Evidence, if relevant and not privileged, is discoverable by the other party, although not necessarily admissible in court. Privileged communications include attorney-client, priest-penitent, doctor-patient, marital, and the privilege against self-incrimination. Law and public policy demand certain matters of evidence be excluded from trial. Hearsay is usually not admitted as evidence, but there are exceptions. Witnesses may be impeached at trial for a variety of reasons, including prior conviction of a crime, bias, interest, prior inconsistent statements, reputation for truthfulness, and contradiction.

The next chapter discusses interview preparation.

Key Terms

Attorney-client privilege
Bluebook
Case facts
Circumstantial evidence
Civil action
Client facts
Comparative negligence
Complaint
Credibility
Criminal action
Damages
Default
Defendant
Deposition
Direct evidence
Discovery
Ethics
Evidence
Formal discovery

Hearsay
Impeachment
Informal discovery
Interrogatories
Lawsuit
Litigation
Material
Plaintiff
Pleadings
Privilege
Procedural law
Relevant
Relevant evidence
Respondeat superior
Statute of limitations
Substantive law
Transaction
Work product

REVIEW QUESTIONS

1. What are the differences between formal and informal discovery?
2. What is the purpose of discovery? Name four of the most frequently used discovery devices and explain the mechanics of each.

3. What is hearsay, and why is it excluded from evidence at trial?

4. Occasionally evidence is refused by the court because of overriding public policy concerns. When might this happen? Explain why.

5. Describe the nature of the relationship between the client and the paralegal.

6. Explain the attorney-client privilege. How does it work? Who holds it?

7. What are the differences between direct and circumstantial evidence?

8. What are some examples that illustrate the differences between direct and circumstantial evidence?

9. What is a statute of limitations and how does it affect a client's claim?

10. What is the doctrine of respondeat superior?

11. Describe the differences between case facts and client facts. How do they influence the relationship between you and the client?

12. What is the work product doctrine and how does it affect discovery?

CHAPTER EXERCISES

Exercise 1-1:   Categorize the following into "case facts" or "client facts." Be prepared to justify your choice:

1. Client McGeorge tells you he wants to sue the trucking company that owned the truck that hit his ten-year-old daughter.

2. Client Lynd wants to keep her attorney's fees as low as possible.

3. Client Gomez tells you that the person who rear-ended him has insurance.

4. Client Merceder informs you that the car that hit him ran the light.

Exercise 1-2:   Using the information sheet from the case file in the Appendix, separate the case facts from the client facts.

Exercise 1-3:   Determine whether your state trial court has rules of civil procedure involving discovery similar to the Federal Rules of Civil Procedure. Compare the federal rules to your state's rules. Make a chart emphasizing the differences. Note where you found the information.

Exercise 1-4:   Using the four scenarios at the beginning of the chapter and the "Discovery Device" chart, list the devices you would use to obtain information important to each of the cases.

Exercise 1-5: Working with a partner and using the exception to hearsay chart above, write examples of the following and describe the circumstances under which a court would admit them as evidence: 1) Dying declaration; 2) Present sense impression; 3) Excited utterance; 4) Admission of a party opponent; 5) Statement against interest; 6) Statement of mental, emotional, or physical condition; 7) Records of regularly conducted activity; 8) Medical treatment; 9) Recorded recollection; 10) Former testimony.

Exercise 1-6: Research the law of evidence in your state to answer the following questions: How is hearsay defined? What are the exceptions to hearsay? What are the policy considerations that curtail the use of evidence? What types of evidence are used to impeach a witness?

Exercise 1-7: Using the information you obtained in Exercises 1-6, make a chart outlining the hearsay exceptions, including whether the declarant has to be unavailable in order for the exception to apply.

Exercise 1-8: Using your state materials, identify what privileges are available to a client in your state.

2

Preparing for the Interview

CHAPTER OBJECTIVES

To interview thoroughly and efficiently, a paralegal must

- discuss case with supervising attorney;
- ascertain relevant law;
- research relevant law;
- draft organization or theory chart.

A.   Introduction

Many of the skills that apply to interviewing a client apply to interviewing a witness. Both interviews are part of the larger investigation process. This chapter addresses the major ingredients of preparing for any interview. Matters applicable specifically to client interviews are covered in Chapter 4 and those peculiar to witness interviews are covered in Chapter 5.

Preparation for the interview is probably the most important aspect of the interview, yet it is often inadequate. Good preparation, including an understanding of the law and your subject, allows for an efficient, focused, productive interview.

A thoroughly prepared interview will yield a wealth of knowledge about the subject of the interview and the person being interviewed. It will also result in a controlled exchange of information between the interviewer and the person being interviewed. Consider the following illustrations:

Ice Cream Contract

This week your supervising attorney has asked you to review a copy of a contract entered into by your client, the town of Windale, and Danny's Incredible Edibles, an ice cream vendor who agreed to provide ice cream for a Fourth of July town party. Proceeds from the "make your own sundae" party were earmarked to support the town park, as had been done for a number of years. Under the terms of the contract, Danny's was to deliver 80 gallons of vanilla ice cream and assorted toppings to the Windale Community Center on July 4 between the hours of 1:00 and 2:00 P.M. When Danny's had not arrived by 2:15 P.M., town representatives went to the local supermarket and bought all the available ice cream, about 39 gallons, only 15 of which were vanilla, and some assorted toppings. Because the ice cream was in short supply and it was 92 degrees in the shade, the town decided to open the swimming pool free to all residents. When the ice cream was gone, people either went to the pool or went home. Danny's arrived at 3:45 P.M. and began unloading the ice cream. Town representatives refused to allow Danny's employees into the community center and the ice cream began to melt. Although the ice cream was reloaded onto the truck, some of the ice cream had melted and could not be sold.

What information do you need from your client to understand whether, as the town alleges, there has been a breach by Danny's? What information can your client provide that will assist your firm in drafting next year's contract?

Personal Injury/Automobile Accident

Harold Madden and his daughter were injured by a "hit and run" late-model luxury car when it jumped the curb in front of the department store where Mr. Madden and his daughter had been shopping. Mr. Madden sustained minor injuries; his daughter's injuries are more serious. She was hospitalized for six weeks, and she will need physical therapy for a number of months. There is a question as to the speed of the car that hit the Maddens and as to whether the driver was drunk. The ambulance and police came to the scene; the car and driver were long gone. Your firm is representing the Maddens and you have been asked to sit in on the interview. How do you prepare for the interview? In addition to the client, what witnesses might there be whom you should interview?

Wetlands

Maggie Winchon, a local business woman and real estate developer, has been a client of your firm for over 15 years. Ms. Winchon is interested in purchasing 250 acres (the "Hall" tract) in the next county for development of single family-luxury homes. When she made the appointment for an interview, she indicated that she has several concerns, one of which is whether part of the land might be wetlands and how that could affect development. She seeks your firm's advice on whether, if purchased, the tract could be developed without delay. She does not want a striped three-toed frog stalling her plans. She also wants to determine whether the builder she has in mind is in good standing with the state agency with contractor oversight. What areas of law are involved? What steps would you take to find the laws associated with the matter? What information do you need from Ms. Winchon?

B.   Purpose of Interviewing

The purpose of interviewing someone, whether a client or a witness, is to gather information. As noted above, it is part of the broader investigation process. In a family case, the information gathered may appear to be as simple as asking when the client was married or asking a witness about the parties' date of separation. In a business matter, the purpose of the interview may be to ascertain what the client wants to include in a lease agreement for a new restaurant.

Interviewing of clients and witnesses falls into two general categories:

- interviews in preparation for litigation; and
- interviews for transactions.

Interviews conducted in preparation for litigation include interviewing the client and witnesses for all facets of trial work. Interviews conducted for transactions include interviewing the client and others for all nonlitigation matters, such as estate planning and contracts.

The interview is one of the most critical aspects of litigation since the complaint, as well as other documents, will be based at least in part on the information elicited from the client. Moreover, the client or witness may be deposed before trial or called to testify at trial about case information. Trial preparation, with all the deadlines and limitations, generates questions that necessitate follow-up interviews in addition to applying the facts to a substantive area of law.

The interview is also critical in nonlitigation. A contract, a will, a patent application, or articles of incorporation are each based on the factual information obtained from the client. Procedures in transactions can be lengthy and complicated with deadlines around every corner; there is usually no immediate legal adversary. Transactions, however, might ultimately result in litigation. Interviews in this context must generate information essential to drafting effective legal documents that protect and serve a client's long-term interests and needs.

Whether the matter is litigation or nonlitigation, clients and witnesses are usually willing suppliers of information. They are not necessarily knowledgeable about the law, though, and so they often do not know what facts are legally important, frequently giving an interviewer conclusions and broad generalizations without articulating specific facts. A good interviewer knows what questions to ask because he or she understands the relationship between facts and law. Although some people have good instincts that help them interview productively, interviewing skills are usually learned. Once basics are learned, these skills take time to develop. The interview itself is a time-consuming process; some interviews take an hour, others take many hours and are broken into sessions. Each case presents new personalities, new issues, and a multitude of facts. Each presents an exciting challenge.

C.   Interviewing and Ethics

1.   Role of the Paralegal

The circumstances under which a paralegal may interview clients or witnesses represented by attorneys are controlled by various regulations. Generally, a lawyer may delegate to a paralegal any task the lawyer would perform except those tasks requiring a licensed attorney. The attorney remains responsible for the work product, which includes any notes or internal memoranda drafted by an attorney or a paralegal under the attorney's supervision while representing a client. American Bar Association Model Guidelines for Utilization of Legal Assistant Services, Guideline 2.

2.   The Paralegal-Attorney Relationship

Rules controlling the relationship between the legal assistant and the attorney are found in the ABA Model Guidelines for Legal Assistant Services. Guideline 1 states that

[a] lawyer is responsible for all of the professional actions of a legal assistant performing legal assistant services at the lawyer's direction and should take reasonable measures to ensure that the legal assistant's conduct is consistent with the lawyer's obligations under the ABA Model Rules of Professional Conduct.

Lawyers have their own ethics section on working with paralegals in the ABA Model Rules of Professional Conduct, Rule 5.3:

With respect to a nonlawyer . . . associated with a lawyer:
. . . (c) a lawyer shall be responsible for conduct of such a person that would be a violation of the rules of professional conduct if:
(1) The lawyer orders or . . . ratifies the conduct;
(2) The lawyer is a partner in the law firm in which the person is employed, or has direct supervisory authority over the person, and knows of the conduct at a time when its consequences can be avoided or mitigated but fails to take remedial action.

In addition to the formal rules governing the paralegal-attorney association, there are other considerations that influence the alliance between the paralegal and the attorney.

First, a paralegal must strive to develop and maintain a good working relationship with the attorneys with whom he or she works. One area in which clarity is needed is in understanding the tasks assigned to the paralegal. Unless the assignment is simple, obvious and clear to both the attorney and paralegal, the assignment should be written. Writing the assignment allows both the paralegal and the attorney to focus accurately on the task at hand. It allows the paralegal to question the attorney as to the issue; it allows the attorney to rephrase or narrow the issue as necessary.

For example, if the attorney asks the paralegal to research the issue of immunity of city police officers for gross negligence before the client comes in for the interview, the paralegal should discuss the task with the attorney, write the assignment as he or she understands it, and read it back or show it to the attorney for agreement. By writing the assignment and showing it to the attorney, the paralegal and the attorney avoid any misunderstanding as to exactly what should be accomplished. Often when presented with the issue in writing, the attorney will add to or modify the assignment, saving valuable paralegal time as well as the client's money. If, during the research, the paralegal finds other issues he or she believes might be important, these should be noted in writing and discussed with the attorney. If the paralegal finds too much information, he or she should discuss with the attorney how to narrow the scope of the research. Written directions help to guarantee a mutual and accurate understanding of the assignment and an overall efficiency in the workplace.

Second, the paralegal should check with the attorney on a regular basis to update assignments. If the firm does not have regular weekly or biweekly meetings, the paralegal should schedule meetings with the attorney as necessary or talk informally with the attorney every day or two in order to review the status of all cases.

Third, the paralegal should keep a copy of all assignments given, including name of attorney, date assigned, date due, date completed, time estimated, and time spent. This will help the paralegal learn to manage time and to document the nature of the work. This technique is especially handy when the paralegal works for more than one attorney. An example appears in Exhibit 2.1.

Fourth, the paralegal should request an evaluation by the attorney on a regular basis. Evaluation areas should include research, writing, interviewing skills, ability to function harmoniously in the office, and analytical

Re: Carrie Weldon, Assignment Sheet

CLIENT	ATT.	ASSIGNMENT	HRS. EST.	HRS SP'NT	DATE ASS'D	DATE DUE	DATE FIN.
Weider, Harold	MSK	gov't/city immunity w/ re to police	5	7.5	1/1/yr	3/1/yr	3/1/yr

Exhibit 2.1 **Assignment Sheet**

ability. The attorney should note areas needing improvement as well as how such improvement will occur and be evaluated.

> **PRACTICE TIP:** As soon as your supervising attorney assigns you a case or task, write in detail what the attorney expects you to do and provide him or her with a copy. By doing this, the attorney can correct any misunderstanding as to the assignment and you can be certain to focus on the correct issue.

D. Finding the Relevant Law

1. Legal Theory

Although problems, like clients and witnesses, come in all shapes and sizes, you will usually have some idea of the nature of the legal theory involved before the interviewing process begins. When a person calls to arrange an interview, he or she usually discusses with the receptionist or an attorney the reason that prompted the call, for example, a business transaction, problems with a contract, a recent criminal charge for burglary, or divorce concerns.

Similarly, before you contact a witness, you are aware of the legal theory involved in the case. If you are unclear about the applicable law, discuss the matter with your supervising attorney to grasp the general nature of the problem.

A legal theory is the legal principle that establishes the rights and responsibilities of individuals. Breach of contract, negligence, assault, defamation, and trespass are examples of legal theories.

2. Legal Sources

Laws are enacted on the federal, state, county, municipal, and town levels. Sources of law include constitutions, statutes, rules, regulations, court decisions, agency opinions, treatises, executive orders, by-laws, ordinances, and charters. These sources can be found in a law library in a courthouse or law school, a college, a public library, or on the computer. Acquaint yourself with these sources.

When the federal or state legislature passes a law, it is printed in a special set of books called general laws or codes. Federal statutes and the Constitution of the United States of America are contained in the United States Code (official) or the United States Code Annotated (unofficial), or the United States Code Service (unofficial).

State laws and constitutions are contained in volumes called "general laws" like the Connecticut General Laws or "codes" like the District of Columbia Code. If one of these laws is challenged in court, the decision of the judges interpreting the law is reported in a series of books called "reporters." There are state, regional, and federal reporters. State and regional reporters generally print only appellate court decisions. Federal reporters print both trial court and appellate court decisions. The trial court decisions are reported in Federal Supplement (F. Supp.). The appellate court decisions are reported in Federal Reporter (F.), Federal Reporter 2d (F.2d), and Federal Reporter 3d (F.3d). A special set of volumes called Federal Rules Decisions (F.R.D.) reports those cases in which a court has interpreted a Federal Rule of Civil Procedure, Federal Rule of Criminal Procedure, Federal Rule of Evidence, or other rule.

If there is no statute on the subject, the controlling law is "case law," which is law made by judges, or "common law," which is law based on the unwritten law of England. Case law and common law will be found only in the state and federal reporters.

The volumes containing laws and statutes have indices to assist you in finding what you want. If you cannot find what you seek, try an encyclopedia or a digest, which lists legal issues in alphabetical and subject order. Also consider state and federal court rules and jury instructions.

Some of these sources, such as statutes and digests have pocket parts in the back of the book to update the bound volume. Occasionally the information is so voluminous that the pocket part is a separate volume. Always check the pocket part to have the most recent amendment or information.

A large percentage of municipal, county, and town laws are published in the state materials; it depends on your state. They are also available from the city or town clerk or local offices. (*See* Exhibit 2.2.)

3. Citators

To determine whether a statute or case has been reversed, modified, or changed in any way, or to locate additional law, use a citator. The best known is Shepard's Citations published by Shepard's/McGraw-Hill. Performing this operation is called "Shepardizing" and is critical to the research process because it tells whether the law you found is still good law. It can also lead you to cases that discuss, distinguish, limit, or expand the law you found.

SOURCES OF LAW	PRIMARY LOCATIONS	COMMENTS
FEDERAL CONSTITUTION	• United States Code • United States Code Annotated • United States Code Service	All federal laws and statutes
STATE CONSTITUTION	• State General Laws • State Code	All state laws and statutes
FEDERAL STATUTES	(Same as Fed. Const.)	Federal laws
FEDERAL REGULATIONS	• Code of Federal Regulations (CFR)	All federal regulations, e.g., Social Security
STATE REGULATIONS	• Code of Texas Regulations (CTR)	All state regulations, e.g., environmental
FEDERAL CASE LAW	• Federal Supplement (trial court) • Federal Reporter (appellate court)	Court decisions issued at the end of a trial or appeal
STATE CASE LAW	• State and Regional Reporter Series	Court decisions issued at the end of a trial or appeal
STATE STATUTES	• State General Laws • State Code	State laws
FEDERAL COMMON LAW	• Federal Supplement (trial court) • Federal Reporter (appellate court)	Judge-made law reported as court decisions
STATE COMMON LAW	• State and Regional Reporter Series	Judge-made law reported as court decisions
MUNICIPAL LAWS	• Charter, Ordinances, Regulations, By-laws	Laws passed by city council
TOWN LAWS	• Charter, Ordinances, Regulations, By-laws	Laws passed by town board/committee
COUNTY LAWS	• Charter, Ordinances, Regulations, By-laws	Laws passed by county board

Exhibit 2.2 **Sources and Locations**

Municipal, county, and town laws are frequently updated by the governing bodies. Notices appear in town offices and on hallway bulletin boards. Local newspapers publish the new laws as well as amendments to the old laws. If your work includes local legal issues, make a point to check frequently for notices of new laws and amendments to old laws.

4. Computer-Assisted Legal Research

All legal sources mentioned in the previous section and many other legally related materials can be found on the computer. If you need current information the computer is the best vehicle—although not always the cheapest—for research.

a. *LEXIS and Westlaw*

The two largest direct dial systems are LEXIS and Westlaw. Both are commercial full-text research tools. Both systems have state and federal materials, periodicals, business and industry information, practice materials, and public records and filings.

Large law firms have one or both systems; smaller firms might have one of them or neither. The systems are expensive to run; charges are passed on to the client. Although these systems are not generally found in public libraries, many colleges have them and you may be able to arrange access to use the system for research. Because the systems are costly, it is wise to focus your search in order to keep on-line time to a minimum.

Access information for a case, statute, regulation, law review article, or other legal material by typing the citation, by searching the selected database with certain terms that appear in the documents (Boolean query), or by using a natural language search (Freestyle for LEXIS and WIN for Westlaw). LawTALK permits certain Westlaw subscribers to search by voice command. Searches can be limited, edited, and run in different databases. Since the databases are updated daily, the material is current.

Shepardizing is accomplished by simply typing in the citation and pressing a button or clicking on an icon. A complete history of the case appears in an instant for your review or printing. (*See* Exhibit 2.3.)

b. *CD-ROM*

Another full-text research tool for state and federal statutes, cases, and regulations are CD-ROMs. Although material is not updated on a daily basis as with the online services, searching on a CD-ROM is much faster than the on-line services. Updates to CD-ROMs are usually provided quarterly, semi-annually, or annually, depending on the service. Many law firms have invested in CD-ROMs instead of purchasing additional state codes, regulations, and reporters.

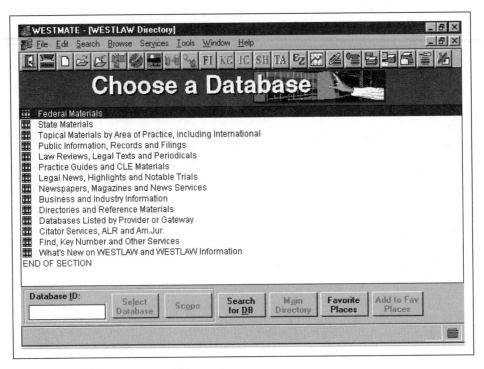

Exhibit 2.3 **WESTLAW Directory**

c. Internet

Legal resources available on the Internet are growing so rapidly that by time this book is published this information will be out of date. Some legal information formerly available only with an expensive subscription to an on-line service is now available free of charge on the Internet. Federal and state governments and educational institutions are moving rapidly to make extensive legal materials—codes, regulations, agency rulings, court rules, court decisions, and legislation—available to anyone with Internet access. A prime example is the Cornell Law School Legal Information Institute, which publishes a vast amount of state and federal legal materials; it also has an impressive index to other legal materials on the Internet. It is one of the most—if not the most—comprehensive free legal research sites on the Internet to date.

Another excellent example is the Government Printing Office Access system, which provides access to the Federal Register, Code of Federal Regulations, the Congressional Record, and other federal materials. All documents are free to print and save; the server provides full text and graphics.

Two full-text subscription services on the Internet are LOIS Law Library and Lawyers Legal Research. Search by words, parties, docket numbers, dates, attorneys' names, or cite. Or use Boolean logic, as with LEXIS and Westlaw. There are links to other cases cited in the original case; click on the cite to read that case before returning to the original case. Purchase on-line time for a year, a week, or a day.

LAW	ADDRESS
Ohio	http://www.sconet.ohio.gov/
Washington	http://www.washingtonstatehelps.com.courts/lawlinks.htm
New York	http://www.law.cornell.edu/ny/ctap/overview.html
California	http://www.courtinfo.ca.gov/
Texas	http://www.courts.state.tx.us/
Massachusetts (links to federal, state, SEC, GPO)	http://www.socialaw.com/
General sources (gopher menu)	gopher://gopher.law.cornell.edu/
Federal codes	http://law.house.gov/usc.htm
State statutes	http://www.findlaw.com/11stategov/index.html
Map to access federal opinions	http://www.ll.georgetown.edu:80/Fed-Ct/
U.S. Government (access cite)	http://access.gpo.gov/su_docs/aces/aaces001.html
Legal Information Institute (Cornell)	http://www.law.cornell.edu/tour.html

Exhibit 2.4 **Internet Sites for Legal Research (Representative)**

Any file downloaded from the Internet can contain a virus. Either install virus protection software or save the material to a blank disk (or both).

Representative Internet sites appear in Exhibit 2.4. If the site address has changed or is unavailable, use a search engine to access your location. See Chapter 8 for a discussion of sites and search engines.

E. Organizing the Law for the Interview

1. Preparing for the Litigation Interview

After you have located the law applicable to your legal issue, you should write out the elements. This can be done in any manner but one of the best methods is on a theory chart. A theory chart is a visual organization of the elements of the law in issue and the facts of your case. By creating one, you will find it easier to design the line of questioning. Theory charts are fluid; they can be modified to suit the case and may include the elements of the cause of action, defenses, sources of proof, applicable law, discovery, and statute of limitations. For example, the elements of negligence are duty, breach of duty, causation, and damages. (*See* Exhibit 2.5.)

In some instances there may be a printed form to guide your questioning. For example, if you are interviewing a client in order to draft a will, you may well use a form that has all the appropriate questions to ask or areas to cover. The questions on the form take into consideration the legal issues involved and are devised to have those issues addressed. Similarly with bankruptcy, some personal injury, and family cases, forms provide excellent, comprehensive questions for the initial interview. For many cases, however, there are no forms to guide the interview questions. In all cases, you should do enough research to determine which legal elements and defenses are important.

Consider the ice cream contract. Your supervising attorney has told you that the client, the town of Windale, represented by town counsel, is coming in for the initial interview. The town had a contract with an ice cream vendor, Danny's Incredible Edibles, to provide ice cream for the town's Fourth of July party. Danny's failed to deliver the ice cream on time and the town is unhappy with the way the company acted under the contract.

Negligence Action		
Client: _____		
Today's date: _____		
Date of incident: _____		
Statute of Limitations: _____		
ELEMENT	**SOURCE OF FACT/LAW**	**EVIDENCE**
1) Duty		
2) Breach of duty		
3) Causation		
4) Damages		

Exhibit 2.5 **Sample Theory Chart**

What does your client, Windale, have to prove to show a violation of the contract? There are several ways to locate relevant law. You can look to the annotated version of state laws under "contract"; that entry will refer you to the law and cases addressing contract issues. You could also look in the state digest to find the law.

Another way to educate yourself quickly is to look in the Model Jury Instructions for your jurisdiction. Jury instructions are statements of law that guide a jury in reaching a decision. Therefore, they are educational on the elements of proof necessary in a case. Jury instructions also include citations to case law in the event you want to research more.

A jury instruction in a breach of contract case in which there is no dispute as to the existence of the contract, but there is a dispute over whether the terms were breached, might be as follows:

> A contract is an agreement that is legally binding. In this case, the plaintiff and the defendant agree that they entered into a contract and that they are legally bound by that contract. You are being asked to determine whether their contract included a provision that required the defendant to [specify]. If you find that their contract did include that provision, you must then also decide whether the defendant "breached"—or violated in a significant way—that provision.

Model Jury Instructions for Use in the District Courts, 1988 ed. (Supp. 1989), Commonwealth of Massachusetts, District Court Department of the Trial Court.

The jury instruction specifies two elements to show a breach of contract. First, was there a particular provision of the contract that required performance on the defendant's part, and second, did the defendant violate that provision in a significant way? A possible defense, such as impossibility to the performance of the terms of the contract, should also be considered. Broken into distinct parts, the organization chart would look like Exhibit 2.6:

Contract Action				
Assumption: contract is legally binding				
PROVISION OF CONTRACT	REQUIRED COMPANY TO:	VIOLATION (BREACHED OCCURRED):	SO WHAT? (DAMAGES):	ANY DEFENSES?

Exhibit 2.6 **Organization Chart**

When you interview the client, you need to determine 1) the provisions of the contract that the parties had to perform; 2) what each provision required the parties to do; and 3) how the breach occurred. Although you may not have had the opportunity to review the contract before the interview, by researching the law and organizing the law into distinct factual predicates, you have an idea of the questions to ask.

During the interview, you learned by talking with the client and reviewing the contract that Danny's was to deliver 80 gallons of vanilla ice cream and assorted toppings on Saturday, July 4, between the hours of 1:00 P.M. and 2:00 P.M. You also learned that Danny's arrived with the ice cream at 3:45 P.M. at which time the town refused delivery because most families had gone home. Your client was unaware of any justification for Danny's failure. After the interview, you placed the information on the chart in Exhibit 2.7.

By studying the chart, you can see the relationship between the elements of the breach of contract and the facts that support each element. Usually a general reading of the law is an inadequate foundation for an interview. By using a chart and listing all the elements it is easy to determine

---

Contract Action

Client: Town of Windale

Date of interview: July 7 (year)

Date of incident: July 4 (year)

Statute of Limitations: 6 years

Assumption: Contract is legally binding

PROVISION OF CONTRACT	REQUIRED COMPANY TO:	VIOLATION (BREACHED OCCURRED):	SO WHAT? (DAMAGES):	ANY DEFENSES?
Para. 2.8 "Delivery of goods"	deliver to Client 80 gallons of vanilla ice cream on Saturday, July 4, between 1:00 P.M. and 3:00 P.M.	Company delivered ice cream at 3:45 P.M.	Client lost receipts in the amount of $600.00	

Exhibit 2.7 **Organization Chart**

whether you elicited all the necessary information, and, if so, whether the facts support the theory.

Had you not researched the law and noted what facts your client needed to show a breach, your questioning of the client may have been scattered. There is no question that without the preparation you would have eventually determined the issues; a follow-up interview, which would have been inefficient in terms of time and money, might have been required.

Organizational charts can vary in format, and each legal theory in a case warrants its own chart. Suppose you are handling the initial interview in the personal injury scenario described at the beginning of the chapter. Your client and his daughter were injured by a car that jumped the curb. One of the theories of relief is negligence.

Each element of the tort will spawn numerous questions, all of which must be addressed in detail. The elements of the tort of negligence are 1) duty to adhere to a standard of conduct; 2) failure to conform to the duty; 3) actual damages resulting from the failure to conform; 4) proximate (legal) cause.

Therefore, you need to establish 1) that there was an obligation on the part of the driver not to hit each pedestrian; 2) that the driver in fact hit the pedestrians; 3) that there were injuries to the pedestrians; and 4) that there was a connection between the "hitting" and the injury. You also want to establish whether any defenses, such as contributory or comparative negligence, might apply.

The completed organizational form in this case might appear as Exhibit 2.8.

In addition to the negligence chart, individual theory charts should be done for assault, battery, infliction of emotional distress, and any other applicable tort theories as well as all potential defenses. Although facts may be insufficient to support a particular theory, charts can help to resolve whether the issue should be pursued.

Make a chart for every interview you conduct. Although there are printed forms and detailed checklists available for extracting information for a variety of causes of action, do not use them unless you are confident you understand the legal theories and defenses involved. If you intend to use a form, review it and consider how each question pertains to the legal theories at issue. If you do not have an opportunity to prepare a chart before the interview, take copious notes and fill one in later.

2. Preparing for the Transaction Interview

Preparing for the transaction interview is analogous to preparing for the litigation interview in that you will generally have an idea of the nature of the help the client seeks prior to the interview. In the transaction interview, however, the focus is less on the legal theory of recovery or defense and more on the laws applicable to accomplish the client's goals. The theory chart, therefore, is inapplicable—at least initially—to this client.

Negligence Action

Client: Harold Madden _____

Date of interview: September 15, (year) _____

Date of incident: May 17, (year) _____

Statue of Limitations: 3 years _____

ELEMENT	SOURCE OF FACT/LAW	EVIDENCE	DEFENSES
1) Duty	common law/statute	cite to law	
2) Failure to conform to duty	car hit pedestrian/ client	witnesses (including client); physical injury	
3) Damages	injury to pedestrian	physical injury	
4) Causation	driver operating car that hit pedestrian/ client	physical evidence	

Exhibit 2.8 **Completed Organization Chart**

Use a different organizational tool that reflects the nature of the transaction and the client's needs. The organizational tool should reflect the issues and laws that affect the transaction.

Some transactions are quite uncomplicated—preparing a simple lease or real estate closing; for those you might use a checklist. Other transactions, involving complicated or multiple legal issues, necessitate a more comprehensive chart.

Consider our client, Maggie Winchon. She is interested in developing 250 acres of property (the "Hall" tract), part of which might be wetlands. She seeks your firm's advice on whether if purchased, the land could be developed expeditiously and without incident. She also wants to know whether the builder she has in mind is in good standing with the state agency with contractor oversight. What areas of law are involved? What steps would you take to find the laws associated with the matter? Legal areas include real property, contracts, business, and environmental. If you were to draft an organizational chart based on the information Ms. Winchon provided over the telephone, it might appear as Exhibit 2.9.

At the interview you would obtain additional information, including the location of the property, the client's time frame for development, and

| Client: Maggie Winchon |
| Date: Today |
| Subject: Development of Hall Tract |

ISSUES/LAWS	SOURCE
1) Determine site boundaries, access, possible easements.	Recorder of Deeds in county where property situated
2) Obtain zoning regulations including subdivision regs.; by-laws, ordinances.	city/town engineering dept and clerk/manager
3) Obtain other regulations.	varies
4) Determine if land protected as wetlands (state EPA).	city/town conservation committees; state environmental dept.
5) Determine if wildlife present and, if so, would it prevent/delay development (Endangered Species Act).	city/town conservation committees; state environmental dept.
6) Obtain building regulations.	city/town engineering dept.
7) Obtain information re: builder.	city/town/state

Exhibit 2.9 **Organizational Chart**

the name of the builder she wants to use. With that information, you could begin your inquiry.

SUMMARY

Preparing for the interview involves understanding where to find the law and how to organize the elements of the particular legal theory into a usable format. Placing pertinent elements on a theory chart is an ideal way to design your line of questioning to obtain the information you need. Make a chart for every interview you conduct and for every separate legal theory in a case. Even if printed forms are available and apparently adequate, the chart establishes the legal theory firmly in your mind. If you are preparing for a transaction interview, use a different type of organizational chart focusing on the client's needs, the issues, and the law.

Key Terms

Boolean query
By-laws
Case law
CD-ROM
Charter
Citator
Code
Common law
Contract
Digest
Encyclopedia
Internet
Jury instruction

Legal theory
LEXIS
Natural language
Negligence
Ordinance
Pocket part
Regulations
Reporter
Shepard's
Statute
Westlaw
Work product

REVIEW QUESTIONS

1. An interview has been scheduled for a client whose case involves a neighbor who might have trespassed on your client's property. What sources of law would you use to learn about trespass in your jurisdiction?

2. What considerations influence the relationship between the attorney and the paralegal? What steps can a paralegal take to develop a strong working relationship with the attorney?

3. What is the purpose of a theory chart? How would you organize one for the tort of battery? Defamation? Intentional infliction of emotional distress?

4. What form of government does your town/city/county have? Are there by-laws? Ordinances? Charters?

5. Under what circumstances is an attorney not responsible for the activities of a paralegal?

6. What is a citator? How does it work? What purpose does it serve?

7. What are the sources of law in your jurisdiction? How many different ways can you access them?

CHAPTER EXERCISES

Exercise 2-1: Assume the following individuals seek legal help from your office:

1. A 58-year-old woman who says she was sexually harassed at work.
2. A 78-year-old great-grandfather who wants to revise his will.
3. A 27-year-old computer programmer who complains of carpel tunnel syndrome.
4. A local business woman who wants to purchase several abandoned downtown buildings for development.

Break into groups of two or three and brainstorm a list of questions you would want to know for each situation.

Exercise 2-2: Pair with another student: one assumes the role of the attorney, the other, the paralegal. The attorney asks the paralegal to research the issue of police brutality as it pertains to security guards for an upcoming interview with a new client. The paralegal should phrase the issue in writing and give it to the attorney. What additional information would you like from the attorney to help clarify your research? Revise the assignment to reflect the issue. Discuss it with your partner.

Reverse roles and repeat the exercise with the attorney asking the paralegal to research the issue of property distribution between two people who never married for an upcoming interview with a new client, the issue of property distribution between two people who never married. What additional information would you like from the attorney to help clarify your research? Revise the assignment to reflect the issue. Discuss it with your partner.

Exercise 2-3: Using the organizational format set out above, what questions need to be asked to support the allegations of negligence in the following example: Dr. Hawes performed abdominal surgery on your client, John Marks, last month. Several weeks after the surgery, Marks was readmitted to the hospital with severe abdominal pain. An examination showed that a small surgical clamp remained in Marks's abdominal cavity. It was removed by emergency surgery; Marks was hospitalized an additional three weeks. He wants to sue Dr. Hawes. List the elements of negligence on one side of a piece of paper. Across from each element, write what fact could support the element.

EXTRA: Find your jurisdiction's definition of negligence in the books or through CALR.

Exercise 2-4: The following are jury instructions involving negligence resulting in property damage. Assume you are about to interview a new client whose house was damaged when her neighbor carelessly cut down a tree that fell onto your client's house. Prepare an organizational theory chart to assist in the interview. From your chart make a list of questions to ask the client for each element.

A representative jury instruction for negligence is as follows:

In this case the plaintiff claims that he (she) suffered some damage to his (her) property as a result of the defendant's negligence. The defendant denies that he (she) was negligent.

The law provides that if a person owes someone else a duty to be reasonably careful, but is negligent in fulfilling that duty and thereby causes the other person some property damage, the negligent person must compensate the victim of his (her) negligence for that damage.

The plaintiff may recover on this claim if, and only if, he (she) proves that four things are more likely than not:

First: That the defendant had a duty to take reasonable care to avoid causing property damage to someone in the plaintiff's position;

Second: That the defendant was negligent in fulfilling that duty;

Third: That the defendant's negligence caused some damage to the plaintiff's property; and

Fourth: The plaintiff must prove the extent or amount of that damage.

The first thing the plaintiff must prove is that the defendant had a duty to take reasonable care to avoid causing damage to the property of someone in the plaintiff's position.

Model Jury Instructions for Use in the District Courts, 1988 ed. (Supp. 1989), Commonwealth of Massachusetts, District Court Department of the Trial Court.

Exercise 2-5: Following the directions from the exercise above, prepare a sheet listing the elements for each of the following actions in your state. Use the volumes or CALR:

1) Assault
2) Battery
3) Trespass
4) Breach of contract
5) Intentional infliction of emotional distress

Exercise 2-6: Using any search vehicle on the Internet, locate the following cites:

1) Your state court system
2) Your state legislative system
3) The federal statutes
4) The federal constitution

3

Interviewing Skills

CHAPTER OBJECTIVES

This chapter discusses

- structuring an interview;
- questioning and listening skills;
- telephone interviews;
- dynamics of communication;
- special circumstances.

A. Structuring the Interview

Construct the initial part of the interview so as to gain an insight into the person's concerns. Witnesses and clients usually want to talk about what brings them to a law office, whether it is an event or series of events underlying litigation or an assortment of needs forming the basis of a transaction. What they say at the outset of an interview, how they order their facts, and how they build their narrative often exposes what is important to them and reveals much about their needs and character.

For a client, introductory questions like "Why don't you tell me what brought you here today?" and "How can I help you?" allow him or her to relax and "tell the story." During this period listen carefully to ascertain what legal issues are involved and what nonlegal concerns the client might have. Interruptions, other than to steer a wandering or rambling client back to the main story, are inadvisable because you want as broad a picture as the client will paint. It is during this initial talking that you might hear issues or concerns that you did not expect.

For a witness, the questions are focused to expand, test, and corroborate the information you received from the client. A witness to an event will have been told generally what information is being sought in an interview. The witness will be prepared to tell what she or he knows or saw but will also need to be guided in order to make most efficient use of the available time.

It is important to recognize the role of the person being interviewed in a transaction or in litigation and to understand, before the interview, how best to structure the interview of this particular person. It is also important to consider what kind of information you want to impart to the person being interviewed. With either a witness or client, if an interview is structured carefully you will be able to control the flow of the interview so that you obtain necessary information, to get the full measure of the person's character and needs and to impart relevant and useful information.

Home Improvement Contract

Morgan and Rita Downey hired Rich Mentor, a small-scale home improvement contractor to enclose their side porch before their daughter's late summer wedding. Mentor had done nice work for some friends of theirs the year before. The Downeys gave him a $5,000 down payment on a total contract price of $10,000. There was nothing in writing. The porch was to be finished in six weeks, in time for the wedding. When Mentor did not start the first week as promised, the Downeys tried to contact him but were unsuccessful. Sometime later, Morgan Downey ran into Mentor by accident. When he asked about the work, Mentor told him he was too busy for the job and for Downey to "get lost; go get a lawyer." The Downeys then hired another contractor to do the job. The Downeys were recommended to your firm by a neighbor. They would like Mentor to return their $5,000.

How should you structure the interview of the Downeys? What legal issues are involved? What personal issues do the Downeys have? How will you know when you have covered the issues? How do you frame the questions?

B. Asking Questions

1. Introduction

People tend to talk in conclusions ("She was driving way too fast." "He stole my painting." "I need a will, not a trust."). An inexperienced or unskilled interviewer adopts the person's conclusions and lets those conclusions provide the basis for additional conclusions.

A skilled interviewer draws out the facts on which the person bases his or her conclusions and uses the facts to support a legal theory or conclusion—whether it matches the person's conclusion or not. In order to be effective in drawing out the necessary information, the skilled interviewer must know the right question to ask and when to ask it.

2. Types of Questions

Paralegals pose questions to clients and witnesses to obtain information. The extent to which you are able to do an effective job for your client depends on the accuracy and reliability of the information you receive from the client and the witnesses. This information is reiterated in pleadings and other court documents, in contracts, in articles of incorporation, and in wills and trusts, to name just a few sources. The information must be correct and precise. The way we ask a question, however, can greatly influence both the content and accuracy of the answer.

Questions may be divided into two main types: Nonleading and Leading.

a. Nonleading Questions

A nonleading question is one that does not suggest the answer in the question. In other words, the person is not "led" to an answer. Open, closed, direct, and indirect questions are types of nonleading questions. Questions posed to a witness on direct examination in a courtroom are generally nonleading questions. Because the answer is not suggested in the question, a nonleading question may produce more reliable information than a leading question. An example of a nonleading question is: "What was the weather like the day of the accident?" In this example, before responding, the client must consider all "weather" possibilities: clear, cloudy, dark, light, raining, snowing, sleeting, hailing, windy, etc. In answering the question, the client must eliminate many possibilities and select one or more descriptions. The question has forced the client to focus on "weather" without suggesting any particular weather condition as the outcome.

Nonleading questions may be open ("Tell me what the weather was like that day.") or closed ("Was the sky clear or cloudy?"), direct ("What color was the sky?") or indirect ("Did you see a weather report that day?").

i. Open

An open question invites a broad response with little structure and allows the person more leeway in answering. The interviewer will be given more information to sort through in order to obtain the information important to the case. Open questions give the interviewer insight into the subject's ability to articulate and into his or her knowledge of the situation. Open questions give the client the opportunity to address issues that are important to him or her. Samples of open questions include:

"How can I help you?"
"Tell me what happened."
"Could you describe the accident?"

ii.   Closed

Closed questions invite a more specific response and focus on a particular subject. They may be used to commit a witness to a particular detail.
Examples of closed questions include:

"Are you positive it was raining hard at the time of the accident?"
"Are you sure the car was bright yellow?"
"What happened at the party?"

Closed questions may also be used to flesh out a person's response
to open questions and to focus the person's recall of a situation to elicit
clear, specific, and often demonstrative details. For example:

"You've said it was raining that day."
["Yes."]
"Was it a hard rain?"
["Yes."]
"Did it rain all day?"
["Yes."]
"Was the rain constant or intermittent?"
["Constant."]

Compare the information elicited by the following two different questions:

Closed

Paralegal: Did you know there was a warrant outstanding for your arrest?
Client: No.

Open

Paralegal: How did you find out there was an outstanding warrant for
     your arrest?
Client: I didn't know. I was just walking down the street with my friend
     and next thing I knew the cops pulled up, grabbed me, and pushed
     my face into the sidewalk. They twisted my arm up behind me hard
     and I heard a "pop." I guess that's when it broke.

iii.   Direct

Direct questions seek particular information and are useful to obtain
information to fill in the factual landscape. Examples include:

"How many people were at the party?"
"What time did you arrive?"
"What was the name of the surgeon?"
"How many officers were there?"

b. Leading Questions

Leading questions control the flow and content of answers. Leading questions contain or suggest the answer in the question. Therein lies the potential for danger. Examples of leading questions are:

"Wasn't it raining the day of the accident?"
"The car was blue, wasn't it?"

The first question, instead of requiring the person to focus on various weather conditions, obliges him or her to consider one condition—rain— and to agree or disagree with the question. If in this instance the answer is "no," the interviewer has learned only that it was not raining, not what the weather was the day of the accident. In the second question, the interviewer has focused the person's memory on one color—blue—and will likely receive a limited response. The person has no incentive to consider the color. Leading questions may influence an answer tending to produce less accurate, less reliable information.

In some interviewing settings, leading questions are appropriate. If a leading question will not taint the accuracy of the answer, the question may be appropriate. In other words, if the interviewer already knows facts supporting the question—for example if the client has given information previously—little harm will result from suggesting the answer. ("Mrs. Smith, you have two daughters, is that correct?") Technically, this is a leading question. But because the interviewer obtained the information earlier, there is little likelihood that the client will be "led" to an inaccurate answer. This technique can be useful when an interviewer wants to "lock in" the answer to a particular question, such as when a reluctant witness is being questioned about a prior statement.

If an attorney is examining his own witness on the stand in a court-room, leading questions are generally not allowed. When opposing counsel cross-examines the witness, however, the rules are different and she may ask leading questions, that is, she may suggest the answer in the question. In fact, conventional wisdom dictates that cross-examination be conducted with leading questions.

Compare "Was the car blue?" with "What color was the car?"

Leading question   >   suggests answer   >   unreliable information

Nonleading question   >   does not suggest answer   >   reliable information

---

Exhibit 3.1 **Leading vs. Nonleading Questions**

The following model interview provides a glimpse of the appropriate use of a variety of questions. The issue is whether or not a civil action in either tort or contract by our clients, the Downeys, against a home improvement contractor will be barred by the statute of limitations. Determining that requires the interviewer obtain a firm date for the legal wrongs alleged by the clients. Mr. Downey has told the interviewer that he contracted with a small-scale home improvement contractor to enclose a side porch. He made a $5,000 downpayment on a total contract price of $10,000 with the understanding that his porch would be finished in six weeks. He can tell you when he made the downpayment, but cannot remember the date when, without having done any work, the contractor told him he was too busy to do the job and suggested he get a lawyer. The Downeys hired another contractor who finished the job; they have only recently been told that they can sue for return of their downpayment. Unfortunately, several years have passed.

Before the interview, the paralegal researched possible causes of action and learned that the facts given by Mr. Downey over the telephone could support a civil suit grounded in both tort and contract theories. Mr. Downey, however, neglected to say over the phone that several years have passed since the events and, when this fact is revealed during the interview, the paralegal realizes that it is critical to determine as accurately as possible the date when the contractor told the client he would not do the job.

Model Interview
Initial Interview of Morgan Downey, September 11, (year)

Paralegal: You told me on the phone the first contractor told you he was not going to do any work. Could you tell me more about that?

Client: Yeah, as I said, I gave him the downpayment for materials and advance wages for his guys. Weeks went by and he never showed up . . . [Interview continues; client explains the history of how he found and hired the contractor, how he could not get him to start the job, and finally how he was told, in an insulting manner, that the work wasn't going to get done.]

Paralegal: Okay, I think I understand how frustrated you must have been when you couldn't get him to come and do the work, and then he told you he wasn't going to do the work, or return your money. Let me get a few details from you before we continue. Could you tell me when he told you he wasn't going to do the job?

Client: Yes, it was some time ago.

Paralegal: Was it last year?

Client: No, it was a year or two before that. I haven't thought about this for a while. I didn't think I could do anything about it.

Paralegal: I see. It is important that we find out when this happened in order to decide what legal options may be available to you. We know from your check when you made the downpayment. Did you pay him at the same time you agreed to have him do the work?

Client: Yes, he came out and looked at the job one day and gave me a ballpark estimate. A few days later he came out and showed me a written estimate that listed materials and showed the costs. Said he'd start in a week or two after that, as soon as we got him the money, which we did that night because we wanted to have the porch finished for August when our daughter got married.

Paralegal: Do you recall the date you gave him the downpayment? You said it was a year or two before last. That would be 1995.

Client: Yes, I think that's right.

Paralegal: Did you sign a contract?

Client: No. I know we should have, but he was recommended by a friend and, well, I just trust people.

Paralegal: Okay, so other than the undated estimate and the check there is nothing in writing. How did you make the downpayment?

Client: I wrote him a check for it.

Paralegal: Do you keep your checks?

Client: Yes, I brought it along. It's dated March 2, 1995 [hands the paralegal the check]. I did talk to the bank, but they said they couldn't help me since they had already paid the check.

Paralegal: Yes, I see.

Client: Well, I'm trying to remember. I know it was after my birthday; I turned 50 that May, May 28.

Paralegal: Okay. Do you remember whether it was before or after the Fourth of July?

Client: I think it was before the Fourth of July because I remember driving by a neighbor's and seeing his truck parked on the street. I went and talked to him. He was so nasty about it.

Paralegal: Why do you think it was before the Fourth?

Client: I remember that we had a party on the Fourth and we used our new gas grill. I remember telling one of our guests about how he treated me and commenting that it would be a long time before I could look at the porch or the grill without getting upset.

Paralegal: Why do you say the grill?

Client: I was on my way home from buying the grill as a surprise for the family, thinking we could use it on the deck we planned for the new enclosed porch when I ran into the guy. The whole thing just left me with such a bad feeling.

Paralegal: Well, I'm looking for information that might confirm the date.

Client: Right. Well, I'm certain that the day I bought the grill was the same day I ran into him and he was so nasty to me. I thought about him every time I used the grill.

Paralegal: How long before the Fourth did you buy the grill?

Client: I'm trying to remember exactly.

Paralegal: Was it more like days or months?

Client: I think it was June or July, but I'm not sure. I know it was hot, real hot, around 95 degrees.

Paralegal: When you bought the grill, how did you pay for it?

Client: Gee, I'm not sure.

Paralegal: Well, how much did it cost?

Client: It was around $450.00.

Paralegal: Well, how would you have paid for it?

Client: I don't remember.

Paralegal: How do you usually pay for things that cost several hundred dollars?

Client: Well, let me think. It wouldn't have been cash for that amount. It must have been a charge card because I have one of those insurance policies on the card and I like to use it for big-ticket purchases.

Paralegal: Do you keep records of your payments, your credit card statements?

Client: I'm sure I do. I hope that I have them that far back.

Paralegal: Do you keep warranty information or a file on appliances or these kinds of purchases?

Client: Oh, I do, I put them in my desk drawer at home. I keep all those receipts too.

Paralegal: Well, proof of payment will establish the date you purchased the grill. So if you happen to have a document, a receipt from the store, a canceled check, a notation in your check register or a credit card receipt, that would be helpful.

Client: I'm sure I could find one of those.

The first question seeks general information about the contractor and the work. It elicits a general answer. The questions that follow pin down the year but the date remains unclear. The paralegal then establishes that it was after the client's fiftieth birthday and before the July Fourth holiday that the contractor said he would not do the job. To ascertain the correct date, the paralegal helps the client focus on details, in this case the date the grill was purchased. The client believes he has information—namely a credit card statement or a receipt reflecting the date of purchase of the grill. These kinds of seemingly insignificant but relevant and verifiable details often add the color of irrefutable truth to a client's story.

PRACTICE TIP: Keep calendars from previous years for reference. If you don't have one you need, your computer or library does.

In any case with the potential for litigation, a client's ability to recall specific facts and details, such as dates and times, is critical. As illustrated above, often a client needs assistance in remembering such details. Skillful and effective interviewing utilizing a blend of questions offers such assistance.

Just as no two people are alike, no two clients or witnesses are alike.

A question that may prompt an outpouring of information from one will get precious little from another. An effective interviewer uses a combination of open, closed, direct, indirect, and occasionally leading questions to elicit all necessary information.

3. Silence

Because silence makes many people uncomfortable, a person may talk to fill a void. Many people also want to tell what they know about a given topic and will respond to silence by filling it with volunteered information. Silence can help to draw out important information and should be considered one of the arrows in your interviewing quiver.

4. Follow-up Questions

As noted, people tend to use conclusory language. People also tend to make judgments. ("He never was a good doctor/driver/accountant anyway." Or, "She stole Mother's money when Mother was in the hospital.") Because you need objective, accurate information, a statement that concludes, generalizes, judges, or contains hearsay must be followed by a series of probative questions. Occasionally no additional useful information will be obtained; usually, however, by asking follow-up questions, the matter can be clarified.

If probing a client's or witness's conclusions elicits hostility or a confrontational response ("Don't you think it's a crime to take money from your mother when she's in the hospital?"), an effective interviewer will patiently validate the person's concerns but say that it is important for the interviewer to have all the facts before arriving at such a conclusion because it is the attorney's and paralegal's responsibility to make sure that all the elements alleged can be proven. Such a response refocuses the roles and purpose of the interviewer and produces facts, not conclusions.

After you have a grasp of the legal area involved, make two lists—one of the topics you need to cover and another of the questions you need to ask to obtain the necessary information. When the person has given you an overview of the case (in response to your nonleading, open questioning), it is time to fill in the information holes by asking direct or closed questions and to follow up answers with questions designed to probe for detail.

For each answer given, you must ask yourself:

1) Does it make sense? Is it logical?
2) Is this answer consistent with earlier answers?
3) Where does it fit in the facts?
4) What element of the substantive law does it support?
5) Can this answer be corroborated or supported by other sources? (Can the client provide the corroboration or the source?)

5.   Obtaining the Chronology

In some instances it is necessary to elicit information concerning a series of events about which your client has knowledge. Usually this is most easily done if you can obtain a time-line, a series of facts in chronological order. The establishment of a time-line is usually attempted after the client has talked generally about the case and his or her concerns. The general overview provides a background for the time-line and allows the client to tell you what is important to him before you focus on the chronology.

For example, suppose your client was pulled over by the police while driving home from a party at which alcohol had been served. In response to "Tell me what happened," the client relates his concern about being stopped by the police, how it will affect his job, his family, and what the punishment might be. Then the client may begin the story at the moment the police pulled him over. Yet the facts of what happened before police involvement are critical, especially with regard to the consumption of alcohol. Therefore, the interview will be more productive if you have the client start at the beginning, when he arrived at the party, or perhaps even before, depending on the circumstances.

Eliciting information in a chronological order might not always be as easy as it seems. Clients may skip ahead to give other information they see as pertinent. In the event this happens, you must gently guide the client back to the time in question. An example follows:

Paralegal: Could you tell me what time you arrived at the party?
Client: Yes, it was around 9:00 P.M.
Paralegal: You seem sure about the time—can you tell me why?
Client: Oh, sure. I got off work at 8:30 that night. I stopped at the package store to buy a bottle of wine, which took about ten minutes, and then I went straight to the party. It's about a 15-minute drive to Bill's house.
Paralegal: So you went straight from work to the party except for a ten-minute stop at the liquor store, correct?
Client: Yes. But the police had no reason to stop me—they can't do that, can they?
Paralegal: Whether or not the police had a reason to stop you is a very important issue; however, that will be up to you and the attorney to discuss. My job is to gather the facts that will help the attorney to make that decision. For now, let's go back to the time you arrived at the party.

The paralegal acknowledges the importance of the question raised, but guides the client back to the chronology. It is important always to return to the time-line to be certain no information is omitted.

As important as a time-line might be, it is equally important that your client be able to discuss freely issues of importance to him or her. Frequently a client wandering off track provides information you had not requested. If this happens, guide the client back to the chronology, but make a note to return to the subject.

Paralegal: When you spoke to the doctor, what did he tell you about your daughter's condition?

Client: Well, he just said that she was conscious, that the operation went as well as could be expected for a little kid who was hit by a car, but there might be some problems—but the nurse had already told us that there were no problems, that she was doing fine. She said that . . .

Paralegal: Mr. Madden, I'm sorry to interrupt but I want to back up for a moment so I don't miss anything the doctor said. What the nurse said is important and I'll make a note to be sure we get back to that, but right now I'd like to finish what the doctor said.

Time-lines are as important to obtain from witnesses as from clients. A client's time-line illustrates a comprehensive story without any voids. A witness's time-line validates the client's chronology, as well as chronologies of other witnesses, through unabridged details. When the time-lines of the client and witnesses are incompatible, additional investigation is required to determine the correct sequence of events. Using the previous example of the party, assume a witness who was at the party states your client arrived at 7:30 P.M., conflicting with the client's statement that he arrived at 9:00 P.M. This detail is important in terms of the length of time client had to consume alcohol. Additional probing is necessary. Questions for the client might include how he is certain he worked until 8:30 P.M. that day; whether he has a time card; whether there is someone at work who might remember. Questions for the witness might include how he determined the time the client arrived—was it his watch or a clock in the house; what time did the witness arrive and how long had he been there before the client arrived; and what was his consumption of alcohol.

Whenever a chronology of events is important to the case, prepare a time-line after the initial client interview and before you begin interviewing witnesses. When you interview witnesses, probe for details sufficient to establish the time of events, whether it conflicts with or corroborates your client's chronology. Request external documentation such as ATM slips, credit card receipts, register receipts, computer calendar print-outs, entertainment (movie, amusement park, swimming pool) receipts, and transportation (bus, train, plane, toll, ferry) receipts, to corroborate statements.

C. Keeping It Simple

Paralegals have a distinct advantage over attorneys in terms of using clear, plain language because they have not had the legal jargon drilled into their heads for three years. Nevertheless, it is important to avoid the use of legal language when interviewing. If you talk with a person about the

complaint, answer, interrogatories, discovery, filing, or statute of limitations, he will probably not understand what you mean. Further, legal terms
are terms of art and may have a meaning in daily usage different from their
legal meaning. Often a person will assume he understands the meaning of
a legal term when in fact he does not. Moreover, people are sometimes
too embarrassed to ask what the terminology means. This situation might
leave the interviewer with the mistaken impression that the person understands the meaning of the terms.

Interviews should be conducted in plain language, without talking
down to a client or witness. Legal terms may be used so long as they are
explained, or if the person already understands them. Care should be
taken to ensure that the person really understands what has been said.
Every substantive area of law has its own peculiar language. Although
you will not usually counsel clients or prepare witnesses using legal terms,
you must familiarize yourself well enough with the terminology to define
and explain it to them.

D. Listening to Your Client

1. Listening Effectively

Listening accurately is one of the most difficult tasks and most important responsibilities a paralegal must accomplish. As an equation, we
might say that "listening equals hearing plus understanding." In listening,
there are implications made, inferences drawn, and conclusions reached
often without information sufficient to support them.

There are several other kinds of listening techniques. The following
section is devoted to two types of listening: active and passive.

2. Active Listening

Active listening is a method of encouraging a person, usually a client,
to become an active participant in the interviewing process. This is accomplished when a paralegal empathizes with the client without judging a
response. Because most clients have nonlegal concerns in addition to legal
ones, a paralegal must be prepared not only for a straight factual response,
but for one laden with emotion as well.

By using active listening, a paralegal can support, without judging,
what a client says. Study the following three responses to the client's
statement:

Mrs. Williams: I called our daughter, Miriam, last week to tell her about
    the new wills and so forth we were writing to make sure our grandchil-
    dren would attend college. Well, she doesn't have any children—I
    didn't think she'd mind so much—she earns so much money—but

she was furious! Things just got worse when I told her I was leaving my diamond broach to her brother, Mitchell. She said she regretted having done anything for me over the years and that from now on, I could just depend on Mitchell and my grandchildren for my needs. I haven't been able to sleep—maybe we're not doing the right thing.

Paralegal:
1) Don't worry about her. I'm sure she'll get over it; sounds like she has her own set of problems.
2) How rude. Who does she think she is anyway?
3) It sounds like you were really upset!

In Answer #1 the paralegal patronizes and plays amateur psychologist. Without justification the paralegal devises a set of problems for the daughter and makes it difficult for the client to formulate a response. If the client agrees with the paralegal, she validates the paralegal's conclusion that her daughter has problems. If she disagrees with the paralegal, she is nonetheless in the uncomfortable position of having to defend her daughter. There is no easy way out.

In Answer #2 the paralegal criticizes the daughter and her actions and places the client in an awkward position.

In Answer #3 the paralegal exhibits "active" listening. He listens to the client and mirrors her feelings in a nonjudgmental way. The answer allows the client to state her feelings and continue with the interview.

Resist the urge to play amateur psychologist, to criticize the other person involved in the conversation, or to impose your own judgment on a client's statement. Your job is to elicit and develop information by listening to your client. Stay professional.

Active listening encourages accuracy and truthfulness. By remaining nonjudgmental, you can be reasonably certain that the subject is not supplying you information he or she thinks you want to hear. Most people like to please by giving you information they think you want or need. Sometimes, people might attempt to manipulate the questioning by telling you what they believe will be the most helpful for the case. For example, in the dialogue above, Mrs. Williams is relaying a conversation she had with her daughter who was upset about her decision to leave the jewelry to her son. She has not given you any information to lead you to conclude that she is not leaving anything to her daughter, that her daughter is a bad person, or that she and her daughter don't love each other. If you judge the daughter and denigrate her, you run the risk of jeopardizing the rapport you have established with the client. The client may trust you less and may seek to give answers she thinks you want simply in order to please you. Furthermore, the client may become alienated or uncomfortable to the point that she takes her case to another firm.

3. Passive Listening

Like active listening, passive listening also encourages a person to divulge information without judgment or manipulation on the paralegal's part. Passive listening techniques include looking up from your notes to make eye contact with the subject, a nod of the head, a smile, a soft "uh huh," a "please go on," or "continue." Passive listening invites a response without substantial verbal interference. As a general rule, if you are talking, your subject is not, and if your subject is not talking, you are not learning any information. If a person is providing a chronology of an event or general information and is staying focused, passive listening is appropriate.

E.   Controlling the Interview

Few people interrupt attorneys or paralegals, but you must be prepared for the one who does. Two types of control apply to interviews: floor control and topic control. Both are important because you must elicit the information in the time allotted for the interview. Having control of the floor means keeping the interview orderly and on time. Attorneys and paralegals generally maintain control of the floor by simply interrupting the person talking. Without floor control, a client or witness can talk on and on without direction. If the interview involves multiple clients or witnesses, maintaining floor control is critical to an efficient interview. In order to elicit the necessary information in the most efficient manner, maintain control of the floor.

Topic control is simply keeping the client or witness focused on the subject at hand. Some clients digress to other subjects, usually another concern or interest they have. Keep the focus on the topic by politely interrupting and returning to the discussion topic.

Occasionally, though, people will need to talk a bit to feel comfortable. Give a little room; listen to them; they will tell you something about themselves.

F.   Telephone Interviews

Although considerable time is devoted to understanding the personal interview, much interviewing, especially that of witnesses, is done over the telephone.

1.   Preparation

Once again, the focus is preparation. Before you place the call, have the case file, especially the theory sheet, in front of you. Draft a list of questions to ask. If you do not have specific questions, what general areas are important? If you imagined that a witness will give you the best information possible for your client, what information would that be?

When you call, identify yourself, your position and the reason for your call. Record the date, time, and length of the call, the witness's name and telephone number. If you are calling from a phone that has call-waiting, avoid distraction by disabling it before you place the call, since interference from an incoming call may be heard by the witness. You may want to ask the person you are interviewing if she or he has call-waiting and ask them to disable it as well.

When you call a client or witness it is a good practice to make sure she or he has time to talk to you without interruption or other distractions. Common courtesy goes a long way toward building alliances. If you are calling a reluctant or elusive witness and you get her or him on the phone, seize the time, but be polite, firm, and persistent.

2. Disadvantages

Because you cannot see the other person, there is no body language to read. You cannot see whether the body position is open and receptive to your questions or closed in defiance or distrust of your questions. You cannot see eye movement, hand gestures, or facial expressions. You cannot see clothes to determine whether the witness cares about appearance, whether the witness is well dressed or poorly dressed. You are unaware of how that witness will look on the witness stand.

You also must find a way to authenticate the voice on the other end of the telephone. Should your interview become necessary evidence in a hearing or trial, it will not be admissible unless you can authenticate the call and identify the person you spoke to with a degree of certainty. Before engaging in a telephone interview with an important witness or a client whose voice you do not know well, discuss the interview with your supervising attorney.

3. Advantages

Telephone interviewing is efficient in terms of time and money. It is easy to take copious notes.

4. Caveats

Avoid using a speaker phone even if the person says he or she is alone; you do not know whether anyone else is present or if anyone walks in during the call. If you have someone else listening to or witnessing the interview, it is good practice to identify that person.

Under no circumstances should a paralegal ever electronically monitor or record a telephone call without the explicit knowledge and consent of the supervising attorney and the consent of the person being recorded. Recording a telephone conversation can involve violations of state and federal law and can adversely affect the outcome of a case—or impact a career.

5.   Considerations

How would you describe the witness's tone? Is it pleasant? Does he sound agreeable? What about language, manner of speech? Is he cooperating in answering your questions? Is he offering information? Does he sound angry? Is this someone with whom we want to schedule a follow-up personal interview? Someone we might call as a witness? Record this information in the form of a memorandum to the file and provide a copy to your supervising attorney. Memoranda to the file are discussed in Chapter 6.

G.   Dynamics of Communication

1.   Assumptions

Clear communication with a client or witness is imperative to the delivery of effective legal services. Yet our ability to communicate with a client or a witness is affected by a number of considerations. Making assumptions, holding stereotypical views, or preconceived notions about people or things are perils threatening clear communication. Consider this old riddle:

> A child was riding her bike when she was hit by a car. Her father rushed her to the emergency room. When they wheeled her into surgery, the surgeon cried, "I can't operate on this child, she's my daughter!"

If you assume surgeons are male, the riddle strikes a dissonant chord. The surgeon is female. Our stereotypical view that surgeons are male prevents us, at least initially, from arriving at the correct answer.

Using a legal example, if your firm represents a client charged with burglary, and the client "admits" the crime, "Yeah, I'm guilty. I did it!" you cannot assume the client is right. Burglary is the 1) entering of a 2) dwelling 3) in the nighttime 4) with the intent to commit a felony. The client may have been caught in the building, but the client's conclusion of guilt is not the consequence of a complete factual and legal analysis of the specific elements. A careful investigation may reveal a missing element, for example, the building was not a "dwelling house," the entry occurred during the daylight hours, or the client did not have the requisite felonious intent on entering the building.

Similarly, if your client has admitted to the police that she stabbed her spouse to death, do not let your preconceived notion convince you that her confession has sealed her fate and that therefore there is nothing to investigate. You may learn, indeed you have an obligation to learn, whether she acted in self-defense.

2. Nonverbal Communication

It is estimated by persons who study kinesics—the relationship between body movement and speech—that over 60 percent of communication is nonverbal. Rolling eyes upward, frowning, smiling, touching fingertips together, touching one's nose with a finger during conversation, all represent examples of kinesics. Correctly reading a person's body language during an interview offers insight into their thoughts, opinions, personality, and even their truthfulness.

A person who feels uncomfortable, threatened, intimidated or is lying might

> fail to make eye contact;
> mumble, or talk to the floor;
> cross his or her arms in front;
> touch a finger to his or her nose; or
> stay physically distant from the interviewer.

A person who feels comfortable might:

> make eye contact;
> speak clearly and audibly;
> keep an open body position;
> keep his or her hands in an open position; or
> lean towards the interviewer during conversation.

A right-handed person attempting to recall a person, place, thing, or event from memory may look upwards to the left; looking upwards to the right signals fabrication instead of a recall. A person's face may appear flushed if he or she is lying, embarrassed, humiliated, or angry.

Body language varies culture to culture. In some cultures, positioning oneself close to another is a sign of respect. In our culture, however, passing too close to another—into the other's "space"—is considered a sign of disrespect. Sitting too close to or too far away from a person may signal lack of interest to that person. Arms folded across the chest is a closed position and may signal to the person that the interviewer is distant, uninterested, or closed to the information the person is providing. Similarly, a client or witness who assumes that position may not be providing complete information, again because of distrust or disinterest.

Occasionally, when interviewing two people, the dynamics between the two will affect the communication. For example, assume that when Mr. and Mrs. Williams (Chapter 1, Third Scenario) arrive for their estate planning interview, Mr. Williams instructs Mrs. Williams where to sit and then pulls his chair slightly closer towards the paralegal than his wife's chair. When you begin the interview, Mr. Williams answers all the questions in a booming voice. As the interview progresses, although he looks to his wife for "approval" ("We're giving Mitchell the broach, isn't that right, Mary Lou?") you discern from her body language (eyes averted, arms crossed, head down, voice lowered) that perhaps she does not agree with his statements. You can usually change this dynamic by aligning yourself with the subordinate person:

Paralegal: Mrs. Williams [smiling at her, leaning towards her, chin in palm], you look a little uncertain about the broach. Could I ask how you decided on Mitchell?

Mrs. Williams: Well [looking at Mr. Williams], I'm not sure. Mitchell has a daughter who could use it . . . Whatever Mr. Williams wants is okay.

Paralegal: But Mrs. Williams, my job is to find out what you want. Would you tell me?

Mrs. Williams: Well I sort of wanted Miriam to have it, but since she doesn't have any kids, well, I don't know . . .

By moving the chair closer to Mrs. Williams, smiling at her, and looking right at her, the paralegal excluded Mr. Williams momentarily from the interview and drew Mrs. Williams into the process. Usually by drawing the quiet or intimidated person into the interview, you establish ground rules for the remainder of the interview. Once the rules are clear to the dominant person, the interview continues with full involvement of both people.

An interviewer who has a open physical posture, good eye contact, and a clear voice will portray a picture of a professional who confidently encourages people to talk. People are generally not reluctant to talk to others in whom they have confidence and who treat them with respect.

As a society we have become more aware of sexual harassment and discrimination. As a rule, you should never touch a client or witness, nor let them touch you, even in an apparently friendly way. Occasionally you will interview someone who during the interview seeks your help or guidance with personal problems. This is beyond the scope of the interview. If it is a client, discuss the matter with your supervising attorney who may provide the client with the name of a therapist or counselor. Your relationship with the people you interview is purely professional and should remain that way at all times.

3. Cultural Differences

In addition to considerations about body language, there are other matters of culture that can affect the relationship. The most common difference is language. A person whose native tongue is not the same as yours may have a difficult time understanding and answering questions in an interview. Moreover, a client may mistakenly believe that she knows enough of your language to explain the case when in fact she is unable to do so in a thorough and accurate manner. It is also true that a client may know enough of your language to appear to understand what you are asking and yet not fully understand. Thus it is always best to use a translator for accuracy.

Frequently a client or witness whose first language is not English, and who is uncertain about her language ability, will bring a friend or family member with her for support and translation. If the interview is with a client, the presence of a third person may affect the existence of the attorney-client privilege. Discuss this with your supervising attorney before proceeding. When language or cultural issues are evident before the interview, it is often possible to ascertain whether there will be a need for a translator or whether the subject of the interview intends to bring someone to sit in with her to provide support or assistance.

Whether the interview is with a witness or client, you may later need the interpreter to assist in using the statements from the interview in preparing the case or transaction. Make sure you obtain identifying information so you are able to locate the person after the interview.

In the event you work in an office in which many clients speak a different language, you would be wise to learn the basics of the language. In some cases, the cultural differences may be insurmountable; in such a case, the attorney should probably decline representation and refer the person to the local bar association for referral in turn to a different attorney.

4. Gender

In her best-selling book, You Just Don't Understand, Deborah Tannen explores the complex differences between the way men and women talk. Just as people from diverse cultures or different parts of the country have very different conversational styles, men and women too have different styles. Dr. Tannen writes that men concern themselves more with status and independence; women with connection to others and intimacy. The interviewer who is aware of the differences in language of men and women can use this awareness to his or her advantage by probing to extract complete, precise, factual information.

H. Special Situations

1. Elderly

The elderly present a unique set of characteristics to the interviewer. An older person may be physically infirm or hard of hearing; do not misconstrue these difficulties for mental impairment. If possible, interview an older person in his or her own home where it is comfortable and convenient. Speak clearly; if you notice that the person is staring at your mouth, it might be that he or she cannot hear you clearly. If the older person is a client and is accompanied to your office by another person, such as a son, ask the son to sit in the waiting room while you interview the client. The other person, if allowed to sit in on the interview, may attempt to speak for the client either by trying to explain the purpose of the visit or by answering questions. A greater concern is that the client might be reluctant to be candid as long as the other person is present.

If a client is brought to the office by a person who will directly benefit from the client's actions—perhaps a transfer of property without compensation—share your insights with your supervising attorney after the interview. Perhaps it is wise for you and your supervisor to talk to the client—alone.

2. Competency

If, during an interview, you begin to question a person's competency, take copious notes, quoting the person as much as possible. Try to make very specific observations as to why you believe the person is mentally impaired. If he responds inappropriately to questions, note the question and the response. If another person from your office is available to sit in on part of the interview, he can make observations. As always, discuss the problem with your supervising attorney.

3. Inability to Read

If you suspect your subject cannot read there are several things you can do. One approach is to ask the person to read something to you such as a police report ("Mr. Bilter, I'd like you to read this police report to me one sentence at a time. After each sentence, I'd like you to comment on what the officer wrote.") Another approach is to watch the person read a document. Frequently, the eyes of a nonreader or a poor reader will not track the written word but will instead jump from one place on the document to another. A third approach is to listen carefully for other cues, such as whether the person has a driver's license, which is not issued without passing a written test. If during the interview it becomes obvious the person cannot read, be sensitive to the issue. ("Mr. Bilter, it looks to me like you're have a hard time reading that. Would you like me to read it for you?")

Unfortunately, the word "illiterate" connotes stupidity. Do not under any circumstances misinterpret an inability to read with a lack of intelligence.

4. Children

To interview children effectively, a paralegal must understand the areas of law specific to children and appreciate related concerns of age and maturity of the child, dynamics of the parent-child relationship, privacy, and the nature of the privileges between lawyers and clients, and between family members.

Laws concerning the representation of children vary from jurisdiction to jurisdiction but are governed generally by broad principles based on promoting the best interests of children and preservation of family relationships. An understanding of the law that applies to the case or circumstance prompting the interview with a child is a prerequisite to any interview with a child.

Interviewing children also involves privileges based on the attorney-client relationship and privileges existing between family members. There is no blanket privilege preventing disclosure of communications between children and parents, but certain limitations have been recognized in some jurisdictions. Also some jurisdictions recognize limited testimonial privileges that prevent children or parents from testifying against each other. A paralegal must understand the rules governing privileges relating to children in the jurisdiction.

There are a variety of circumstances in which children will be represented or interviewed by lawyers. These include appointments from the court to represent children as clients or witnesses, such as representation of children as a guardian *ad litem* (GAL); appointment or assignment by a court as a Court Appointed Special Advocate (CASA); representation of a child in a juvenile court proceeding such as a delinquency matter, or what is known in some jurisdictions as a "child" (or "person") "in need of supervision" (CHINS) or (PINS), or "child in need of assistance (CHINA)." In these instances the attorney represents the child, not the family.

When the older child has been charged with a criminal or delinquent act, or the interests of the minor client may be adverse to the parents' interest, the interview should be bifurcated with part of the interview involving the parent and child and part with just the child. This is a delicate state of affairs because often parents will be upset that they cannot be present during part of an interview with their child. It requires tact, compassion, and considerable patience to tell a parent that the attorney-client relationship will be compromised if the parent is present during portions of the interview and therefore, it will be necessary to speak with the child privately. In conveying this information, it is desirable not to offend or alienate the parent or guardian. When the child charged with a criminal or delinquent act tells the interviewer his version of the events or recounts his story for the first time the parent should never be present.

Having the parent or guardian present during part of the interview offers the interviewer the opportunity to observe interactions that may be essential to understanding your client or witness. Observe the interplay between these individuals carefully and note your observations after the interview.

Interview young children with caution and always with another person from your office present as your witness. Under most circumstances, a parent or guardian should be present as well. Do not ask any leading questions; young children can be very susceptible to suggestion. After asking a question, wait patiently for a reply. Take the time to establish a rapport with the child; talk with the child about something he likes to do. Tell him why you are asking questions. Engage the child and make sure you ask questions directly to the child, not the adult accompanying the child. By the same token, be sure to let the child answer questions fully; do not finish the child's answers.

Older children need not necessarily have a parent present during the interview, for example, where the parent is disruptive and the parent-child relationship is strained. Although the interest of the child may not necessarily be adverse to a parent's interest, the interests are different. It is still advisable to have a second adult present during the interview. Interviews with children should be prepared carefully and the legal and ethical issues relevant to each interview should be reviewed in advance with the supervising attorney.

I. Flexible Thinking

Learn to think "flexibly," just as you learned to think analytically. "Flexible" means that you are not bound by your own beliefs, that you are willing to move outside the walls of your mind, outside the box. Part of thinking flexibly is thinking creatively. It can be hard to think creatively, to shake off what we "know" from our experience and environment. But a good investigator has to do that. Sometimes "creatively" can simply mean "differently." To think differently about a problem, look at it from all angles. Remember the brain teaser about the bear who walked one mile south, turned east and walked another mile, and then turned north and walked the last mile, which brought it back to the starting point? The question is: What color was the bear? By approaching the problem from different angles, you begin to understand the issues. In order to travel one mile south, one mile east, one mile north and end where it started, the bear would have to travel in a triangle. The only place this could happen is the north pole (you can't walk south from the south pole, and bears don't live there anyway). You really don't need to know much about geography or bears to answer the riddle. Thinking creatively leads to the answer.

While flexible thinking will not answer all your questions and is not a substitute for solid preparation or good factual investigation, it can help solve a puzzling problem.

PRACTICE TIP: Do crossword puzzles, play chess, or any thinking games. Write poetry, music, or stories to encourage creative thought.

J.   Ethical Considerations

While interviewing a client or witness, a paralegal may not suggest or encourage a person to commit a fraudulent act such as lying, preparing a fictitious document, or leaving the jurisdiction to avoid testifying. Nor may the paralegal sanction an illegal act such as violating a court order by removing children from the jurisdiction when custody is at issue. ABA Model Rules of Professional Conduct, Rule 3.3 and 3.4 and Ethical Canon 7-26. Paralegals, like attorneys, must avoid even the appearance of impropriety.

As noted above, unconsented interception or recording of wire or oral communications might implicate violations of federal or state criminal statutes. *See, e.g.,* 18 U.S.C. §2510; Mass. Gen. L. ch. 272, §99 (1997). Even inadvertent violations of the law have serious consequences for paralegal, attorney and client. Do not record conversations without first talking to your supervising attorney.

SUMMARY

Interviews should be structured to gain insight into a client's concerns and to a witness's possible motives. Asking nonleading open-ended questions provides better accuracy than leading questions. Closed and direct questions are useful as follow-up techniques to elicit specific details. Where appropriate, time-lines should be obtained and corroborated by other chronological information. Telephone interviews have the advantage of efficiency in terms of time and expense, but present different considerations, including an inability to assess fully the witness. Communication is effected by body language, gender, age, physical and mental infirmity, cultural differences, and stereotyping. You must be aware of your own biases and prejudices to become an effective interviewer.

Key Terms

Active listening	Direct
Chronology	Indirect
Corroboration	Leading
Floor control	Nonleading
Passive listening	Open
Questions:	Time-line
Closed	Topic control

REVIEW QUESTIONS

1. Describe the differences between leading and nonleading questions. When do you use leading? Nonleading?

2. Why is silence an effective interview technique?

3. How do you deal with the "rambling" client? How can you tell whether his or her diversions are important?

4. What are the dangers of using legalese?

5. Consider the differences between active and passive listening. How do the two types differ in the way they are used?

6. Why is controlling the interview important? What is the difference between floor control and topic control?

7. What are the advantages and disadvantages to the telephone interview?

8. What is the value of eliciting information from a client and a witness in chronological order?

9. What things do you consider when conducting an interview through a translator when you and the client speak different languages?

10. How can gender and cultural differences influence an interview? What steps can you take to prevent the differences from affecting the quality of legal services?

11. What are the special circumstances that surround the interview of a child?

CHAPTER EXERCISES

Exercise 3-1:   Consider the following questions. Classify them as leading or nonleading and explain your answer.

1) Where were you last Saturday night?
2) Wasn't the man tall and balding with a limp?
3) Can you tell me what happened after you arrived at the office?
4) Would your sister be able to testify for you?
5) Weren't the Wilsons your neighbors?

Exercise 3-2:   Choose partners. One of you is the client, the other the paralegal. Practice asking nonleading and leading questions. Write each question down on paper. Review them with the class. What makes them leading or nonleading?

Exercise 3-3:   Explain the following legal terms in lay language:

Complaint	Motion
Contract	Personal injury
Costs	Pleading
Deposition	Statute of limitations
Evidence	Subpoena
Element	Summons
Filing fee	Tolling
Indictment	Tort
Judgment	Will

Exercise 3-4: Translate the following paragraph into plain language:

Well, Mrs. Jones, Attorney Woodruff has informed me that the statute of limitations won't bar the filing of your complaint. Once the complaint is filed, of course, the statute is tolled and that triggers the time they have to file the answer. Then of course there's the discovery—interrogatories, requests for production, depositions, and so forth, and probably a request for admissions. We'll keep you posted as we do status checks. Don't forget, we need the filing fee before you leave today.

Exercise 3-5: How well do you listen? Bring in a newspaper article from the community, social, or obituary section of your paper. Choose a partner from the class and read a paragraph to her or him. Have your partner recite it back to you verbatim. Read another paragraph, taking notes this time. After you have tried twice, switch roles and try again. Repeat the same exercise using the business section of the paper.

Exercise 3-6: Try the following exercises for mental gymnastics.

1) List all the legal terms you can think of in five minutes. How many are on your list? Compare yours with other students' lists. What terms did you miss?
2) Draw the floor plan of your house or apartment, estimating measurements. Measure and determine how close your estimate matched the actual measurement.
3) Draw ten different traffic signs.

4

The Client Interview

CHAPTER OBJECTIVES

This chapter discusses

- establishing a rapport with a client;
- preparing the client for the interview;
- physical setting and tone;
- motivators and inhibitors to interviewing;
- difficult clients;
- helping theories.

A. Introduction

Paralegals interview to gather information in order to accomplish a task, such as drafting a complaint, an answer, interrogatories, or a will. In order to accomplish the task efficiently and effectively, the information obtained must be complete and accurate. During the course of the interview clients must disclose highly personal information. Sensitive areas include:

- Finances (assets and liabilities)
- Difficult family matters
- Criminal behavior

> Rapport, from the French, rapporter, to report talk. . . . [a] relationship, especially one of mutual trust . . .
>
> ---
>
> He [the interviewer] seemed concerned not only with my obvious legal problems, but with my personal problems as well. Here I was, a social worker, arrested for possession of drugs. I was horrified to think what the charges would do to my family, my reputation in the community, and my career . . .

> When the interview started, he explained confidentiality to me. I felt much more relaxed knowing I could be forthright and not worry that our conversation would be repeated to outsiders . . .

The relationship you establish with your client greatly influences the kind, quantity, and quality of the information you acquire. Much of the information on which attorneys and paralegals rely comes directly from the client. Although you must verify independently all information from whatever source, you will generally be able to obtain reliable information from a client with whom you have established a good rapport.

B. The Paralegal-Client Relationship

1. Introduction

Paralegals work for the client to perform a task or a series of tasks on the client's behalf. The relationship between the paralegal and the client is a professional one, much like the relationship between a patient and a doctor. Law is a service industry in which the paralegal, under the supervision of an attorney, works for a client. The client is not the paralegal's friend. The paralegal should not give a client his or her home telephone number. If the client obtains it and calls the paralegal at home, the paralegal must tell the client to call the office during business hours. If it is an emergency, the paralegal should call the supervising attorney and let the attorney handle it. If someone's life or safety is in jeopardy, the paralegal should have the client call the police or other appropriate official or make the call for the client.

The basis for the paralegal-client relationship is mutual trust and respect. The client should trust and respect the attorney and the paralegal; the attorney and the paralegal should respect and trust the client. The paralegal is part of a problem-solving team, made up of the client, lawyers, and experts such as accountants, doctors, or document examiners. The team takes the information provided by the client, analyzes it, verifies it and applies the law to the emerging facts. (It is at the verification point that the paralegal's trust of the client may evaporate—when two or more conflicting sets of facts have to be reconciled.)

2. Ethics

a. *Scope of Paralegal Responsibility*

An attorney is responsible for ensuring that a paralegal's conduct is consistent with the attorney's obligations under the ABA Model Rules of Professional Conduct. ABA Model Guideline 1. Although ABA Model

Guideline 2 allows the lawyer to delegate to a paralegal "any task normally performed by the lawyer," certain matters may not be delegated by an attorney under any circumstances. ABA Model Guideline 3. They are

1) responsibility for establishing the attorney-client relationship;
2) responsibility for establishing a fee; and
3) responsibility for rendering a legal opinion to a client.

Thus a paralegal may not decide whether the firm will accept or decline the case; nor may a paralegal inform the client as to the fee structure. Finally, the paralegal may not give legal advice to a client. These issues are addressed again in the context of an actual interview later in this chapter.

b. Confidentiality

Under ABA Model Rules of Professional Conduct, Rule 1.6, a lawyer "shall not reveal information relating to representation of a client" without the client's consent. Under the ABA Model Guideline for Legal Assistants Services, Guideline 6, it is the lawyer's responsibility to ensure that the legal assistant preserve all client confidences. Client confidences include all information necessary in the representation of the client and not simply verbal or written statements from the client. The rule is designed to encourage clients to divulge embarrassing or legally harmful information without fear of disclosure by the attorney. The rule also covers communications made before the establishment of the attorney-client relationship, whether or not the lawyer is retained, and extends indefinitely after the relationship is concluded. For the rule to apply to a communication, the communication must have been made to an attorney or an employee of the attorney for the purpose of obtaining legal advice or services.

Two exceptions to the rule allow the lawyer to disclose confidential information. The first exception arises if the lawyer believes the client is about to commit a criminal act that might result in serious physical harm or death. The second exception occurs when a lawyer is sued by a client, when the lawyer must sue a client, or when the lawyer is defending herself against a criminal or civil charge based on the client's conduct. Under these exceptions, an attorney may disclose confidential information to establish a claim or defense.

A paralegal should keep the client's identity and all information obtained from the representation confidential. Methods used by firms to ensure confidentiality include

1) assigning all client files a number in lieu of recording the name on the file;
2) maintaining the files in cabinets with numerical designations;
3) storing files in a separate locked room;
4) maintaining the integrity of a computer network system so as not to be compromised by an outside source;

5) blanking computer screens when not in use or when others are present;

6) keeping sensitive documents or files closed or secured when they are not in use; and

7) putting files or documents related to client matters out of view when clients, witnesses, or other people from outside the firm are in a working area.

c. Conflicts of Interest

One of the most common examples of a conflict of interest is the representation by the same firm of two or more clients with adverse interests. If the basis for the attorney-client relationship is loyalty and trust, how could the attorney represent adverse or even competing interests? ABA Model Rules of Professional Conduct, Rule 1.7, states the general rule: A lawyer

> shall not represent a client if the representation of the client will be directly adverse to another client, unless . . . the lawyer reasonably believes the representation will not adversely affect the relationship with the other client, and each client consents after consultation.

Depending on the size of the firm and the volume of clients, different processes are used to cross check all potential clients with current clients. Firms with multiple branches and hundreds of clients use networked computers to perform daily checks; firms with few clients may check for conflicts at their weekly meeting. With a computer, conflicts checks are accomplished in a matter of seconds by typing the name of the potential client and referencing it to the other names in the client database. An example of a software program that performs this function is ABACUS LAW +:

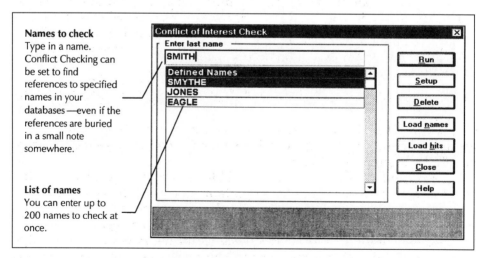

Exhibit 4.1 **Conflict of Interest Check**

Other behavior prohibited by the ABA Model Rules of Professional Conduct includes entering into a business deal with a client unless the lawyer has made full disclosure of the terms, has given the client the opportunity to seek independent legal advice, and has obtained the client's consent in writing. Although a lawyer may not generally provide financial assistance to a client for litigation, he or she may pay court costs and litigation expenses for an indigent client, and may advance costs and expenses to a client with repayment contingent on the outcome of the litigation. ABA Model Rules of Professional Conduct, Rule 1.8.

Finally, lawyers are disqualified from representing a client in a similar or related matter if the lawyer represented an adverse interest in a former firm. Disqualification to one lawyer in the firm is generally disqualification to all. A paralegal moving from one firm to another or working for several firms simultaneously must be on guard for possible conflicts. Prohibiting the paralegal from working on a particular case or obtaining written consent from the client may avoid attorney violations of ABA Model Rules of Professional Conduct, Rules 1.9, 1.10 and 1.11. ABA Informal Opinion 1526 (1988) allows a paralegal with knowledge of confidential information to move to a new firm that represents an adversary of the former client so long as the firm isolates the paralegal from all confidential material.

A paralegal, like any employee in a law office, must be aware of the potential for conflicts of interest to arise. Should a paralegal suspect the existence of a conflict of interest or other ethical problem, he or she should promptly report it to a supervising attorney. Never assume that these issues will disappear or take care of themselves.

3. Client Rapport

a. Attorney-Client Relationship

In most instances, the client will meet the attorney first and discuss general facts, needs, and concerns. The attorney decides whether the office will take the case and, if so, discusses issues of confidentiality and fees with the client. After the firm has been retained, the paralegal is brought in to perform certain functions involving the case.

If the paralegal is involved with the client from the first interview, the stage is easily set for subsequent interviews and fact-gathering by the paralegal.

Clearly it is the responsibility of the attorney to decide which cases are appropriate for paralegal involvement and at what stage the paralegal should be brought into the case.

As a general rule, if a paralegal will have significant contact with the client or will be responsible for important aspects of the case, he or she should be present at the first interview to begin to establish a good working relationship, or rapport, with the client. When the paralegal is present at the inception of the attorney-client relationship, the importance of the role of the paralegal as a complement to the attorney-client relationship is underscored.

b. Establishing Rapport

Rapport is established on trust. It is a comfortable connection between people, an essential part of the paralegal-client relationship and the interviewing process. Establishment of a "good rapport" allows for truthful thorough reporting of facts and feelings. Begin establishing a rapport with the first client contact.

Think of what makes you comfortable—direct eye contact, a smile, a handshake, a simple acknowledgment of presence. We tend to take these things for granted in our everyday lives. Some people are reluctant to shake hands—perhaps they have arthritis, "clammy hands," are "germ-conscious," are restricted by their religion from such contact, or simply not comfortable doing so. Do not be put off by a person who refuses your extended hand; offer a smile instead.

In a professional environment, such as a law office, you must learn to help make people comfortable as quickly as possible. Generally, what makes you comfortable will make another person comfortable as well. But this might not always be the case. Anticipate your client's arrival. What do you know about this person? A young person may be more comfortable with a casual approach; an older person may expect, and be more comfortable with, greater formality. Observe the client, look for clues about how he or she feels, and act accordingly. Draw on your own experience in relating to others. How do you relate to youthful or elderly members of your own family?

Consider the social worker arrested for possession of drugs in the opening scenario. How do you establish a relationship to help him trust you—trust you enough to tell you that the drugs, in this case heroin, belong to his 21-year-old son who will lose his college scholarship if he is convicted of possession of drugs?

c. Dress

Try not to be influenced by the way someone dresses. Studies show we tend to respond more favorably to people who are well dressed and articulate. We tend to believe that a well spoken, nicely dressed person has higher "status," or has a disciplined personality because we tend to see those attributes as evidence of personal pride and caring. Clients, however, come from all strata of society and all walks of life. There are many reasons why a client dresses the way he or she does for an interview with an attorney or paralegal. There may be many legitimate reasons for a client to appear for an interview casually or even inappropriately dressed. These reasons may become apparent during the course of the interview or later as the relationship matures. Similarly, awkward or strange mannerisms or inarticulate speech may have numerous explanations or causes. While it is important to take clues from and to be informed by the actions, mannerisms, or dress of a client, it is essential for a paralegal to treat all clients with respect and with dignity. As a professional, a paralegal must look beyond the clothes, speech, and idiosyncrasies of the client and be careful not to prejudge.

C. Preparing the Client for the Interview

1. Initial Contact

If your first client contact is to schedule the interview, call the client to schedule. In the event the appointment has been scheduled, call the client to confirm. Do not have a staff member (secretary or receptionist) call the client unless it is impossible for you to do. Your call to the client shows him or her the importance you attach to the case. It is the start of developing a good rapport.

Although you may not be aware of pertinent documents in the client's possession until the interview is completed, ask the client to bring any documents which he or she thinks might be necessary or pertinent. You should give the client the following practical instructions: how to get to the office; where to park and how much it will cost, if anything; and the appropriate bus or subway stop and walking directions from the stop. You should also give the client a quick overview of the meeting: the topic(s) of discussion; the length of time the meeting will take; and any documents or information the client should bring. If time permits write an introductory letter to the client with the above information and include your business card. A sample letter is in the Appendix.

Allow enough time for the interview. If you expect it to take one hour, allow for two. Always allow for time after the interview has concluded to write a summary. This process is discussed in detail in Chapter 6.

Treat the first and any later interview with a client as though it were the last. This consideration will help you to prepare and concentrate on the information you need to elicit.

2. Greeting the Client

When a client arrives for an appointment, be certain to go to the waiting room promptly to greet her or him. A personal greeting emphasizes the importance the client has to the firm. Although not intended as a script to follow, a sample introduction appears below:

Paralegal: Hello, Ms. Andrews. I'm Michael Gonzales.
Client: Hello. It's nice to meet you.
Paralegal: Let's go to my office [or the conference room or the library] so we can get started.

[As you are walking to the room:]

Paralegal: I hope you didn't have any trouble finding our offices [or that my directions were okay, or parking wasn't too difficult, or traffic was manageable, etc.].

Client: No, it was okay, although the traffic seems to get worse every
   year.
Paralegal: Yes it does, doesn't it? Here we are. Why don't you have a seat
   over there . . .

If you know a bit of information about a client's personal life, like
hobbies or children, use it as an ice-breaker.

Paralegal: Hi, Mr. Sorens, I'm Sarah Engles. Mr. Nestor tells me you're a
   real soccer fan, is that true?
Client: Oh, my yes. I've loved the game all my life. My kids played and
   now my grandkids play. Do you play?
Paralegal: I played a bit when I was little, but then it seems I got too busy
   doing other things and it dropped by the wayside.
Client: I know how that is!

This initial informal conversation relaxes both you and the client and sets
the groundwork for a productive interview.

3. Physical Setting

Your interviewing room should be a comfortable inviting place where
one is not offended by the art or decor. A paralegal who is lucky enough
to have an office should hang her or his diplomas on the wall, bring in a
plant, and frame a poster for color. A lamp or two may serve to soften
harsh overhead lights and provide a calming effect for the interview.
Finally, always have a box of tissues on the desk or table for client use;
your client will be grateful.

Although it is preferable for a client to leave children at home, it
occasionally happens that the sitter cancels at the last minute and children
accompany your client. Because children can be a distraction and interfere
with the purpose of the interview, it may have to be shortened or resched-
uled. A client with children may be very impressed by your forethought,
however, if your bottom drawer reveals a variety of toys, books, pens,
pencils, markers (washable) and some paper for her or his children to play
with during the interview. If you do not have readily available playthings,
you can make do with office supplies (a paper punch is a wonderful device
for making confetti).

If a client arrives with a friend or acquaintance, ask the friend kindly
to wait in the reception area since the presence of a third person in the
interview could destroy the confidentiality of your interview with the
client. If the client insists on having the third party present, take the client
aside and explain to her or him that the third person could be subpoenaed
by the other side and made to answer questions about the interview.

Most offices have a limited range of available furniture; however, a
hard straight-back chair is a must for an elderly client or a client with a
back problem. If you do not have one, borrow one for the interview. Meet

in the conference room or the library if you do not have a private office or if your office is messy or uncomfortable.

The way you choose to seat your client and yourself might encourage or hamper the establishment and maintenance of good rapport.

Seating arrangements fall into two general categories: formal and informal. Formal arrangements are conventional, conservative, and reserved; they are used most frequently with new clients. Informal arrangements are casual, relaxed, and unpretentious; they are generally used after you have developed a relationship with the client.

Study the four configurations in Exhibit 4.2.

In Illustration 1, the setting is formal, with the paralegal and client sitting across from each other at a desk or table. Taking notes is simplified; eye contact is easy to maintain. Office settings of attorneys, paralegals, doctors, and executives could be characterized as formal. The desk suggests that the person sitting behind it holds a position of authority or power. But this desk, seen as a statement of authority, might serve to obstruct the development of the relationship between you and your client because it could intimidate your client. In other words, it might hinder your ability to elicit information from your client in a timely and exacting manner. When you first start as a paralegal, this position may be desirable and provide an element of security and comfort for you. As you become more confident with your knowledge and abilities, however, you will no longer feel the need to use the desk as a buffer.

Frequently the initial meeting with your client will take place in the formal setting of Illustration 1, with later meetings held in a more casual setting, after a relationship has been established.

In Illustrations 2, 3, and 4, the settings are less formal; these arrangements are frequently used at later interviews. In Illustration 2, the expanse of desk is gone, yet note taking is still easy. This is an ideal set-up to review documents with the client.

Illustrations 3 and 4 portray the least formal settings and allow you and the client to have direct contact with each other. These arrangements are often used with clients to help them feel comfortable while dealing with difficult or nonadversarial issues. For example, a spouse who is about to sue for divorce or a parent who seeks custody of a child or a widow

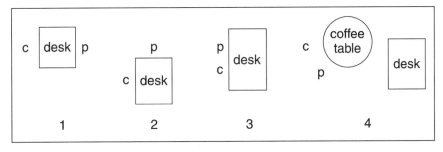

Exhibit 4.2 **Seating Configuration**

seeking help to probate her spouse's will might all be more comfortable in a less formal setting.

You should use the setting that best suits your client's needs and the one in which you and your client are the most comfortable. Remember the client has the information you need; making her or him comfortable will help to establish the rapport that will encourage the client to be forthcoming with information.

Of course, any seating arrangement may be modified by other considerations. For example, the conference room or library may be the best place to meet with a client who has considerable paperwork that you need to review together. A client who is unable to make it to your office because of a physical disability may ask you to come to his or her home.

Regardless of your initial arrangement, be aware that even a slight modification, like moving your chair closer to the client, may change the dynamics of the interview.

PRACTICE TIP: Before you meet with a client, be certain that all confidential material concerning other clients or the firm is put away. Remember that even the fact of your firm's representation or potential representation of a client may be confidential, so all materials should be removed or covered; your computer screen should be blank. Do this *before* your client arrives so that you do not run the risk of breaching the confidentiality of another client. You also do not want the client to witness the last minute reorganization of your office or the conference room. Clients want the offices of their attorneys and paralegals to appear neat and organized.

---

4. Setting the Tone

Before your client is comfortably seated, instruct the staff that you do not wish to be disturbed by telephone calls or visitors. Tell your client that you will be taking notes during the interview in order to ensure that you have all the information. Both of these steps let the client know the importance you attach to the interview.

Begin the interview with a brief introduction of yourself and your role in the process. It might start as follows:

Paralegal: As I told you on the telephone, Mr. Murati, my name is Carmen Hernandez. I am a paralegal working with your attorney, Adrian Morrisky. I will be doing the initial interview in this matter today; it should take approximately one hour.

   Let me start by saying that everything you tell me is confidential. By that I mean that as a paralegal I am bound by a code of ethics—just like an attorney—not to discuss your case with anyone outside this firm without your permission. You should also know that everyone who works here, including our receptionist, secretaries—all the staff— are covered by the same rule.

As you probably know my role as a paralegal is very different from that of an attorney's. The major difference is that I cannot give you legal advice. In other words, I can't make suggestions or counsel you as to what you should do legally. Decisions about the legal/procedural aspects of this matter will be discussed with you by the attorney.

My job today is to gather information from you. After today I will be keeping you advised on the status of the case. [And whatever else your attorney has asked you to do.]

During the interview, I will be taking notes so that I can be absolutely sure of the information you're providing me today.

Do you have any questions?

Client: No, that seems clear.

Paralegal: Okay, then let's get started. Why don't you begin by telling me what brings you here today.

Client: Well, I believe my mortgage company is overcharging me interest . . .

Inevitably, at some point during the interview, the client will seek legal advice of some sort. For example:

Client: What are my chances of winning? Do I have a strong case?

Paralegal: Those are good questions and I wish I could answer them for you. But as I told you I am prohibited from giving you any kind of legal advice. However, the attorney will be able to discuss that with you when you meet. Now if I may, I have a few more questions before we conclude . . .

Remember the client does not pose these questions to test your strength of character or allegiance to the Code of Ethics, but because he wants answers to questions that are important to him. In the model answer, the paralegal affirmed the client's question ("Those are good questions"), expressed an understanding of the client's need to know ("and I wish I could answer them for you"), assured the client the matter would be addressed ("the attorney will be able to discuss that with you"), and reiterated his or her position as paralegal ("I am prohibited from giving you any kind of legal advice").

In an effort to establish rapport with a client, it is common to feel the urge to tell the client something positive about his or her position. While it is important to affirm a client's feelings and not be judgmental, it is equally important not to offer judgments or opinions about the likelihood of success or the value of a case. It is critical that a paralegal not create unrealistic expectations for a client. Plaintiffs will often ask what a case is worth or how much they can get and defendants will similarly look for guidance on their potential exposure. Establishing the monetary value of a civil case for the parties requires a grasp of all the legal and factual nuances of a particular case together with an accurate assessment of the strengths and weakness of the other side. Predicting the outcome of any legal problem is an extremely difficult exercise. If done improperly or hastily it may create unrealistic expectations that will significantly affect the ability of a lawyer effectively to represent a client. Consequently a paralegal should resist the temptation to build a bridge to a client by offering encouragement about the worth or potential success of a case. A paralegal should never tell a client what he or she thinks a case is worth or offer encouraging suggestions about how a case is a "sure winner."

PRACTICE TIP: At the conclusion of the interview, provide the client with a business card with your name or the name of the law firm. ABA Informal Opinion 1527 approves of business cards for paralegals. While most states approve of cards for paralegals, not all do, and some have restrictions. Check your jurisdiction.

D. Maintaining Rapport

1. Correspondence

Once you begin to establish a good rapport with your client, both through the personal confirmation of the interview appointment—by letter or telephone—and through the interview itself, it is imperative that you continue to build trust in the relationship.

One way to do this is to write the client a letter summarizing the main points of the interview. This follow-up letter serves numerous purposes. First, it underscores the importance of the client to the firm. Second, it lets the client know you understood the facts and circumstances of the case as discussed in the interview. Third, it allows the client to correct any erroneous information contained in the letter. (For example, suppose your notes indicate the client, Mrs. Williams, wants her will to reflect a bequest of her jewelry, a pearl necklace, to her daughter, Morgan; you reiterate this in the letter. When the client receives the letter, she realizes that there is some confusion because she wants the necklace to go to her daughter, Mirian. She will write or call you to clarify the matter.) Fourth, the follow-up letter may provide details as to your expectations from the client. (For example, it may list documents the client needs to locate for the case—her will, insurance policies, correspondence, deeds, etc.) Fifth, the letter may clarify for the client the status of the case by pulling together and organizing the matter to date. And sixth, the letter lets the client learn some legal aspects of the situation. Samples of various types of letters appear in the Appendix.

2. Telephone Calls

Another way to maintain rapport with a client is to keep in touch by telephone. Often clients call to inquire about the status of the case or to offer additional information they believe might be helpful. If the client leaves a message, return the call as soon as possible, but no later than the following day. If you are unable to return the call personally within 24 hours, ask another staff member if he or she will call on your behalf to advise the client as to when to expect your call. Note the date you intend to return the call on your calendar and do not forget to do it. The most frequent complaint lodged by clients against lawyers is failing to return telephone calls. Make certain this complaint never applies to you.

3. Electronic Mail

Once considered inappropriate, electronic mail (e-mail) is quickly becoming a popular method of contacting clients. Experts in computer security, however, remain adamant that e-mail is not secure. As technology changes to provide additional security, e-mail will become commonplace for confidential client communication. Until such time as the systems are secure, hard-wire phones and letters are the best way to keep client contact confidential.

E. Motivators

Clients, like all persons, have physical and emotional needs. By recognizing those needs, you can encourage a client to talk openly during an interview. Several of the more common methods to encourage clients to participate in the interview are empathizing with the client, appealing to the client's sense of benevolence, enticing the client with a reward, and praising the client when information is provided.

1. Empathy

Empathy is compassion towards a client and his or her situation, displaying sensitivity to the client's needs and fears, and an understanding of the situation. Empathy is listening to a client, without giving advice, without telling the client what to do, and without passing judgment. In some respects the easiest part of interviewing is getting the facts. The difficult part is untangling the facts from the emotional baggage that comes along with those facts. Think of it as the client having two small and one large reservoirs in her brain. In one of the small reservoirs there are the facts as the client perceives them. In the other small reservoir are the feelings. These two small reservoirs feed into the large reservoir, which mixes them both together. When it comes out, it is jumbled. The interviewer has to sort it out, carefully, while being aware of the array of feelings a client has.

For example, our client, Mr. Jamison, is in the position of having to sue his trustee, Mr. Burnson, who is also his uncle. Mr. Burnson assumed control of Mr. Jamison's inheritance as a trustee when Mr. Jamison was

12. Although Mr. Jamison has long been legally able to manage his own affairs, he allowed his uncle to continue because he knew little about the stock market in which his money was invested. For 25 years Mr. Burnson managed the trust fund profitably; however, in the past two months he has made several bad trades losing 20 percent of the portfolio. Mr. Jamison seeks legal help as a means to an end—to stop the erosion of his portfolio— yet he does not want to hurt his uncle's feelings. In fact he is concerned that removing his uncle from control of the account will "push him over the edge" and contribute to an early demise. Like many clients who are pulled in one direction by intellect and another by feelings, he needs an empathetic listener.

2.   Doing the Right Thing

A client might be motivated by knowing that she is doing the right thing. For example, a client who has been burned by the local used-car company might be willing, even excited, about being the named plaintiff in a class action. The idea that her action could help other consumers may be very appealing. There are clients who want to see justice done.

3.   Winning the Prize

A client who has much to gain from the case, especially financially, will usually be very forthcoming with information. The motivation is the client's desire to be rewarded with a money judgment or settlement. If Mary Stockton wins her medical malpractice case against Dr. Wizzen she will reap a considerable financial reward; she will win the prize.

4.   Praise

Every person responds favorably to praise. Praising a client during an interview encourages the client to provide more information and reaps great rewards in the form of information. When the client has provided relevant material, praise him. Tell the client he is doing a great job, that what he is telling you is very helpful and encourage him to continue.

F.   Inhibitors

Just as some clients are motivated quite easily to provide information, other clients feel constrained to share information. A variety of factors may influence the client's willingness to be frank during the interview. The client might feel personally threatened, might withhold information in order to manipulate the interviewer or the case, might feel a need to be in charge, or conversely, for the interviewer to be in charge, or might be under the influence of a traumatic event.

A client with whom you have developed a good rapport is less likely to be inhibited during the interview. Even when you have a good rapport, however, a client can be reluctant to share information.

1.   Threat to Self-Esteem

A client might be unwilling to offer information, even when specifically solicited, if the client is embarrassed. Consider the following examples: A client consulting you in a family case might be a victim of abuse, but might be unwilling to discuss it because she believes it reflects poorly on her. A client who has signed a contract without benefit of legal counsel might be ashamed of having made a bad deal. A client who has a substance abuse problem might not want you to know about it.

A client wants respect from the interviewer; he does not want an attorney, a paralegal, friends, or family to think less of him—to think perhaps that he was stupid. Rather than airing the truth and looking bad, the client might lie to preserve an image.

If you suspect a client is being less than forthright because of a threat to her ego, there are several methods to use to encourage her to talk. First, remind the client of the attorney-client privilege. You might handle the situation as follows:

Paralegal: Did you expect the company might go under?

Client: Well, no, I mean their reputation was excellent.

Paralegal: But one of the documents you provided me was their most recent financial statement, which shows they're in trouble.

Client: Yeah, but I never really looked at it, I mean, well you know . . . I've been so busy with the Merkins deal.

Paralegal: Remember everything you tell me is confidential. If you're not experienced at reading a financial statement, I can understand how you believed the company was in good shape. The cover sheet gives that impression. But my job is to help you by getting all the information I can. I need you to be completely forthright with me. We all make mistakes.

Client: I'm so embarrassed. I didn't want to admit I didn't understand it. I've been so foolish. I don't want anyone to know.

Paralegal: I will keep all the information confidential as I am required to do. Thank you for telling me. Let's talk with Attorney Zomat about how to handle this information.

2.   Jeopardy to the Case

In this situation, the client withholds information because he believes the case will be jeopardized if he is forthright. For example, it is quite common for clients to give a bottom-line settlement figure much higher than what they would actually take, believing that if they give a realistic settlement figure, the attorney will simply settle for that amount.

3. Authoritative Client

The authoritative client believes the client's job is to tell you what to do—after all, you do work for her. This client provides information that she deems relevant and refuses to give other information requested. The authoritative client must be convinced that the information sought is relevant to the case.

4. Subservient Client

The subservient client occupies the other end of the spectrum from the authoritative client. This client believes that if you have not requested the information, it is irrelevant. Because he or she volunteers nothing, the interviewer must ask many more questions, continually motivating the client to talk.

5. Embarrassment

A client might not wish to provide information if the process of telling the information is embarrassing. For example, a victim of a racial assault or discrimination might not want to provide the details of the incident because it is embarrassing. He might be too uncomfortable to provide you with exact language. The client might say they called him "names" without being explicit. Although the client eagerly shares this information with friends and family, telling the paralegal is too uncomfortable. The client must be gently reassured that it is critical information for you to know. If the client remains unwilling to speak certain words, suggest he write them down on a sheet of paper.

6. Inability to Focus

A client might have a difficult time focusing on your questions because she is concentrating on other issues. For example, in a divorce matter, the client might be concentrating on custody issues to the extent that she appears disinterested in the property issues. In fact, the client might tell you that the only thing she cares about is the child; that there is no interest in the house. Or a client might have come to your office with the intention of making revisions to her will now that the spouse has died; but in fact the client is in the midst of the grieving process and is unable to focus on the task at hand. The interviewer must address the other issues either before or within the context of the interview.

A client required to relive a painful event during an interview might "shut down" during the interview. For example, in a case involving a claim of negligent infliction of emotional distress against a driver who killed the client's child when she exited the school bus, the client might have great difficulty talking about the incident. The client who comes to see you to discuss probating his or her recently deceased spouse's will might be too grief-stricken to provide information.

The paralegal should acknowledge the client's other concern and then proceed to the reason for the interview. For example, "Mr. Collins, I know the custody of your child is of paramount importance to you, however, it is very important that we have an accurate picture of your financial situation." Or, "Ms. Meddon, the death of your husband must have come as a great shock to you. If you prefer we could reschedule for next week. I know that you're concerned, however, about several of the provisions of your current will, so if you want to continue now, I'll be happy to."

7. Unaware of Importance of Information

Because a client often does not know what facts are important, he leaves out items he believes are not important. For example, a client might not know that a person is important as a witness or that a document is an important piece of evidence. This is supported by the often-heard client statement, "I don't know if this is important, but . . ." Let the client know that his job is to give you as much information as possible; your job, along with the attorney, is to decide what information is useful or important. Remind the client that information that appears irrelevant to him might in fact be relevant or may lead to relevant information.

The inhibitors listed above are the most common, but the list is by no means exhaustive. Be aware that there might be other reasons why a client is not forthcoming with information, and it would not be unusual for a client to be affected by more than one motivator or inhibitor. Although motivators and inhibitors can affect the relationship with a witness as well as with a client, it is usually to a much lesser extent.

MOTIVATORS	INHIBITORS
1) Empathy	1) Threat to self-esteem
2) Doing the right thing	2) Jeopardy to case
3) Winning the prize	3) Authoritative client
4) Praise	4) Subservient client
	5) Embarrassment
	6) Inability to focus
	7) Unaware of what is important

Exhibit 4.3 **Motivators and Inhibitors**

G. Clients Accused of Crimes

A client charged with a crime is in a significantly different circumstance than a client in a civil matter. Under our system of justice an accused has no obligation to prove his or her innocence or to establish a defense. The burden of proof in a criminal matter rests entirely on the prosecution. A defendant in a criminal matter need not testify and certainly cannot be called to testify at trial by the other side. The accused has an absolute right to remain silent and the exercise of that right cannot be commented on or considered in determining guilt or innocence.

When interviewing a client accused of a crime it is important to bear in mind that in a criminal trial it matters little whether your client "did it." Rather, it matters whether the prosecution can adduce sufficient evidence to establish the existence of each element of every offense beyond a reasonable doubt.

A criminal trial, seen in this context, is as much a trial of the prosecution's evidence as it is a trial of a particular defendant. With this in mind it becomes easier to understand why many experienced defense attorneys and their legal assistants will refrain from asking the first question that comes to the minds of others—"Did you do it?" It is more important that a defendant understand that a criminal trial occurs in stages, stages that begin with pretrial motions, extend through motions to suppress evidence, and end with the trial itself.

The purpose of a client interview in a criminal case is to learn essential facts about the client, about the events surrounding the alleged crime, and about the interactions between the client and the police and others. It is also important to be aware of available defenses and to identify facts and circumstance applicable to the available defenses. Obviously, in some cases it is important to know what the client did and that will involve knowing whether the client actually committed the acts attributed to him or her.

Take for example a case involving a killing attributed to your client. Murder is the killing of another in the absence of justification, mistake, or excuse. The client might have killed in self-defense or in some other manner excused by the law, and thus the killing is not murder but justifiable homicide. In this case it pays to know what the client did because without that knowledge the defense cannot be used.

Usually in a criminal case the attorney will meet with the client and explain the elements of the offense and the defenses available to the client before eliciting the client's version of events. This approach allows the interviewer to educate the client about the nature of each charge and illuminates the significance of facts in the context of the charge and the relevant defenses.

Preparation of the defense of a client accused of a crime also requires developing a fact-based analysis of suppression issues. For this reason the client interview must focus on all the details of the client's arrest and interrogation by police.

H. Difficult Clients

1. The Client Who Lies

Clients intentionally distort the truth; they lie. Not all the time, not all clients, but clients do lie. They lie to avoid liability, to increase the amount of a settlement, to stay out of trouble. Lying must be distinguished from the "client's truth." For example, a client might tell you the car was green; later the evidence shows it was yellow. This evidence does not necessarily show the client was lying, but that the client was mistaken. The client gave you his or her "truth." In other words, the client told you what she or he believed even though it was factually incorrect. A "client's truth" is affected by many extrinsic factors, including observation skills, memory, environment, and stress. By comparison, the client who lies is not mistaken. She or he has intentionally distorted the truth.

Clients who lie to their attorney often do so because they believe that if they get their attorney to believe their fabrications, their attorney will be able to convince a judge or jury of the truth of the fabrications. Often these clients will infuse their fabricated stories with significant inconsistencies. When these inconsistencies are identified, the client can be confronted with them. It is important to recognize that the purpose of the confrontation is not to make clients admit that they are lying; rather it is to make them understand that the inconsistencies will be fatal to their cause. Sometimes it will take several separate confrontations, or sometimes separate interviews, to move the client from the original false version of events to something closer to the truth.

There are several other ways to handle clients who you believe to be lying. First, reminding them of the attorney-client privilege and its extension to paralegals and office staff might be enough to discourage dishonesty. Second, the paralegal can suggest the possibility of deposition or trial to uncover the truth. For example:

Paralegal: Ms. Client, I know some of these questions are uncomfortable for you to answer, but if the opposing party deposes you, or you are called to testify in court, these are the questions that will be asked. If you tell me the answers now, we can work with them—no matter what the answers are. If you don't, it could spell some real trouble for you down the road. Let's try again.
Client: Okay.

This method is frequently used by attorneys to deal with a difficult client. The attorney will examine the client as though he or she were being cross-examined in court. And third, finish the initial interview, share your concerns about truthfulness with the attorney and let the attorney follow up with a second client interview.

2. The Angry Client

Legal interviewing will bring you into contact with clients who are angry. They might be angry over a loss they've suffered, a loss of a loved one, or loss of property. Active and passive listening techniques can be used to defuse an explosive situation. Letting a client yell or cry for a bit may relieve the stress and allow the interview to continue. There is nothing wrong with a client showing anger at an injustice, a wrong. Suggest a break in the interview; get the client a cup of tea. Acknowledge the anger, let him or her vent, and then go on.

I.   Helping Theories

This chapter would be incomplete without a brief overview of various methods of helping clients. Law is a service industry; we provide expert services to our clients and receive compensation in return. Understanding what a client tells us is the basis for good service; it is also colored by a variety of complicated factors. In order to provide the best service possible to the client, we must strive to understand the background on which they sketch their story. In the previous section, we considered the "client's truth"—the client's relaying of circumstances as influenced by history, environment, and beliefs, as well as legal and emotional needs. The "client's truth" is not necessarily the same "truth" as the one that can be corroborated. It is not a lie because the client intends no deceit. A client might repress the truth because it is painful; a client might actually lie because the truth is too humiliating.

It is important for us to have an understanding of the various theories of helping in order to provide the best service possible. Although most lawyers and paralegals are not trained to conduct therapy under any theory, if we acquaint ourselves with the theories, we can understand ourselves and our clients. We can understand why clients say the things they say and why they sometimes distort the truth.

In their book, Interviewing, Counseling, and Negotiating, Bastress and Harbaugh identify five main theories of helping clients:

- Psychoanalysis
- Person-centered theory
- Behaviorism
- Rational-emotive therapy
- Transactional analysis

1. Psychoanalysis

Developed by Sigmund Freud, psychoanalysis divides the personality into the id, ego and superego. The id connotes our primitive instincts, the superego, our morality, and the ego mediates between the id and the superego and the outside world. Because human beings seek pleasure to avoid pain, the ego may "repress" an unpleasant experience or "rationalize" an event to make it appear it was really for the best. Repression and rationalization are two of the defenses that, when used by a client, might distort the truth.

2. Person-Centered Theory

Developed by Carl Rogers, this theory, in contrast to Freud's, maintains that individuals are basically good and can reach their full potential with the help of an empathetic, nonjudgmental person. A client who knows you will not judge him or her is more likely to share information that is embarrassing or unfavorable. This theory focuses on a person's intrinsic worth.

3. Behaviorism

Behaviorists believe that external stimuli provide the basis for an individual's actions and behavior. In contrast to psychoanalysis and person-centered theories, behaviorism concentrates not on a person's feelings and thoughts, but on a person's actions. By changing a person's response to external stimuli, the therapist can alter the person's behavior.

4. Rational-Emotive Therapy

Developed in the 1950s, the premise of this theory is that an individual's emotional system, that is, anxiety, can profoundly affect how he or she deals with an event and that emotional problems are a result of faulty thinking. RET assumes all individuals are born with rational and irrational potential. These tendencies might be aroused and intensified by the environment.

5. Transactional Analysis

The premise of transactional analysis is that individuals have three separate personality or ego states: parent, adult, and child. TA was developed by Eric Berne in the 1960s and combines various perspectives. Its proponents believe that each individual is inherently good and can control his or her own life. A "transaction" occurs whenever two people interact and may involve any combination of ego states. The adult state is logical and rational. The parent state is based on behavior inherited from parents and other authority figures. The child state is creative, playful, and spontaneous. According to Berne, individuals need a good combination of all three states. If one state is underemphasized or overemphasized, problems of personality might result.

Lawyers and paralegals are not therapists. If we work to understand our clients, however, our relationship with them will be more productive and our service to them, more effective.

SUMMARY

Interviewing is a sequence of contacts between a client and a lawyer or paralegal that results in a body of information and insights about the case and the client. Establishing, fostering and maintaining the relationship between the paralegal and the client is of the utmost importance in the delivery of legal services. Establishment of a good rapport is a basis for productive questioning. Clients lie; clients get angry. Understanding a client's emotional needs is important to a successful interview and relationship.

In the next chapter we discuss the witness interview.

Key Terms

Behaviorism   Person-centered theory
Confidentiality   Psychoanalysis
Conflict of interest   Rapport
Inhibitors   Rational-emotive therapy
Motivators   Transactional analysis

REVIEW QUESTIONS

1. Why is it important to establish a good rapport with a client?

2. What would you do if a client arrived at the interview with two small children?

3. What do you say when a client asks you for legal advice?

4. List five "motivators" and seven "inhibitors" and state how they can influence the interview.

5. Once a good rapport is established with the client, how do you maintain it?

6. How do you handle the client who lies?

7. How do you contend with an angry client?

8. What is a helping theory? How does one affect our relationship with a client?

9. Should you use electronic mail to contact a client? Why or why not?

10. What matters may not be delegated by an attorney to a paralegal?

11. How is confidentiality defined and applied in a legal setting?

12. What is a conflict of interest? If one is uncovered, what steps are taken?

CHAPTER EXERCISES

Exercise 4-1:   The managing partner of your law firm, Mercer, Alvarez & Peabody, has assigned you the task of writing directions to your office for clients who walk, drive, or take public transportation. These directions will be mailed to clients before their first appointment. Use any format you think appropriate. For purposes of this assignment, assume your classroom is the office and write instructions accordingly. Be certain to have the costs correct. Trade with another student and check for accuracy and clarity.

Exercise 4-2:   Henry Winslow, a businessman new to the area, has contacted your firm to do some tax and estate planning. You have an appointment with him two weeks from today. Draft the initial client letter.

Exercise 4-3:   Design your interviewing area, whether it is the library, conference room or other space. It should be comfortable and flexible for interviewing. Use a rectangle to show the desk, other shapes to show chairs and Xs to place clients. Write a paragraph explaining why you chose this arrangement.

How would you modify it if you were to interview:

a) an elderly client with a will problem?
b) a husband and wife with an estate problem?
c) a mother with a juvenile (teenage) son?
d) a business woman with a corporate problem?

Write a paragraph explaining each arrangement.

Exercise 4-4:   Choose a partner from the class. One person assumes the role of the client, the other the paralegal. Begin the interview as in the above example. State your role as a paralegal; discuss confidentiality. Switch roles; repeat exercise. Discuss and critique.

Exercise 4-5:   Assume the inevitable happens and the client asks you for legal advice. Practice what to say. Switch roles; repeat exercise. Discuss and critique.

Exercise 4-6:   You have just finished the initial client interview from Exercise 4-7. Draft a letter to the client advising her of the date and time of the next interview and reminding her to bring the following documents: current will, deed to house, and life insurance policy.

5

The Witness Interview

CHAPTER OBJECTIVES

In this chapter you will learn

- how to evaluate a witness;
- how to handle a reluctant witness;
- how to find and evaluate an expert witness.

A. Introduction

Although the interview of a witness contains many of the same considerations as interviewing a client in terms of cultural differences, communications, and the psychology of interviewing, there are differences of relationship, purpose, and level of interest that can influence the quality of the interview.

1. Relationship

The depth of the interviewer's relationship with a witness depends on the importance of the witness to the case. For example, if you are assisting in a simple real estate transaction, spending an hour developing a relationship with the appraiser is probably a waste of your time and your client's money. If you are investigating a medical malpractice case, however, and the witness is the only nurse who was present in the operating room when the doctor performed the Cesarean section and hysterectomy, time spent developing a relationship with her is time well spent. How important is this witness? Could another witness—for example another appraiser—fill the same role or does your case rely on a single witness, such as the nurse?

Usually the relationship is limited. The client has given the overview of the problem during a lengthy interview or series of interviews. The interviewer has established a rapport with the client that allows for a efficient working relationship. For the interviewer, developing a professional relationship with the witness is less important and in some cases even inadvisable. The interviewer-witness relationship is limited to the information the witness has and the interviewer needs.

2. Purpose

The witness provides information generally in the form of corroboration of the client's (or other witness's) statements, or of new information about the case. The client has provided facts that support a theory of relief; you seek to corroborate the facts to support the theory. Occasionally the witness will provide information that contradicts your client. You might have expected the information or it might come as a surprise. Either way it is information you need to know.

3. Level of Interest

Because clients invest time, money, and emotion in their own cases, they have a lot at stake. They can swim (win), sink (lose), or surface somewhere in between (settle). A witness usually takes no such risk.

B. Ethical Considerations

1. Overview

Generally you may not speak with anyone who is represented by counsel without permission from his or her attorney. This is especially applicable in multiple-party civil lawsuits and criminal cases where witnesses are more likely to have their own attorneys. There are, however, circumstances where it is permissible to talk to people who are "represented" by attorneys. In order for the bar against communication to operate, counsel's representation must be related to the cause at issue, and there must be actual representation. Often corporate counsel will communicate with attorneys suing the corporation and forbid them from interviewing employees of the corporation without counsel present. Because the attorneys represent the corporation and not the individual employees, there is no ethical bar against talking with employees who are not in a position to speak for or bind the corporation. The question to ask is, "Who does the attorney represent and what is the purpose of the representation?"

With regard to records, unless you are instructed otherwise, you should always identify yourself and your purpose and have appropriate authorizations before attempting to secure confidential documents. Sample authorization forms appear in Chapter 8.

While some ethical problems are clear, others are not; you should discuss difficult issues with your supervising attorney and allow him or her to make the final decision.

In the unlikely event you are faced with a situation in which you believe your supervising attorney has made an unethical decision or has exhibited unethical behavior such as talking with a person the attorney knows or reasonably should have known is represented by counsel, call the bar association and explain your dilemma. They will provide you with guidance.

2. Guidelines and Rules

Under the National Association of Legal Assistants Model Standards and Guidelines for Utilization of Legal Assistants, Chapter IX, a legal assistant may "locate and interview witnesses, so long as the witnesses are aware of the status and function of the legal assistant." Article 4 of the ABA Model Rules of Professional Conduct provides additional guidance with regard to an attorney's relationship with persons other than clients in issues such as truthfulness, contact, and respect.

a. Truthfulness

Under ABA Model Rules of Professional Conduct, Rule 4.1, an attorney is prohibited from knowingly making a false statement of fact or law to a third party. The Comment to the Rule illustrating the meaning of the Rule, however, makes clear that this prohibition does not mean that an attorney has an affirmative duty to disclose relevant facts to the third party. Thus a paralegal may not make a statement he or she knows is false to a witness, yet is under no obligation to supply any pertinent information about the case. Some facts about the case may need to be disclosed in order for the paralegal to properly interview the witness. The question to be answered is, "Must I disclose this information to this witness in order to elicit the information I seek from the witness?" Do not disclose more than is absolutely necessary.

b. Contact with Unrepresented Persons

As discussed earlier, an attorney may not speak with a person she knows, or learns during conversation, is represented by counsel without permission of the attorney. When the person is unrepresented by counsel, however, the attorney may talk with the person but must explain her role as the attorney for another person and may not give advice except to advise the witness to obtain counsel. ABA Model Rules of Professional Conduct, Rule 4.3. A paralegal must explain his or her position so the witness is clear about the role the paralegal has.

If the witness is important to the case and is unrepresented at the time of the interview, the paralegal should be prepared to obtain all relevant information because the initial interview might be the only opportunity to interview this witness before formal discovery begins. This is particularly true in cases in which the witness might have a legal or financial interest in the case. In cases like this, a witness's availability or willingness to talk might be significantly affected by the witness's consultation with an attorney. Also, when a witness has a potential legal interest in the events or transaction, what the witness says or does not say might be affected by information obtained from his or her attorney.

c.   Respect for Rights of Third Persons

Under ABA Model Rules of Professional Conduct, Rule 4.4, an attorney may not "embarrass, delay, or burden" a witness for the sole purpose of doing so without any other legitimate justification. Nor may an attorney violate a person's legal rights in the collection of evidence.

3.   Payments to Witnesses

Both the ABA Model Rules of Professional Conduct and the ABA Model Code of Professional Responsibility forbid an attorney from paying a nonexpert witness for testifying and from agreeing to pay a contingent fee to any witness. An attorney, however, may reimburse a nonexpert witness for expenses of testifying (such as parking fees) and may pay an expert witness a reasonable fee. The fee paid to the expert is not for his or her testimony, but for work performed—such as reviewing medical records—in arriving at a legitimate opinion. *See* Rule 3.4(b) and Comments of the ABA Model Rules of Professional Conduct and EC 7-28 and DR 7-109 of the ABA Model Code of Professional Responsibility and Disciplinary Rules.

C.   Arranging the Interview

Call the witness to schedule the interview at her convenience. If you believe it is important to assess the witness's appearance and demeanor, schedule a personal interview at your office or, if she is reluctant to come to your office, at a neutral place where you cannot be overheard. In some situations you might want to interview a witness in her own home, among comfortable surroundings where she may be more likely to be forthcoming with information. There may be times you want the element of "surprise" on your side. In that case, find out where the witness lives and drop by the house at a reasonable hour.

In other cases, you will want to interview by telephone. If your client is unable to provide the witness's number, use the phone book, directory assistance, or the Internet to locate it. Sometimes numbers are either unlisted or listed in another's name and it is necessary to send the witness a letter requesting a meeting.

If a telephone interview is satisfactory, discuss with the witness the most convenient time to call, and conduct the interview at that time. For a nurse working the midnight shift, the best time may be about 1:00 A.M. after she or he has checked on all patients and administered medications. *See* Chapter 3 for more on telephone interviews.

D. Witness Evaluation

First consider the circumstances. Is this witness sympathetic, hostile, or neutral to your case? What has your client indicated about this witness? Does your client know this witness? If so, what is the relationship? What information would you like the witness to provide?

E. Strategy

Unless there are exigent circumstances, you should have theory charts prepared *before* you interview a witness. The charts will give you an idea as to whom you should interview and what information you hope to obtain from them. The charts will help you prepare a list of questions to which you need answers. The chart should *not* accompany you on your interview; it is a privileged and confidential work product to be used as an "in-house" organizational tool.

1. Dress

You should dress appropriately—a suit for one type of interview (for example, the bank executive) and jeans for another (for example, the saw-mill operator). What do you want to convey to the person you are interviewing? Will he feel comfortable enough to talk to you?

2. Manner

Be polite and pleasant but firm. Tell the witness who you represent and why you want to talk to her. Sometimes, if a witness is made to feel important to the case, she is more likely to share information. Conversely, sometimes a witness will want to talk with you because it makes her feel important; she may embellish the story or distort the facts to satisfy her ego.

Assume you found the person you want to interview. When you meet the witness, the exchange might be as follows:

Paralegal: Hi, Ms. Paul? Melissa Paul?
Witness: Yes.
Paralegal: I'm Terry Williams; I work with Maggie Watkins, an attorney who represents the Rodriguez family [handing her your card]. You may recall two of their children were seriously injured when they were hit by a car several months ago at the intersection of 16th and Hopkins Streets. Your name appears on the police report as an eye witness to the accident. May I have a few words with you?

If the witness seems unsure or doesn't want to be bothered, be firm and persistent.

Witness: Yes, but I'm busy now.
Paralegal: Gosh, aren't we all! This will only take a few minutes, I promise.
Witness: Look, I just don't have the time right now.
Paralegal: Ms. Paul, those kids really need your help.
Witness: Well, okay, I guess, if you hurry.
Paralegal: Thank you so much—I'll be as brief as possible.

Sometimes a little encouragement or a combination of encouragement and making the witness feel important is all that is needed to get the interview started.

Remember to avoid leading questions. In other words, do not suggest an answer to your question in the question itself. Nonleading questions take more time, but yield more accurate information. If what the witness tells you hurts your case, it is better to know early on—even before the case is filed—because it tells you something about your adversary's case. The information most harmful to your case will likely come from an unknown witness or from a known witness who has information you failed to elicit. The person you are interviewing may next appear on the witness stand destroying your case. Although you cannot prevent such testimony, if it is expected, the attorney can deal with it through a deposition or by presenting a rebuttal witness to call into question the witness's credibility.

3. First-Hand Knowledge

First-hand knowledge is what a witness knows because he has heard it, seen it, touched it, smelled it, or tasted it. He has experienced it first-hand. First-hand knowledge does not necessarily guarantee accuracy since it is the witness's powers of perception that are being tested. But it tends to approach the truth more closely than anything else we have. *See for example, State v. Bloodsworth,* 313 Md. 688, 548 A.2d 128 (1988), a rape case in which the jury believed the "positive identification" testimony of the complainant and found the defendant guilty. Thereafter, in post-conviction proceedings, DNA testing proved the witness was wrong.

Consider the statement: "She was driving way too fast." Taken at face value, it is of little use to your case. There is no objective measure of what it means. A follow-up question might help. Compare the following two dialogues.

Dialogue 1

Witness: She was driving way too fast.
Paralegal: Okay, anything else?
Witness: No, that's about it. I'm in a hurry.
Paralegal: Okay, thanks for talking to me.

Dialogue 2

Witness: She was driving way too fast.
Paralegal: When you say "way too fast," what do you mean?
Witness: She was just speeding.
Paralegal: Help me get a clearer idea of her speed. What made you believe that she was speeding?
Witness: Well, there's a curve in that road—nothing too much, but she went around it on two wheels! She came up on the cars in front of her real fast—they looked like they were stopped, but they weren't.
Paralegal: You saw her go through the curve on two wheels?
Witness: Yep—and tires squealing too. I thought she was going to flip over.

By probing the witness, you learn that the witness has objective criteria—what he saw and what he heard—which tends to support his conclusion of speeding. Consider another ending to the interview:

Witness: She was driving way too fast.
Paralegal: When you say "way too fast," what do you mean?
Witness: She was just speeding.
Paralegal: Help me get a clearer idea of her speed. What made you believe that she was speeding?
Witness: Well, that's what Cliff said and he's been driving a long time. I didn't really get a good look.
Paralegal: You've been very helpful. I'd like to talk to Cliff if he's around.

Further questioning alerts you to the fact that the original contact witness actually did not see the driver. Therefore, he has no first-hand knowledge of the incident and will not prove helpful to your case. Cliff is the person who apparently saw the driver; he is the witness with the information.

4. The Reluctant Witness

Witnesses not parties to the proceeding, be it litigation or a transaction, are sometimes reluctant to talk to the interviewer. The reluctance may stem from any number of factors, including:

- general distrust of strangers;
- fear of reprisal from another;
- protection of another;
- unfamiliarity with the process; and
- guilt for being involved.

If we can understand the basis for a witness's reluctance, we can attempt to allay any fears or concerns he has and encourage him to talk with us. There are times when a little coaxing, such as in the example above, simply will not work. Be certain he knows exactly who you are and what your role is. Be sympathetic and persistent. Talk about the process to make it less personal. ("All the interviews have to be concluded as soon as possible," not "You have to talk to me today.") If you have the opportunity, ask him why he does not want to talk with you. You might send a colleague to see if he or she fares any better. Perhaps explain to the witness that he might have his own reasons why he doesn't want to be involved, but that he would be doing an enormous service to your client if he would talk; you are simply trying to determine exactly what happened.

It might be that your adversary has already interviewed him and subtly (or not so subtly) suggested that he refuse to talk to you. If you believe this might have occurred, report it immediately to your attorney. Of course, you could always inform him that if he chooses not to talk with you, he might be served with a subpoena, which will force him not only to talk, but to do it under oath, outside his home, in a court or an attorney's office.

F. Writing about the Interview

Any contact with a witness or a potential witness must be documented, either by a statement from the witness or by a memorandum to the file detailing the circumstances of the interview. This should be done whether or not you believe the witness has any importance to the case. Because others in the office may work on the case, failing to note your contact with a person you deem unimportant to the case could result in another person contacting the person a second time. Preservation of information is addressed in Chapter 6.

G.   Expert Witnesses

1.   When Used

An expert witness is a witness who possesses more knowledge or expertise in a certain area than the average person. An engineer might be qualified to testify as an expert in a case involving bridge construction. A neurologist might be qualified as an expert witness in a case involving a brain disorder. Expert witnesses are generally used to help prove a cause of action or to establish the appropriate amount of damages in a case. Experts are commonly retained before a complaint is filed to avoid violations of FED. R. CIV. P. 11. After a complaint is filed, experts aid in the planning of discovery and might testify at trial.

Federal Rule of Civil Procedure, Rule 702, regulates use of experts. "If scientific, technical, or other specialized knowledge, will assist the trier of fact to understand the evidence or to determine a fact in issue, a witness qualified as an expert by knowledge, skill, experience, training, or education may testify thereto in the form of an opinion or otherwise."

Although usually not witnesses to the event or occurrence, experts may be qualified by a judge to apply their knowledge to the facts of the case and render their opinions. For example, an accident reconstruction expert can help to establish liability in a multiple car crash. A psychiatrist could testify as to which parent, in his or her opinion, would be a better custodian for the children. An appraiser would testify as to the value of a piece of real estate. Usually each party employs an expert if specific expertise is necessary.

2.   Yours

Although the attorney usually prepares the expert for testifying, your tasks might include locating, interviewing and evaluating the potential expert. The most brilliant scientist in the world will not make a good expert witness if she cannot explain information to the average person. It is important for you to be aware of the expert's position and expertise. Will she establish causation for the accident? Establish the value of the property? What questions do you have for her? How can she help your case? How can she hurt it?

3. Theirs

Each party is required to divulge to the other party the identity of any expert witness that party intends to call at trial. This allows the other party the opportunity to depose, or examine under oath, the witness during the pretrial phase. In some states the pretrial deposition of an expert witness can only be accomplished by agreement of the parties or by court order.

4. Finding Experts

Locate expert witnesses by contacting:

- other lawyers who take similar cases;
- local or national trial lawyer organizations, such as the American Association of Trial Lawyers;
- a business entity or educational institution that studies or researches the area; or
- an on-line service such as the Industrial Defense Library (products-liability experts).

Experts should be contacted and interviewed as soon as the decision to retain them is reached. Review the expert's curriculum vitae and any published materials she has written. If there is a contradictory view, review that information as well. If the expert has testified previously, and transcripts are available, review them to determine whether the expert was a good witness. The Industrial Defense Library publishes transcripts of products-liability experts.

The best expert does not always make the best witness. Sometimes the expert is unable to explain a matter to a judge or a jury in such a way that is understandable for the fact-finder.

Paralegals should familiarize themselves with the area of expertise so that an interview will be productive.

SUMMARY

The extent of your relationship with a witness depends on his or her importance to the case; it is governed by various rules of ethics. If a witness is reluctant to talk to you, apptempt to discern the source of the reluctance and assuage the witness's fears.

Familiarize yourself with experts available for your case and the area of expertise in order to make the interview productive. Remember that the best expert does not always make the best witness. Sometimes the expert is unable to explain a matter to a judge or a jury in such a way that is understandable to the fact-finder.

Key Terms

Curriculum vitae   **First-hand knowledge**
Expert witness   **Reluctant witness**

REVIEW QUESTIONS

1. What is an expert witness and how is one used?
2. How does one find an expert?
3. What is first-hand knowledge? Why is it important to your case?
4. What steps should you take if you believe your supervising attorney has done something unethical?
5. In what ways does interviewing a witness differ from interviewing a client?
6. Do the ethical rules prevent you from interviewing a witness who is represented by counsel? Why or why not?
7. Under what circumstances can nonexpert witnesses be paid? Are the rules different for expert witnesses? How?

CHAPTER EXERCISES

Exercise 5-1:   Return to the scenarios at the beginning of Chapter 1. For each scenario, prepare a list of witnesses you would interview.

Exercise 5-2:   Review the Model Standards and Guidelines for Utilization of Legal Assistants (National Association of Legal Assistants) and determine which ones apply to contact with witnesses. What provisions do the Guidelines make?

Exercise 5-3:   Choose a partner from the class. One of you is a paralegal representing Greg Welsch who has been charged with the theft of a motor bike belonging to Mary Ann Morgan. Morgan had been shopping at a local drugstore when the bike—which had been parked outside—was taken. The paralegal's job is to interview Morgan who is very hostile to Welsch. The paralegal simply wants to establish dates and time of the incident.

6

Preserving Information

CHAPTER OBJECTIVES

This chapter discusses the importance and methods of preserving information, and specifically how to

- take accurate notes during the interview;
- draft the interview summary;
- draft the interoffice memorandum;
- record audio and video information;
- use diagrams and photography;
- meet evidentiary standards.

[P]reserve case information as though when you walk out of your office you are hit by a bus; somebody else has to come in and take over where you left off.

Annonymous

A. Introduction

It is hard to over-dramatize the importance of preserving information about a case. In this chapter, we turn to a discussion of the nature of the information obtained from clients and witnesses and the methods of preserving that information. We consider the importance of taking notes during the interview, summarizing the interview, different methods of preserving information, the interoffice memorandum, and, finally, maintaining the file. Many cases, especially civil cases in state courts, take years to complete. Lawyers and paralegals with different writing styles and organizational skills might work on the same case. Therefore it is imperative that each person who works on the case file strives to create and maintain as thorough and accurate a record as possible. Furthermore, information in a case file is important even after the case is "over."

Burglary

Last week Gladys Winston was arrested for the burglary of an apartment. Immediately after the arrest, her family retained Kris Zucker, one of the attorneys in your firm who handles criminal defense work; Ms. Zucker represented Ms. Winston at her arraignment. Ms. Winston met briefly with Ms. Zucker, in the presence of family members, when she was released after she posted bail at arraignment. Because there were third parties present at the first meeting with the client, Ms. Zucker did not ask Ms. Winston for her version of the events leading to her arrest; nor did they discuss possible defenses to the charge. Ms. Winston was advised not to discuss the case with anyone except Ms. Zucker or paralegals working for the office. Ms. Zucker explained to Ms. Winston's family that this advice protects Ms. Winston's rights. Ms. Winston scheduled an initial interview for today and Ms. Zucker has asked you to be there. Shortly before the interview was to begin, Ms. Zucker was called to court on an emergency matter. She asked you to conduct the initial fact interview with the client.

B. The Importance of Preserving Information

Whether the interview is conducted in person or by telephone, with a client or with a witness, it is important to have a record of what was said. Information is preserved for different reasons, the most important of which is to retain a complete and accurate record. An accurate record might be relied on in a different forum, including a malpractice claim against your firm by a disgruntled client.

1. Accurate Record

It is imperative to create an accurate record while memories are fresh, while people are able to recall detail. Because cases can take years on their journey through the court system, because lawyers and paralegals come and go, and because clients and witnesses die or become otherwise unavailable, we have to be able to reconstruct the case from what we, or others, have preserved. An attorney or paralegal new to a case should be able to pick up the file and by reading it gain a thorough and accurate understanding of the nature of the case and the parties involved. Consider the cases against a major chemical company by women who developed complications from silicone breast implants. Many years have passed since the first suit was filed; many different paralegals and attorneys have handled the same cases, and many parties and other witnesses have become unavailable to testify because of death, infirmity, incompetency, or because they are beyond the jurisdiction of the court.

2. Reliance on Information in Another Forum

Preserving accurate information guarantees a clear and complete record in the event a client relies on case file documentation in another forum. In fact it can be a matter of life or death. For example, an experienced criminal defense attorney was asked five years after a trial in a death penalty case to recall pretrial interviews with a client to determine whether he had properly advised the client as to certain rights. The issue was whether the defendant-client had the right to make an unsworn statement at sentencing to the judge or jury. The attorney was able to determine by looking at his notes that he had in fact not properly advised the defendant with regard to this critical information. The attorney testified that although it was his practice to discuss the issue with a client in cases in which the death penalty could be imposed, it was also his practice to make specific notes of such a conversation in the file. Since his notes reflected no such conversation, he was confident that he had not discussed it with his client. Therefore the court found that the client had a valid ineffective-assistance-of-counsel claim in a post-conviction hearing and ordered further proceedings. The attorney was able to give the court this information in spite of the fact that over five years had elapsed between the time of the interview and the time the issue arose.

3. Malpractice Claim

An attorney must be able to present an accurate record in the event of a malpractice action against the attorney. Good legal practices, including excellent record keeping, help to avoid problems of client suits. Even the best attorney, however, may find himself or herself as a defendant in a malpractice action. If that happens, well-kept records might well be the basis of vindication.

For example, in a case involving custody of a child, let's assume the losing parent sues the attorney for malpractice, alleging that she should have talked with the child's teachers and hired a psychiatrist as an expert witness. The issues are valid because these are concerns a competent attorney would have discussed with the client. If a review of the attorney's file indicates that she in fact talked to the teachers, but made a tactical decision not to call them as witnesses at trial because they clearly did not favor the client as the custodial parent, the claim is very weak. If the notes showed further that the attorney recommended to the client that she hire a psychiatrist and that the client was vehemently opposed to it because she was afraid the psychiatrist would favor the child's father, the second claim is weak and recovery against the attorney is unlikely. Note that in cases in which the attorney's handling of a case is placed in issue by an unhappy client, the client waives her right to have the attorney's material kept confidential under the attorney-client privilege.

C. Preserving Client Information

1. Preliminary Information

Before you begin to interview the client, it helps to explain the process—that you will be taking notes to have an accurate record of what was said, that you may interrupt the client from time to time, or that you may ask him or her to slow down. Some firms use a special Intake Form to gather preliminary information, such as the client's full name, address, telephone number, and referral source.

Intake forms provide essential information. For example, in a domestic violence case, the form may indicate that the client wants you to contact her through her sister or mother, but not at her home. Ignoring the restriction in a case like this could jeopardize a client's safety. If the case involves a divorce, the client might not want his spouse to know that he has contacted an attorney. Whatever the instructions, you must be certain to follow them. Other important information on the Intake Sheet includes any upcoming court dates or filing deadlines and whether the client needs a translator.

PRACTICE TIP: The Intake Sheet provides insight into the nature of the case and any instructions/restrictions regarding contacting the client. Remember the relationship the client has with your office is confidential.

If the client has already completed an intake sheet, you need not review it in detail with her, but you should give it a cursory review together to be certain the information is correct and complete. If the client has not completed a sheet and you are the first person interviewing her, it might be your responsibility to obtain the information. More than one client has left an initial interview without ever being asked her address and phone number, which might be unlisted.

A sample intake or preliminary information form appears in Exhibit 6.1.

A completed Intake Form is in the Appendix in the "Sample Client File." If your office doesn't have one, you might want to design one to meet your purposes.

INTAKE SHEET

Name _____

Address _____

_____

Mailing Address _____

Phone: Home _____

          Work _____

How to contact _____

When to contact _____

Special instructions/restrictions on contact _____

_____

Referred by _____

Date of first contact _____

Date of first interview _____

Billing rate _____

Responsible attorney _____

Court date/filing date _____

Name of adverse party _____

Other information _____

_____

_____

_____

Exhibit 6.1 **Sample Intake Form**

2. Taking Notes

After the preliminary information has been gathered, you begin the actual interview. If you have an idea of the issue(s), your theory chart will help guide the questioning. Take copious notes in outline form as to what the client says, using her words to the extent possible. Although recording the client's words might seem tedious, it is important that your conclusions and your judgments not be substituted for your client's facts. Use quotation marks to mark the client's words. If she is talking faster than you can collect the information, ask her to slow down. If necessary, stress to the client the importance of your having an accurate account of the case. The client knows it is in her interest that you record the information correctly and thoroughly. At the same time, however, you must balance the need for accurate note taking with the client's need to tell a narrative. Too many interruptions may result in lost detail and a frustrated client.

As you write the notes during the interview, look up at the client intermittently to make eye contact as a way of preserving rapport and of acknowledging with approval the amount and kind of information she is providing. Remain nonjudgmental; nod your head and utter "uh huh" to show understanding and perhaps empathy, not agreement.

PRACTICE TIP: Gather information as though you have only one chance to talk with the client. Preserve information as though your client's case depends on it.

Good note taking is a skill that must be learned and mastered and it can be a difficult task under some circumstances. One way to make it easier is to use two legal pads at the interview, one to record the outline and details of the interview, the other to note items to which you need to return or explore further. After the client has given her narrative, return to those items on the second pad, adding the information to the outline. On the second pad, you should also note things the client needs to do ("find last year's tax return"), and things you need to do ("title search 901 Peach Street—ASAP"). Before the client leaves, copy the things she needs to do on a separate sheet of paper and give it to her.

3. Writing the Summary

The summary is a synopsis of the interview prepared from the outline notes. It is for internal office use only, protected by the work product rule and not discoverable by the other party. It should be completed for either a personal or telephone interview. Draft it as soon as possible after the interview has ended. Referring to your notes, write a narrative about the interview, putting into context the information the client has given. Keep it factual and clear; precision is absolutely critical. If you find it necessary to make assumptions, note what assumptions you are making and why.

The sooner the summary is prepared, the more accurate and thorough it is. The longer the wait, the more the risk of inaccuracy, especially if another interview concerning a similar cause of action occurs between the time you interview the client and the time you prepare the summary. Allow extra time for preparing the summary immediately after the interview when scheduling appointments.

The summary is comprised of four parts:

1) Interview specifics (date, interviewer, and length)
2) Statement of the problem
3) Narrative summary (client's description of events)
4) Impressions of client

The date of the interview is important because it tells the reader how long after the incident the interview took place. Certainly an interview conducted a year or more after an incident leaves open to speculation the accuracy of the client's memory, whereas an interview conducted close in time to the incident—when the person's memory of the incident is fresh—suggests a more accurate reporting. The interviewer's name should appear on the face of the summary since the attorney responsible for the case will want to discuss the case with the interviewer. The length of the interview might indicate the thoroughness of the interview and whether a follow-up needs to be scheduled. A matter involving multiple theories of recovery may require more than one interview; thus a follow-up would be scheduled.

The statement of the problem should be brief and clear. For most cases, one to three sentences will be adequate. The narrative summary is the heart of the document. It is a summary of the client's description of events. It is a retelling of the client's story using as many of the client's own words as possible. It should be as long as necessary to tell someone unfamiliar with the case what the client said.

The summary should also include your impression of the client. In developing your impression consider whether the client was articulate. Did she seem clear about what happened? How did she present herself? Was she calm? Fidgety? Did she seem truthful? Your observations will help the attorney determine what kind of witness the client will make at a deposition and at trial.

Write the summary, either by hand or on your computer, as soon as possible after the interview. You may dictate your summary using a dictaphone; some large firms in metropolitan areas have a secretarial pool available to type what you have dictated. Dictating is another skill to be learned; if you want to pursue the dictating option your firm offers, start with short memos and letters until you become proficient enough to dictate an interview summary. Attach your interview outline and notes to the summary since those are the only notes that were taken contemporaneously with the interview and are the basis for the summary.

> **PRACTICE TIP:** If you use a computer, be certain to back up your work on a disk. If you intend to give that disk to someone else to work on, back up a second copy on another disk.

4. The Follow-Up Interview

Writing the summary brings to mind additional questions for which you need answers, documents you need to obtain, and perhaps other issues you need to explore. Depending on the length of time necessary to elicit the additional details, the follow-up may be done by telephone or in person. Regardless of the method, the procedure is similar to that described above—copious note taking followed by a summary.

5. The Interoffice Memorandum

After you have interviewed the client, summarized the interview, and researched the law, you should prepare the Interoffice Memorandum.

The Interoffice Memorandum contains the facts and information obtained from the Intake Sheet and the interview, your legal analysis of the case, the client's goals, the alternatives discussed and the proposed follow-up. It must be well organized and easy to read so that the results of your interview and research are clear. Attach the litigation/theory chart containing the elements of the law important to the case, making a chart for each individual cause of action or theory of relief at issue. *See* Chapter 2 for a discussion of the role of substantive law in the interview process and the value of preparing a litigation chart listing the elements of the cause of action.

While the Interview Summary focuses on the factual description provided by the client, the Interoffice Memorandum focuses on the application of the facts to the law. To prepare the memorandum, study the interview facts from the summary and the law from the litigation chart, and combine them in narrative form. The following example illustrates the entire process, pre- to post-interview.

6. Gladys Winston File: From Theory Chart to Interoffice Memorandum

a. Pre-Interview

Gladys Winston is arriving for her initial interview today. Before the interview you consult the statute and case law of your jurisdiction and learn that burglary is defined as the breaking and entering of the dwelling of another in the nighttime with the intent to commit a felony therein:

N.C. GEN. STAT. §14-51 (1994)

There shall be two degrees in the crime of burglary as defined at the common law. If the crime be committed in a dwelling house . . . and any person is in the actual occupation of any part of said dwelling house . . . at the time of the commission of such crime, it shall be burglary in the first degree. If such crime be committed in a dwelling house . . . not actually occupied by anyone at the time of the commission of the crime . . . it shall be burglary in the second degree. . . .

At common law burglary is defined as the breaking and entering of the dwelling house of another in the nighttime with the intent to commit a felony therein.

State v. Jones
249 N.C. 642, 243 S.E.2d 118 (1978)

To constitute burglary in either degree . . . the breaking and entering [must] occur in the nighttime.

You prepare a theory chart that looks like this:

Theory Chart

Client: Gladys Winston
Charge: Burglary
Date Chart Prepared: Today's date

ELEMENTS	SOURCE OF PROOF	INFORMAL FACT INVESTIGATION
1) BREAKING		
2) ENTERING		
3) A DWELLING		
4) OF ANOTHER		
5) IN THE NIGHTTIME		
6) WITH INTENT		

> **PRACTICE TIP:** Ask yourself "What do I have to prove?" or "What do they have to prove against my client?"

b. Interview

Because the attorney handling the case was called to court on an emergency matter, she was only able to speak with the client for a moment before going to court. You have been asked to handle the interview.

Interview of Gladys Winston

Paralegal: [Meeting client in waiting room] Ms. Winston? I'm Mickey Marino, a paralegal working with your attorney, Kris Zucker.

Client: Oh, yes. She told me you would be talking to me.

Paralegal: She is in court this morning and has asked me to meet with you.

Client: Okay.

Paralegal: Let's go to the conference room so we can talk [walking back to the room]. Did you have any trouble finding the office?

Client: Oh, no, your directions were fine.

Paralegal: Here we are. Could I get you some coffee or tea?

Client: Not right now; maybe later, thanks.

Paralegal: Why don't you sit here, Ms. Winston.

Client: Thank you.

Paralegal: Ms. Winston, I know you want to tell me your side of this but before we do I have a few things I have to go over with you. All right?

Client: Sure, I don't mind.

Paralegal: Ms. Zucker, your attorney, has asked me to review some of what she covered when she met you and your family outside court the other day. First of all, I want to tell you that I am a paralegal, I am not an attorney. I work for your lawyer and therefore everything you say to me is confidential, just as though you are saying it to your lawyer. I am here to help your lawyer help you. I cannot practice law or give you legal advice, but I am helping Ms. Zucker work on your case for you. Okay?

Client: Sure.

Paralegal: I understand that you have never been in any kind of trouble with the law before, is that right?

Client: No, I've never been in any trouble before. Not arrested or anything, even for a traffic ticket. But I'm in a whole lot of trouble now. The police are saying I robbed some lady's apartment and I didn't do anything. I don't even know how I got into this mess, it's just crazy!

Paralegal: I understand that you are upset; this is a very scary and difficult process to be caught up in. Let me tell you a little bit about where you stand right now.

[The paralegal tells client that she has been accused of committing a crime, that she has no obligation to prove she didn't do the crime but that the prosecutors must prove what they say happened. The paralegal reminds the client that generally she should not talk about the case to people outside the attorney-client relationship because those conversations are not privileged. The paralegal tells the client that the lawyer will advise her throughout the proceedings, which will involve pretrial discovery and motions for which the client will need to be available to the attorney for consultation; she will likely have to appear in court. The paralegal then obtains addresses for the client including back-ups and contact numbers who would know where the client could be reached in an emergency.]

Paralegal: A few minutes ago you said that you were charged with robbing an apartment. Let me use that expression to show you what I mean about what the prosecutor has to prove in your case. You are charged with burglary, not robbery. You cannot rob an apartment, even though people always talk about houses getting robbed. Crimes are made up of parts and without those parts all being there, without evidence to prove each part, the crime doesn't exist. Those parts are called elements. They are like the parts of a bicycle; the frame, wheels, handlebars, seat, pedals and chain. Without all the parts you don't have a bicycle, you just have parts. Same with robbery or burglary or any other crime. Robbery is the taking of property from a person with force or violence. So you see, you can't rob a house, because a house can't be made afraid. Do you see?

Client: I think so.

Paralegal: You are charged with burglary which is [holding up six fingers] 1) the breaking 2) and entering 3) the dwelling house 4) of another 5) in the nighttime 6) with the intent to commit a felony. So in order to prove the case against you the prosecutor must prove that you, and not someone else, broke and entered the dwelling house of another in the night with the intent to commit a felony. Do you see what I mean about the parts of the crime the prosecutor has to prove?

Client: Yes, I do, but does that mean that if I prove they didn't see me go in I'm not guilty, because I didn't break in, you know?

Paralegal: I can't answer that question because I can't give you legal opinions or advice. I can tell you that right now you are presumed innocent and that we have no burden to prove anything. If you have questions like that I will be happy to pass them on to Ms. Zucker. Only your lawyer should answer legal questions for you. For now, let me review with you what's in the police report because that sets out the general facts that will make up their case against you. Okay?

Client: Yeah, okay. What does it say?

[The paralegal reads the police report that recites that Ms. Winston was arrested following a complaint of a breaking and entering at 222 Renfrew Street, at approximately 12:00 P.M. She was seen leaving an apartment in an apartment building by a neighbor who knew the resident was in the basement laundry. When Ms. Winston was detained for questioning she broke into tears and said she was only in the apartment to visit a friend and watch soap operas. The owner of the apartment arrived and told police that he did not know Ms. Winston and had not invited her over for any reason. Ms. Winston was arrested and searched and a $50 bill was found in her pocket that the apartment resident identified as one he'd left on a table. Ms. Winston was transported to the station for booking.]

Paralegal: Do you understand what they say you did?

Client: Yes, but that's not what happened. They got it all wrong. I tried to explain it to the policeman in the car but he kept calling me a liar and a thief and said I was just like all other drug addicts.

Paralegal: Why don't we go back to the beginning and you can tell me what happened.

Client: Well, I went over to my friend's apartment on Renfrew Street to watch the soaps.

Paralegal: Who's your friend?

Client: Lucy Kowalski.

Paralegal: What apartment number does she live in?

Client: 222 Renfrew, apartment 817.

Paralegal: When was that?

Client: September 11, around noon.

Paralegal: How do you remember the time?

Client: That's easy: The soap we watch—One Chance at Living—comes on at 1:00 P.M. and we thought we'd eat a bit first. Well, I was walking down the hall and I saw a door to an apartment open. I thought it was Lucy's apartment and I walked in. When I called her name, no one answered. I looked around and realized it wasn't her apartment and I went to leave.

Paralegal: Okay, go on.

Client: Well, I don't know what got into me. I got a good job, I don't need the money.

Paralegal: I know this must be hard for you; take your time and tell me what happened then.

Client: Well, I saw this $50 bill lying on the table right by the door and I just reached and took it. I'm not a bad person, and I've never done anything like this before. I can't tell my friends . . . I've never been arrested before.

Paralegal: After you took the money, what did you do?

Client: Well, I panicked and started to run down the hall—but some guy came out of another apartment and yelled "Hey, thief!" So I stopped—I thought I could just explain it to him, but he grabbed me and took me to another apartment and called the police. The police came right away and handcuffed me, emptied my pockets and handbag. They just poured it out on the floor and started asking me questions. This guy came up and said he didn't know me. I started crying, trying to explain it was all a mistake . . . I was so scared.

Paralegal: Okay, Ms. Winston, let's go over this again, one small step at a time. When you saw the door, was it ajar, slightly open, or wide enough to walk in without touching?

Client: Oh it was open wide, that's why I didn't read the number, I thought Lucy left it open for me, so I just walked right in. . . .

The notes from the interview might look like Exhibit 6.2.

Gladys Winston
September 15, (year)/1 hr.
Cl chrgd w/ burg.
[Address, phone, contact names/addresses/phones.]
reviewed process & rights per instructions.
elements of offense.
read 911 reprt [police report].
Client version:
    To friend's apt to watch soaps.
    F = Lucy Kowalski.
    March 1, @ 12:00 P.M.; 222 Renfrew St., apt. 817; to see soap
        at 1:00 P.M.—"1 Chance at Living," have lunch first.
    walk dwn hall; saw dr to other apt open.
    went into apt; thought was F's; realized mistake & as leaving
        saw $50 bill on tbl near door; took it.
    guy out of apt yelled "Hey thief"; chased & grabbed Cl; he
        called cops.
    PD arrived fast, handcuffed, searched & questioned cl.
    Cl's pockets & purse emptied at scene.
    Apt resident arrived & sd he didn't know cl.
    Cl taken from scene.
    Cl charged; no arrest record; never in trouble; "I don't know
        what got into me; I've never done anything like this
        before; I got a good job; don't need the money."
    Reviewed facts of entry: Door open; cl. just walked in; not
        push or ajar bec. door open; Cl. thought F left open for
        her; didn't read apt # & just walked in.

Exhibit 6.2 **Interview Notes**

c.   Post Interview

From the interview notes you write the summary that appears in Exhibit 6.3.

Summary of Interview of Gladys Winston

Date of Interview: September 15, (year)
Interviewer: Paralegal
Length of Interview: 1 hour
Statement of Problem:

Ms. Winston states she was charged with burglary allegedly committed on September 12, [year].

Client's Description of Events

I interviewed Ms. Winston on September 15, [year], three days after she was charged with burglary. I reviewed the arrest narrative [police report] with her. She stated she had gone to the apartment of friend, Lucy Kowalski, of apt. #817 at 222 Renfrew Street, to watch the soaps. She arrived at the apartment around noon; she had planned to have lunch with her friend before the soap, "One Chance at Living," which starts at 1:00 P.M. As she was walking to her friend's apartment, she passed an apartment with an open door, which she entered. She said she went in the door believing the apartment was her friend's apartment, and that the door had been left open for her. When she realized she was in the wrong apartment she left. Near the door was a table; on the table she saw a $50 bill and took it. She was pursued by man who called her a thief, grabbed her, took her back to the apartment, and called police. The police came quickly. She was hand-cuffed, her pockets and purse were emptied, and the $50 found. She was questioned. She stated she "has a good job," doesn't "need the money," doesn't "know what got into" her. Never been arrested/in trouble before. [At this point the summary would continue to track the rest of the facts elicited in the interview with the client.]

Impressions

Ms. Winston appeared truthful and seemed genuinely distressed with her situation. Per my instructions, I identified myself, explained my role as a paralegal assisting Ms. Zucker. Ms. Winston was advised of the procedural status of the case and elements of burglary were identified for her. I also explained the prosecutor's burden of proof. She said she understood.

Exhibit 6.3 **Interview Summary**

The facts you elicited during the interview allow you to fill in the theory chart in Exhibit 6.4.

Theory Chart

Client: Gladys Winston
Charge: Burglary
Date Chart Prepared: September 15, (year)

ELEMENTS	SOURCE OF FACT	INFORMAL FACT INVESTIGATION
1) BREAKING	Client says door open—no break	cl. interview
2) ENTERING	client	cl. interview
3) A DWELLING	client/bldg. witness	cl. interview
4) OF ANOTHER	client/apt. owner/bldg. witness	cl. interview
5) IN THE NIGHTTIME	client/witness incident occurred @ 12:00-1:00 P.M.	cl. interview (interview witness)
6) WITH INTENT TO COMMIT FELONY	client intent formed after entry	cl. interview

Exhibit 6.4 **Theory Chart**

d.   Interoffice Memorandum

Although you have not had the opportunity to investigate the case, you have seen the initial incident report and the charging document. The client has stated with certainty that she entered the dwelling in the afternoon and that she was in the building to visit a friend for lunch. You note that, based on that disclosure, elements five and six cannot be satisfied—the client entered the apartment during the day and formed the intent to take the money after she was inside the apartment.

After a thorough review of the notes, theory chart, and summary, you turn to drafting the Interoffice Memorandum, shown in Exhibit 6.5. The memorandum is the written culmination of the initial client interview and preliminary research process. It addresses the client interview, the relevant law, and proposes the steps to be taken.

Interoffice Memorandum

To: Supervising Attorney
From: Paralegal
Date: September 16, (year)
Re: Gladys Winston

I interviewed Ms. Winston on September 15, [year]. A copy of the Intake Sheet and Interview Summary are attached.

Legal Analysis

The charging document in this case is a complaint charging client with common-law burglary. The elements of this crime are:

1) breaking
2) entering
3) a dwelling
4) of another
5) in nighttime
6) with felonious intent

1) *Breaking:* Client says the door was open and entry effected without touching the door. If the door was open and client did nothing except walk in, there is no breaking;
2) *Entering:* Client admits she went into the apartment and she was seen leaving. There is evidence of entry;
3 & 4) *Dwelling of another:* Client stated it was an apartment in the apartment building she believed belonged to her friend but that actually was the residence of another;
5) *Nighttime:* Client seems clear that she was there around noon, planning to have lunch with her friend before they watched the soap operas. This element is dispositive of the charge if the client is correct because the element of nighttime cannot be met;
6) *Felonious intent:* Client says she formed the intent to steal the money after she was already in the apartment. She must testify, however, for this to come into evidence.

[At this point the memo would list facts relevant to possible search and seizure issues and might address other possible charges, like trespass or theft.]

Nonlegal Concerns

Client is very concerned the effect this charge will have on her job. She is also very worried about attorney's fees and costs.

Follow-up

1) Check for prior arrest.
2) Get additional police reports and reports of interviews by police with witnesses and victim.
3) Interview Lucy Kowalski and apartment owner.

Attachments

Interview Summary and Notes
Litigation Chart
Intake Sheet

Exhibit 6.5 **Interoffice Memorandum**

As you can see, each item builds on the next, yet each stands alone in satisfying its purpose. A sample case investigation file appears in the Appendix.

D.   Preserving Witness Information

1.   Should You Preserve the Information?

Before you decide how to preserve information, you must decide whether to preserve it because once you have the statement, it might be discoverable by the other party. Under certain conditions, information should not be preserved. If the witness has not signed a statement and you do not want your opposition to learn of the existence of the witness, you might not want a statement.

2.   Written Statement

The statement of a witness should contain the name of the person interviewing, the person interviewed, other persons present, and the date, time, place, and circumstances of the interview. As with client interviewing, the interview should be memorialized as soon as possible after it occurs, even writing it as the witness talks and having the witness sign it, if this is desired, at the end of the meeting. A strong, clear statement from a witness may lead to a favorable early settlement for the client.

Under some, but not all, circumstances you will want a witness to sign his or her statement. First, you might want a signed statement from a witness to preserve testimony in case the witness moves, disappears, or for any reason is beyond the subpoena power of the court. Second, you might want to preserve the witness's information because the trial might be years away, and it is likely the witness will forget some or all of the information he knows now. Third, you might want to preserve the witness's statement in order to perpetuate the story in the statement at trial, or to impeach the witness at trial should the witness change his statement. Fourth, you might want a hostile witness to sign his statement (if he will) to lock in his story. Just because a witness is hostile to your case, is not truthful, has a police record, has a motive to lie, or simply is unsure of the accuracy of its contents does not mean that you should not preserve the statement. The old saying "the devil you know is better than the devil you don't know" applies here.

In the event you want a witness to sign the statement, be certain the statement carries the date, and attach a declaration that the document was "signed under the pains and penalties of perjury." If the statement is more than one page, number the pages, and have the witness initial each one. For example, "page 2 of 4." This protects the integrity of the document.

In addition to having a witness sign a statement, you want to have some indication that he has read every word of the statement and has adopted it as his own. If the witness hand-writes his own statement, review it with him, reading it very carefully and asking questions where it is not clear. If additions or changes are made, have him initial each one. If you write the statement while the witness talks, make certain you do the same review. Some investigators will intentionally make mistakes on every page and have the witness initial the "corrections." This technique ensures that the witness will read and initial every page within the text, which can later be used at trial to prove the accuracy and care with which the witness made the statement. This particular technique works very well with a hostile but patient witness who makes a statement helpful to your case. The appearance of his initials in the text can be used to prove not only that he made the statement, but that he took the time to review and correct it. The witness will be less likely to disavow a statement made with this technique.

For example, according to Gladys Winston's theory chart, one of the elements of burglary—in the nighttime—cannot be met because, according to Ms. Winston, she entered the apartment during the day. Ms. Winston has told you that she was on the way to her friend's apartment to watch the soaps at 1:00 P.M. To corroborate Ms. Winston's statement, you interview Ms. Kowalski. As she talks, you write her statement, shown in Exhibit 6.6.

PRACTICE TIP: Become a Notary Public. In the event the statement needs to be notarized, you can do so, then and there.

Statement

Statement of: Lucy Kowalski
Taken by: Leslie Dupree
On: 6:00 P.M.; September 17, (year)
At: Law Office of Murray and Brown
Present Were: Ms. Kowalski and Mr. Dupree
Special Circumstances: none

My name is Lucy Kowalski. I live at 222 Renfrew Street, Apartment 817, Any City, State. On September 11, [year], at about 9:00 A.M. I called Gladys Winston to invite her to my apartment to watch the soap operas. I have *known* Gladys for about four years. We are both part-time students at the college. We have done this before, usually at her place, but I just *moved* to a new apartment so I invited her over. The soap we really like is called "One Chance at Living," which comes on at 1:00 P.M. She answered the telephone and said she'd like to come. I told her to come early, around 12:00 P.M., so we could have a bite to eat. She asked if she could bring anything; I said no, "just yourself." About 12:15 P.M., I heard a commotion in the hallway. I *opened* my door and saw a man running after Gladys yelling "Hey thief!" He grabbed her and said she took some money. I couldn't believe it. Then police came and took her away.

LK

LK

LK

SIGNED UNDER THE PAINS AND PENALTIES OF PERJURY.

Lucy Kowalski

Lucy Kowalski

page one of one

Exhibit 6.6 **Statement**

3. Memorandum to the File

After you interview the witness, you should write a memo to the file with a copy to your supervisor detailing the interview regardless of whether any information is obtained. The simple fact that you contacted this witness warrants a memorandum.

You should state the circumstances under which you interviewed the witness, including the place, time, and conditions of the interview. Use the witness's own words as much as possible, placing quotation marks around them. This method serves to underscore the accuracy of the statement. While you and your supervisor may disagree on what particular words mean, at least you have not substituted your own conclusions for the witness's. Impressions you form and observations you make should also be preserved, but should be in a separate document because it is protected by the attorney-work-product rule.

When preparing the memo, avoid the use of conclusory or judgmental language. Write objectively using clear, concise language. To the extent possible, use the witness's own words and be certain to use quotation marks for those words. Nothing else should appear in quotations. Although it is always the hope that your reports will be protected by the attorney-work-product rule, that might not always be the case. Therefore, reports should be treated as though they will be discovered by your adversary. Reports of witnesses should not generally contain any case information, such as strategies, the role of this witness in the case, or comments on the credibility of the witness. Analyses should be written separately in a memo format and with the notation "Attorney Work Product/Privileged and Confidential." If you believe there is a credibility issue with the witness, discuss it with your supervisor.

> **PRACTICE TIP:** Label all documents discussing or analyzing the case "CONFIDENTIAL/ATTORNEY WORK PRODUCT" to help prevent them from being discovered.

As a final note, if you are unable to interview a witness for whatever reason, that fact too should be documented as completely as possible.

E. Diagrams

In certain cases, such as motor vehicle accident cases, the client and witnesses should draw diagrams of the accident. It is best to do this at the scene on a day when conditions are similar to those of the day of the accident; if that is impossible, it can be done elsewhere. The author should mark on the diagram where she or he was positioned, where the motor vehicle or vehicles were, where people were, where the impact occurred, and whether her or his view was obstructed in any manner. The author should fill in the date, time, weather, street and traffic conditions. The diagram should be referred to in the follow-up memorandum, and a copy attached to the memorandum. An example is shown in Exhibit 6.7.

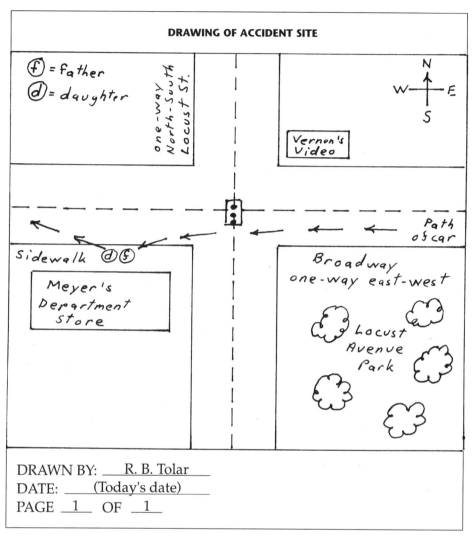

Exhibit 6.7 **Diagram of Accident Scene**

F. Other Methods of Preserving Information

1. Audio Recording

Client interviews and witness statements can be tape-recorded. This method is not recommended, however, for several reasons. First, the tape might be running but not recording for some reason, leaving you to believe you just obtained important information, but on replay there is nothing. Second, good tape-recordings are difficult to get, especially if there is background noise. Third, transcribing the tape can be a lengthy and tedious task and the transcription must be completed before the interoffice memo can be written. Fourth, recording can affect the candor of the interview since people are often reluctant to be taped.

Notwithstanding the factors against recording, there are times recording is called for. One is if the interviewer is unable to take notes. Another is if the client or witness is gravely ill, with death imminent, and further interviewing opportunities for clarification will be impossible. If you have to tape, check the recorder and microphone before you interview. Use a brand new tape and have an extra one on hand in case the first one malfunctions. Test the mike by taping test words or numbers and replaying it before beginning.

Should you decide to tape the conversation, you must obtain the person's permission. Under federal law and most state laws, it is illegal to tape a person's conversation without consent; criminal penalties might be imposed. Be sure to check with your attorney about the law in your jurisdiction before taping. If you intend to tape, it is an excellent idea to have the person consent to the taping at the beginning of the tape and again at the end in case the issue of permission arises.

2.   Video Recording

Previously, video taping was a significantly more cumbersome process to use than audio; it was generally restricted to those cases where the client or witness was expected to be unavailable for trial because of poor health, for example. It was seldom used by investigators to document a scene or a witness's statement; there was no provision in the rules of civil procedure for video use.

Advances in video recording have changed how we use videos. The new, small, light, user-friendly camcorders have made taking videos convenient. An investigator can shoot the scene of the accident or, with the witness's permission, tape a statement.

Under some circumstances courts will allow a tape of the scene of the accident with a narration of the driver, or a tape depicting a "day in the life of" a client who alleges the defendant caused his disability through negligence or products liability. An attorney might want to tape a client's will if competency is an issue. A recent amendment to FED. R. CIV. P. 30 provides for the video taping of depositions. As with audio taping, have your equipment ready and in excellent working order before starting. If you intend to use the tape at trial, it is wise to engage a professional who is experienced at documenting information in a clear, clean, noninflammatory way to handle the taping.

As with audio taping, have the person you are video taping consent to the videotaping both at the beginning and again at the end of the tape.

3.   Photographs

A picture can be worth a thousand words—if it's a great picture! Too often, investigators rely on photographs to tell the story and neglect recording their observations. When developed, the pictures are too dark, too light, or somehow just do not convey what you saw. Some years ago a museum wanted to reproduce a wooden sculpture. The directors sent a photographer to take pictures of the original piece so that it could be reproduced. The photo, however, contained no yardstick to show the scale. When the reproduction was finished, it was a good ten inches taller than the original.

If your supervising attorney wants an accurate picture of an intersection or of the bridge span, for example, she or he should hire a professional who has the appropriate equipment. A small cheap camera or even a large expensive camera with the wrong lens or operator will provide disappointing results.

Nonetheless, every law office should have a 35 millimeter single-lens-reflex camera available for photographing at the interview or investigating the scene; an extra roll of film should always be kept on hand. If the office does not have one, make arrangements for one to be available the date of the interview. Use one roll of film per case, and for every picture record the f-stop, film speed, and lighting conditions. Take numerous shots, as least two from each angle and at least two for each f-stop you use. On the back of the photo record the name, date of the incident, and the date of the photo.

Pictures should be taken if the client has been in an accident and has injuries, for example, or if the client is a victim of domestic violence or police brutality. Many hospitals and domestic violence centers now take pictures of injuries to preserve the information as a matter of course in the event of litigation. Be certain to have enough light or use a flash and add a figure or other object to show scale.

Often clients are embarrassed by their appearance and will not make an appointment for legal assistance until the swelling has gone down and the wounds have begun to heal. Photograph anyway to preserve the client's appearance on that particular date. If the client is embarrassed because the location of the injury is private, remind the client that a picture is worth a thousand words. Ask a female or male colleague to assist if that would make the client more comfortable. As a last resort, you might ask the client to have a friend or family member take the picture. Of course if the client refuses to have the picture taken, that is the client's prerogative. If the client is adamant, however, note in the file the reasons you gave the client for taking the photograph and the client's reasons for refusing.

If you are photographing an accident scene—an intersection, streets, motor vehicles—or any other scene, take a Polaroid shot first before capturing the image with the 35-millimeter camera. The Polaroid shot develops within seconds and allows you to see exactly the picture you have captured. Make adjustments in the angle of the shot, the lighting, positions of objects, and the distance. Include in the shot, a telephone pole, street sign or other reference point and use a tape measure to show distance. If the tape appears in the photo, it reflects the work of a professional investigator and adds credibility to the work. Photographs might be discoverable, however, and discrepancies between the Polaroid shot and the finished product might cause evidentiary concerns.

Have your prints or slides developed immediately to ensure adequacy. Complete a Photo Sheet for every picture you take. Affix the photo with rubber cement or other adhesive that will not affect the surface. A sample appears in Exhibit 6.8.

G. Evidentiary Considerations

1. Real and Demonstrative Evidence

Real evidence is generally physical evidence directly involved in the litigation. The Colt .45 determined to be the murder weapon is real evidence. The syringe used to stab the victim is real evidence. Demonstrative evidence is not the actual evidence involved in the case; rather it is evidence prepared by a party to demonstrate something to the judge or jury to help them understand a fact in the case. A Colt .45 used to demonstrate the size of the gun when the actual gun could not be found, or a syringe of the same size and type when the genuine one was inadvertently destroyed, are examples of demonstrative evidence.

Audio and video recordings and photographs are examples of demonstrative evidence that can provide very accurate portrayals of case facts. If you intend to use them as evidence, under FED. R. EVID. 901(a) they must be authenticated by the person who made them before they can be admitted. The person responsible for the recording or photograph must testify to the authenticity of it and is therefore open to cross-examination. The court must be satisfied that the circumstances of taping, and the integrity of the tape itself, are beyond reproach. The person taping will have to testify about the process and the "chain of custody" to assure the court that the tape was not altered. If the attorney intends for a jury to see it, the recording or photograph should be professionally done in spite of the expense. Under certain circumstances a court might not allow the recording or photograph into evidence if the client is available or if the video might unfairly prejudice the jury.

2. Other Evidence

If your case involves an original document, such as a contract, make duplicates of the original. Keep the original in a fire-proof safe. Provide your client with a copy and keep a copy in the client's file. In the event an original is destroyed, a duplicate can be substituted. *See* FED. R. EVID. 1001, 1003.

Surveillance tapes, 911 tapes, pathology reports, and television news stories are four examples of potential evidence that are not preserved by their custodians for any length of time. If you know you need one of these

---

PHOTO SHEET

Client Name: _____

Date of Photo: _____

Photographer Name: _____

Describe location: _____

_____

_____

_____

_____

Describe circumstances/conditions: _____

_____

_____

_____

_____

AFFIX PHOTO HERE

PHOTO ____ OF ____.

Exhibit 6.8 **Photo Sheet**

items or any similar item, you must request them early on in the case before they are destroyed. Sometimes a court order is necessary.

Under no circumstances should you write on, or mark in any way, an original document. Marking on the document jeopardizes the integrity of the document as evidence.

> **PRACTICE TIP:** When you obtain information, whether you believe it is important to the case or not, write it down. The writing should take the form of an interoffice memorandum and should contain the details of the facts or other information you have uncovered. You should state the circumstances under which you obtained the information, including date, time, place, and circumstances. If it involves information from a person, place his or her own words in quotation marks to promote accuracy.

H.   Preserving the Files

Proper set-up and maintenance of files is a task often given short shrift by attorneys who frequently rely on others to care for the files. Both set-up and maintenance are integral parts of a legal practice. Although portions of such work are clerical in nature, much is careful documentation of the life of the case, especially contact with your client, witnesses, and opposing counsel. A well-organized case file is essential to the smooth handling of a case and is the basis for the litigation or trial notebook prepared before trial. Although the "paperless trial" has found its way into the courtroom, it is not the norm in most jurisdictions.

The styles vary, from paper to electronic, but a typical client file would contain multiple files, including case status, correspondence, court filings, research, documents, witnesses, and miscellaneous items. Depending on the type of case, the file might be three thin paper folders, a room full of file cabinets, or a diskette or a CD-ROM. Regardless of the size, the strategy is the same and organization is the key. A complete file is reprinted in the Sample Client File in the Appendix.

In a "paperless" firm, all correspondence and documents are scanned and included in the client's computer file. The original hard copies are stored. If the office computer terminals are net-worked, this procedure allows quick and easy access to files by multiple users (for example, you and two attorneys). The advantage of using a computer is that data can be retrieved in an instant. Although depositions come with an index, scanning a rather long deposition onto a disk gives you immediate access to specific details, such as how often the deponent used a particular word or phrase.

A variety of software programs are available to maintain client files.

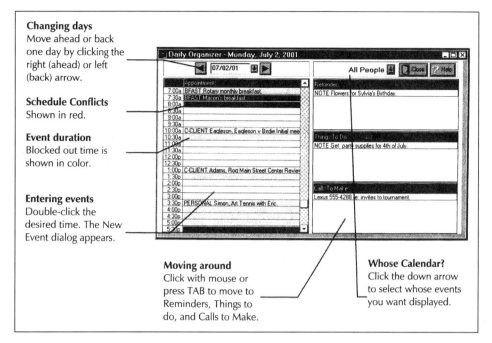

Changing days
Move ahead or back
one day by clicking the
right (ahead) or left
(back) arrow.

Schedule Conflicts
Shown in red.

Event duration
Blocked out time is
shown in color.

Entering events
Double-click the
desired time. The New
Event dialog appears.

Moving around
Click with mouse or
press TAB to move to
Reminders, Things to
do, and Calls to Make.

Whose Calendar?
Click the down arrow
to select whose events
you want displayed.

Exhibit 6.9 **Abacus Law Plus**

One, "Abacus Law Plus" (*see* Exhibit 6.9), is a popular, outstanding example
of how software can streamline calendaring and case management tasks.
With it one can access client, case, or calendar information while running
another program; track all events, including appointments, court dates,
depositions, and reminders; print reports and calendars for people or
matters; maintain mailing lists; retrieve and dial telephone numbers; and
check client and scheduling conflicts.

Various files serve to organize the case.

1.   Status/Notes File

The Status/Notes File contains a chronological documentation of each
action taken on the case. It can be a separate manila folder with individual
paper sheets, or computerized. Once the initial interview has been conducted, and the preliminary information sheet and summary completed,
it will then be necessary to document every action taken on the case.
Entries of each activity are kept on a "status" or "running" sheet. The
sheet should note the date of the initial client contact and all subsequent
contacts, the date of any court proceedings, the date any pleadings or
documents are filed, and the date any pleading or document response is
due to be filed.

Also included on the status sheet is every client contact or attempted
contact. Whether the client calls you or you call the client, a memorandum

Status Sheet		
Client: Brown, Alice		

DATE	ACTIVITY	INITIALS
10/15/yr	Initial client interview Summary completed Req. Cl provide tax returns for last three years	*JL*
10/18/yr	Cl brought tax returns	*JL*
11/1/yr	Answer to Complaint filed	*JL*
6/12/yr	Telephone call to client at 524-6543 re court date for hearing on 8/30/yr. Cl said she would take time off from work for the day.	*JL*
8/13/yr	t/c to Cl at 524-6543 to remind re court; no answer.	*JL*
8/14/yr	t/c to Cl at 524-6543 (3x); no answer.	*JL*
8/15/yr	t/c to Cl's mother at 524-9087; will give message for Cl to call ASAP; tickle for 8/17.	*JL*

Exhibit 6.10 **Partially Completed Status Sheet**

of the call *must* be made and placed on the status sheet whether you and the client talked or not. Note the inclusion of the phone number to memorialize the number called. If the client is difficult to reach, note the number of times the phone rang before you hung up. If the client called you, the message slip should appear in the file, stapled to the side of the file sheet. The first page of a partially completed status sheet might look like Exhibit 6.10.

All activity on the case is reflected in the Status Sheets. The Intake Sheet should be placed on the bottom of the folder, underneath the first Status Sheet.

The other side of the folder would hold the Interview Summary, to which the Outline Notes have been attached.

2. Correspondence File

In a simple case with one plaintiff and one defendant, the *correspondence* file might consist of a single manila folder with correspondence between the client and your firm on one side (privileged) and all other correspondence on the other side. In complex cases with multiple parties,

more than one file might be needed. For the paperless office, correspondence can be scanned with the original archived. Always keep the envelopes
with the original letter in case they are needed to show mailing dates or
addresses. If the correspondence file contains many letters, an index with
the sender, addressee, date, and topic will be useful.

PRACTICE TIP: Retain envelopes and mailers in the correspondence
file since information regarding name, address, postmark, and can-
cellation mark might become important. Handwritten envelopes
may be used for a handwriting exemplar.

---

3.   Court Documents File/Pleadings

Unfortunately the term *pleadings* has come to be used as a catch-all
phrase meaning "anything filed in court." According to FED. R. CIV. P. 7(a),
however, pleadings are claims for relief and responses to those claims.
Pleadings include complaints, counterclaims, cross-claims and third-party
claims, answers and replies. Motions, discovery requests, and other documents filed with the court are not pleadings.

This file should contain a copy of each and every document filed
with the court. There should be no difference between the file the judge
reviews and the file in your office. In a simple case, the "documents folder"
would contain all the documents filed with the court on the right side and
the status sheets on the left. In a more complex case, multiple folders or
a different type folder that holds one to four inches of documents might
be used.

The top sheet in the folder should be a "Document Index" showing
the name of the document, the date the document was filed, and the date
it was served or received. Again, the pleadings can be scanned for inclusion
in the client's computer file.

4.   Research File

This file should contain a copy of each theory chart and all pertinent
law (statutes, case law, rules, and regulations). You should have a separate
research file for each claim, defense, or issue. Again depending on the
complexity of the case, you might have one file or twenty. If there are
multiple files, prepare a master sheet and use tabs to index them.

5.   Documents File

This file should contain originals and copies of all relevant documents.
Examples include contracts, deeds, licenses, and certificates.

6. Deposition File

As described earlier, a deposition is testimony taken under oath, before an authorized reporter, usually as part of pretrial discovery. A transcript of the proceeding is prepared and retained for trial preparation. Various summaries of the transcript, including chronological, subject matter, topic index or narrative, are prepared before trial.

The deposition file contains the original transcripts and summaries. If the transcripts are too numerous or too bulky, they would be placed separately in an accordion file or file box or scanned for computer use.

7. Witness File

Names, addresses, telephone numbers (work and home), statements, notes, and summaries of all witnesses should be in this file. If the witness has been served a subpoena, a copy should be in this file. If there are multiple witnesses, index with tabs and a cover sheet listing all witnesses.

8. Miscellaneous File

Any document that does not have its own file should be placed here. It might be a duplicate record or document.

9. Other Files

Make other files, for example, for evidence or expert witnesses as the nature of the case demands.

Attorneys might need any of the files on short notice—in court, before a jury. The ability to find the right part of the right file at the right time shows strong organizational skill and fosters the appearance of credibility on behalf of the client and attorney.

I. Case Management/Calendaring

An important aspect of managing cases is the use of a reminder system or *tickler system*. It "tickles" your memory or reminds you of something you need to do. Law involves deadlines imposed by the court or other third party, by the client, or by your firm. Some deadlines, if not met, like a statute of limitations, have grave consequences and extinguish a person's rights. Others, like responding to a demand letter, might be less serious, but nonetheless should not be forgotten.

In order to meet those deadlines, every law firm has some sort of reminder system. The system can be paper or electronic. For those without a computer program, the system itself can be as simple as a box of 366 index cards, one for each day in the year (and leap year) divided by a card for each month. On January 1, the first card appearing as you open the box would be the divider card, *JANUARY*, followed by 31 cards, or one for each day. Then the *FEBRUARY* divider would appear, followed by 28 or 29 cards. At the beginning of each day, the card for that day is checked for activities, (for example, "Answers to Interrogatories due in *Franklin v. Moses*"). After the activity is completed and a notation to that effect made in the case status file ("5/17—Answers to Interrog. filed"), the item is crossed out and the card is returned to the box. At the end of each day, the card in the front is moved to the back of the box.

As "due dates" become available, they are entered onto the card and the card is reinserted in the box. For example, on March 15 your client is served with a summons and complaint for which the answer is due in 20 days, excluding the day of service. The client brings the complaint to your office on March 16. When you open the box, the first card is for the current day, March 16 (the "March divider" and the first 15 cards for the days in March have already been moved to the back). You select the card for April 4, which is the date the answer is due. On the card for April 4, you write "*Lord v. Abbott*, Answer to Complaint due." You should also tickle an earlier date, say 10 days before and note "*Lord v. Abbott*, Answer due in ten days."

If your office uses a computer, a variety of programs are available for calendaring and case file management. "Abacus Law +" provides case management and calendaring for everyone in the office. (*See* Exhibit 6.9.) It has a daily organizer input screen to organize every part of your day. The process is the same as by hand but instead of writing the information, it is keyed into the program. You simply enter all the case information, including names, addresses, dates, tasks, and more and "Abacus+" will organize it for you.

Remember to back-up your work frequently and keep your batteries charged so that when the power goes out, you can access your calendar and information.

Regardless of the type of program you keep at the office, it is helpful to have your own appointment calendar to keep track of important dates.

Note that attorneys are generally required by the terms of their malpractice insurance policy to keep two separate tickler/reminder systems. If an attorney had only one reminder system, missed an important date and was sued for malpractice by the client, the insurance company would attempt to deny coverage since the attorney did not comply with the terms of the policy. With two systems in place, the possibility of error is reduced.

Many court rules also require that a attorney appearing in court bring a calendar in the event there are scheduling issues. *See, for example,* D.C. Supr. Ct. Rule 104, which states ". . . Attorneys are expected to carry with them at all times they are in court a calendar of their future court appearances."

> **PRACTICE TIP:** Make a paper copy of everything you write for your own files. If the original cannot be located, you have an extra.

SUMMARY

Information is preserved to have a complete and accurate record of the entire case. Methods of preservation include note taking, audio recordings, video recordings, and photographs. If information is valuable to your case, it must be preserved with accurate note taking in the form of an outline and then put into narrative summary form. Interviewing skills are combined with researching skills to prepare the interoffice memorandum. All components of the client's case are organized into a case file—paper, computer, or a combination of the two—so that you can find what you need at a moment's notice.

In the next chapter we explore the process of investigation.

Key Terms

Case management
Correspondence
Court documents
Demonstrative evidence
Deposition
Deposition file
Documents file
Intake form
Interoffice memorandum

Interview summary
Litigation chart
Outline
Pleadings
Real evidence
Research file
Summary
Tickler system
Witness file

REVIEW QUESTIONS

1. You have just been given a case that has been around the firm for two years. What kinds of things do you want to know about it and why?

2. What are the advantages and disadvantages of audio and video recordings?

3. What are the parts of the interview summary and why are they important?

4. Why is it valuable to attach your notes to the summary?

5. What's the purpose of an Interoffice Memorandum?

6. What purpose does it serve to photograph an accident scene with a Polaroid camera?

7. What are the evidentiary considerations with audio and video recordings or a photograph?

8. What is the difference between real and demonstrative evidence?

9. What does it mean to "authenticate" evidence?

CHAPTER EXERCISES

Exercise 6-1: Choose a partner. One of you is the paralegal, the other the client. Using the Sample Intake Sheet, gather the information from the client who assumes the role of a battered spouse. Switch roles. Again using the Intake Sheet, gather information from a 22-year-old client who lives with his parents, but does not want them to know he's been charged for possession of a small amount of marijuana.

Exercise 6-2: Pick a partner from the class; one assumes the role of the paralegal, the other, the client. Using the fact sheets supplied to you, conduct an interview, drafting an outline as you go. Reverse roles and use a second fact pattern to conduct the second interview. Review the outlines. Do they make sense? Are they well organized?

Exercise 6-3: Using the outline of information you obtained in the previous Exercise, draft a four-part summary of the interview.

Exercise 6-4: Choose a partner. One of you is the paralegal and the other, a female client with severe bruises from an altercation with the police. The client is resisting having her picture taken because the bruises are on her back. The paralegal's job is to try to convince the client, with sensitivity and compassion, to let her (or someone else in the office if the paralegal is a male) take the picture. Switch roles and repeat.

7

The Investigation Process

CHAPTER OBJECTIVES

In this chapter you will learn how to

- define the scope of an investigation;
- plan the investigation;
- recognize the limitations of investigation;
- investigate ethically.

A.   Introduction

Investigation is the gathering and preserving of information. The process is like an archeological dig. The landscape may hold few obvious clues on the surface. Only by digging, slowly, carefully, layer by layer, does one unearth the factual secrets of a case. Case investigation is a factual expedition that is fun, exciting, demanding, and sometimes nerve-wracking. Like a good archeologist, a good investigator has an idea of where he or she might be going and keeps eyes, ears, and mind open to possibilities and relationships. Truth is, after all, sometimes stranger than fiction.

The Swimming Pool

Last week two teenage brothers drowned in a hotel swimming pool. The family was on vacation in the United States and after an exhausting day of driving, arrived at the hotel where they had reservations. According to the boys' parents, while they were checking in at the registration desk, the boys were looking around. After the parents finished registering, they did not see the boys and began looking for them. Eventually they found the boys floating face down in the pool. The pool was located just off the registration area down a short hall behind a set of heavy double doors. The pool area itself was noisy

because of two industrial exhaust fans that were on and sounded like
they were in need of repair. There was a sauna on one side of the pool
with warning signs posted on the door limiting access to those over
the age of 18; a large red "X" appeared on the head of a picture of a
child.

   The family was a foreign family and spoke little English. They
have retained your law firm to investigate their belief that the hotel
was negligent and could have prevented the boys' deaths.

   Your supervising attorney has assigned you to the case. You have
been asked to conduct some preliminary research to determine whether
there are sufficient facts to support a complaint that would withstand
the "reasonable inquiry" requirements of Rule 11 of the Federal Rules
of Civil Procedure.

B.   The Unexpected

On an archeological dig, you might unearth unexpected rare artifacts while
looking for other artifacts you had expected to find. Similarly, while investigating a breach of contract action or wrongful eviction, you might uncover
facts to justify a discrimination or tort claim. While investigating a claim
for false arrest, you might unearth facts to support a police brutality claim.
Consider all possibilities; do not be blinded by your own preconceived
notions of what the case involves.

   Investigation falls into two general categories: formal and informal.
Formal investigation is discovery, regulated by court rules. Under these
rules, parties request information from other parties and witnesses through
interrogatories, requests for documents and admissions, depositions,
and other discovery tools. Formal investigation is fully discussed in
Chapter 1.

   Informal investigation involves factual inquiry and analysis performed outside the scope of formal discovery. The major portion of informal
investigation is conducted before filing a lawsuit, for many reasons. First,
you cannot be sure your client has a claim until you have completed your
informal fact investigation. Second, the allegations in the complaint must
be supported by facts learned through informal investigation. Rule 11 of the
Federal Rules of Civil Procedure requires this inquiry. Third, information
obtained close in time to the incident or occurrence is more likely to be
available and to be more accurate than information obtained later since,
as time passes, people forget, move or die, and physical evidence may be
disposed of or destroyed. Fourth, information is often easier to obtain from
witnesses before a suit is filed because they are often less apprehensive
about talking when the event is current in their minds and the likelihood
of having to testify seems remote. Moreover, a witness who might later
lie to cover facts or protect an interest or person might tell the truth
soon after an event simply because he or she might attach no particular

importance to the information imparted. Later, after a lawsuit has been filed and the legal and factual issues are brought into focus, these facts become colored by the lawsuit and might be distorted or hidden by witnesses who have chosen—or been assigned—sides in the litigation. And fifth, informal investigation is inexpensive compared to formal discovery.

Too often attorneys and their colleagues mistakenly assume they will obtain the facts necessary for a successful prosecution or defense of a claim through formal discovery. Frequently complaints are drafted and the discovery process initiated years after events supporting or underlying the claim. By this time, details are lost to memory, documents are lost or destroyed in the course of business, and facts that seemed so obvious when they were fresh are irretrievably lost. There is no effective substitute for prompt, creative, and thorough investigation.

PRACTICE TIP: Under Rule 11 of the Federal Rules of Civil Procedure an attorney must certify to the court that he or she has made a reasonable inquiry and that the claims and defenses in the pleading are warranted by law.

C.   Paralegal-Attorney Relationship

1.   Getting Good Instructions

Good instructions facilitate sound, efficient investigations. If you know why the information is important, if you understand how the information is to be used, the investigative process will be fruitful. Ideally, you will have been present at the initial interview. If you were not, you must be thoroughly briefed about the case and understand your role in the investigation. Research the legal theories you believe are involved and develop a theory or organizational chart for each one. Prepare lists of witnesses; prepare questions to ask those witnesses. Meet frequently with your supervising attorney and others assigned to the same case and compare notes. Most importantly, begin your investigation as quickly as possible while memories are fresh.

2.   Understanding Limitations

Investigations are limited by time and money. Before accepting a case, the attorney and potential client will have a full and frank discussion about the costs of the case, including legal fees, the chances for recovery and the time frame for the case. If the client is being billed at a fixed fee (for example, $1,500 for a bankruptcy case), the cost is clear to the client. If the client is being billed at an hourly rate, the attorney might attempt to estimate the overall cost, although that might be difficult. A simple civil action—for example a complaint for failure to pay a fixed amount of money—might require a single court appearance and take a limited amount of time. More complex cases require more legal time and attention. It is critical that the attorney knows the amount of resources the client is willing to commit to the case; it is equally important for the client to understand that many things are beyond an attorney's control. The attorney will explain this clearly before accepting the case.

If it is a contingency case, the attorney knows the amount of resources the firm is willing to advance the client. Although personal injury plaintiffs are ultimately responsible for the costs, they are usually unable to reimburse the attorney if the case is unsuccessful. Therefore, costs must be considered carefully. Will the case require expert witnesses such as engineers, doctors, or accountants? Will accident reconstruction be necessary?

Regardless of the type of retainer agreement your firm has with the client, your investigation must correspond to the time and money allotted. Keep your expectations in line with this allotment. Ask the attorney how much time you should commit to the case. Advise the attorney as to the amount of time you are spending, the results you're getting, and what you think should be done. You can't always fly first-class.

D.   Legal Identities

Answering the question "Who do we sue?" or "Who's involved?" is not always as simple as it looks. Yet before an attorney files a complaint or prepares to assist a client with a transaction, he or she must know the legal identity of the parties involved. Types of legal identities include: an individual person, a partnership, or a corporation. Typically, the client provides a substantial amount of information about the case and the parties involved. You will still need to investigate, however, to obtain more extensive information. What follows is general information about identities. Specific sources appear in Chapter 8.

1.   Individuals

For an individual the legal identity is the person's legal name. Generally this information is provided by your client. If your client is uncertain of the accuracy of a person's name, you can check birth, marriage, or citizenship records. If the individual owns a business under a fictitious name (for example, "Friendly Flowers"), but has not incorporated, the county where the person works might have an "Application for Registration of Fictitious Name" on file. Many municipalities issue business licenses or permits in the names of businesses, cross-referenced with owners or operators. Applications of this kind will typically contain the person's name and address. They often contain other important information such as Social Security numbers or tax identification numbers.

2. Organizations

a. Partnership

A partnership is an unincorporated business relationship involving two or more persons (including an individual, a corporation, trust, or another partnership) who contribute to the partnership in property or labor and share the profits and the risks of the business. Partnerships do not pay federal income tax since income is allocated among partners who pay individually. But partnerships must file federal, state, and sometimes local tax returns. If there is no local return available, there might be a record of payment of a fixed assessment or licensing fee.

b. Corporation

A corporation is a large or small group of people who incorporate under state laws to run a business for profit (or nonprofit, discussed below). A corporation is owned by shareholders who usually cannot be held personally liable for the wrongdoing of the corporation. A corporation's liability is usually limited to the value of its assets. State statutes require that a corporation file certificates of incorporation, have annual meetings, and produce reports. Some states, notably Delaware, are more generous with corporate requirements in order to encourage incorporation in their state.

c. Closed Corporation

This organization is similar to a regular corporation, but has fewer people as shareholders, and by statute is not required to adhere to the same formalities as the regular corporation.

d. Nonprofit Corporation

A nonprofit or a not-for-profit corporation is an organization whose main purpose is something other than moneymaking. There are over one million nonprofit organizations in the United States. Schools, religious organizations, and some hospitals are nonprofit corporations. Because of their missions, the Internal Revenue Service grants them a tax exempt status. Nonprofits are also called 501(C)(3) or (C)(4) corporations, after the IRS Code section that grants the exemption. Simply because a corporation is nonprofit does not mean the corporation takes in no money. Some nonprofits are multimillion dollar operations, paying their executive directors annual salaries in excess of $200,000 with perks of cars, boats, and club memberships. Nonprofit simply means that the main purpose of the corporation is nonprofit.

e. Limited Liability Company

The Limited Liability Company (LLC) is a relatively new form of business structure recognized by nearly all states. An LLC is a hybrid organizational structure that provides tax advantages of a partnership with the liability protection afforded corporations. Under IRS rules an LLC might be classified as a partnership (no federal tax imposed) or a corporation (tax imposed). Regardless of classification, an LLC must file a federal return.

3. Governmental Unit

Governmental units include states, counties, cities, townships, parishes, and other such units within a state. It also includes the federal government and its agencies like the Equal Employment Opportunity Commission and the Social Security Administration. States (and their subordinate units), like the federal government, are immune from suit except to the extent they allow themselves to be sued under statutes called "tort claims acts." When suing a governmental entity, early notice to the entity (for example, either thirty days or six months), is required before a lawsuit can be filed. This notice allows the entity to investigate and settle a claim before litigation begins. Under federal laws and the laws of some states "notice" to the entity is a "jurisdictional prerequisite." If it is not given or not given on time, there can be no recovery for the plaintiff because the court has no jurisdiction to hear the case. Mail it "Certified Mail, Return Receipt Requested." A example of a state statute that requires timely filing of claims appears in the Appendix.

> **PRACTICE TIP:** Some states require business entities to file documents with the Secretary of State where they are formed as well as where they do business. These documents are public records. When obtaining such records it is advisable to obtain certified copies of the documents, unless the cost of the documents is prohibitive.

E. Defining the Scope of the Investigation

Having discerned the nature of the case or matter and considered the identities of the parties involved, you can now define the boundaries of the investigation. Initially you must clarify the purpose of the investigation. Accomplish this by answering one or more of the following questions:

1) Who is involved?
2) What happened?
3) Where did it happen?
4) When did the incident happen?
5) How did the incident happen?
6) Why do you need the information?

Consider the introductory scenario of two teenage brothers who drowned in a hotel swimming pool. According to the boys' parents, while they were checking in the boys found their way to the swimming pool and drowned. The family was foreign and spoke little English. The scope of the investigation is:

- Who: Hotel/parent corporation
  Hotel employees/others who may include the manufacturer of the fans, pool maintenance company, architectural or engineering firm that built the hotel
- What: Drowning of boys
- Why: To determine who, if anyone, is liable for the deaths
- When: Two weeks ago
- Where: Our fair city
- How: What chain of events or causal relationships led from acts of potential defendants to the deaths of the two boys

1. Who?

The hotel is the obvious place to start. But who is the hotel? What is its identity? Is it locally, nationally, or internationally owned? Is it a corporation, a partnership, or another type of business entity? If it is a corporation, is it a subsidiary of another corporation? What is its financial health? Does it have a reputation, perhaps created through advertising, for catering to families?

Others who might have liability are the employees or contractors hired to maintain the pool or pool area, the manufacturer of the noisy fan, the architectural or engineering firms who designed and built a hotel pool accessible to children but inherently difficult to see or supervise. The questions asked above will apply to these entities as well. Additionally, a clear line establishing legal responsibility will need to be drawn from the hotel to these other persons or entities.

2. What?

The boys were found in the pool, but did they drown? Could there have been foul play? Does it matter how they died as long as they died in the hotel? Did they die in the hotel?

3. Why?

Does the hotel have a duty to its guests? What is the nature of the duty? What is the relationship between the hotel and its employees? Is the hotel responsible for the actions of its employees under the theory of *respondeat superior*? Does the hotel have a duty to provide safe premises? What if another guest or other nonemployee played a role in the boys' death?

4. When?

When did the deaths occur? Is there a statute of limitations issue? At what point will it become an issue? What is the latest date a complaint can be filed within the statute? Is there more than one applicable statute of limitation? If so, what are they? Are there any procedural requirements? Is there any reason the city should receive notice?

5. Where?

Did the deaths occur at the hotel? Did the deaths occur in this city and state?

6. How?

What were the causes of the boys' deaths? What are the events or factors that, when taken together, can be said to have caused the deaths? Were the fans of faulty manufacture or was the design deficient in light of their intended use? Were there architectural faults that permitted access by children but prevented or impaired supervision? Was the hotel negligent in not providing lifeguards or leaving the pool area unguarded or un-locked? Were employees of the hotel negligent in their supervision of the pool area or was the area maintained in a manner that rendered it danger-ous to children? Were the parents negligent in their supervision of their own children?

Determining the scope of the investigation precedes developing the investigation plan. The scope informs us how broad or narrow, how com-plex or limited, the investigation should be. As the investigation progresses, the scope might be expanded to include other issues, or constricted to limit the issues. As the scope of the investigation is altered, the plan is modified.

F. The Investigation Plan

Understanding the scope of the investigation allows one to plan a thorough and efficient investigation. The plan should include the steps necessary to develop the case, including interviews of the clients or witnesses, the gathering of documents, field investigation, and follow-up. As the investi-gation progresses and evolves, the plan is revised and refined, adding or subtracting witnesses and documents. Information and documents not obtained through the informal aspect of the process will be sought through formal discovery. A sample plan is shown in Exhibit 7.1.

Investigation Plan

Preliminary
    (research applicable law; prepare theory chart)
    (prepare questions for interview)
Interview client
More legal research/additional theory charts
    Find/Interview witnesses
    Visit site
    Obtain documents
Refine legal research based on facts
Follow-up with client (personal/telephone)
Interview new witnesses, experts
Other documents

Exhibit 7.1 Investigation Plan

Based on your review of the law of negligence in your jurisdiction, you prepared a theory chart in the Traveling Family case before the first interview:

Traveling Family Case
Theory Chart and Investigation Plan

Theory of Relief: Negligence
Client: Traveling Family
Date of Preparation: Today's Date
Statute of Limitations: Three Years

ELEMENT	SOURCE OF PROOF	INFORMAL FACT INVESTIGATION	FORMAL (DISCOVERY)
1) Duty			
2) Breach			
3) Causation			
4) Injury (Damages)			

With the chart prepared, you focus on three things: the law that creates the duty, the breach of the duty, and causation. Specifically you will determine whether through your investigation you can find facts to support each element of the claim. If your investigation reveals law and facts that support each of the elements, your complaint will pass muster under Rule 11.

Look at each of the elements and draft a list of questions for each element. Your list might appear as follows:

Duty:
>   What duty, if any, did the hotel have to the boys?
>   Duty to keep safe premises? How is "safe" defined?
>   What are the laws, rules, and regulations applicable to the hotel?
>   If the hotel serves many foreign guests, is there a duty on the part of the hotel to post warning signs in other languages?
>   Did the boys' parents actually register as guests at the hotel? Does it matter? What if they were only asking directions?
>   Did the boys speak or read English? If yes, how well? Does this matter?

Breach:
>   Is there a requirement that a lifeguard be on duty when the pool is open?
>   Does the law require fencing?
>   Was the pool open?
>   If it was closed, how did the boys enter?
>   Is it fenced?
>   Did the boys climb over the fence?
>   How did the boys find the pool?
>   Were they directed to the pool? Enticed?
>   Were there signs written in English? With pictures?
>   What type of warning signs, if any, were at the pool? Language? Pictures? Where are they posted? Height? Painted on the pool?
>   Are there notations of the depth (for example, 6') around the pool? If so, are Arabic numerals sufficient warning in a hotel catering to international travelers?

Causation:
>   If the hotel had a duty to the boys and it breached its duty, was the breach the direct and proximate cause of the boys' deaths by drowning?
>   Did the boys die from drowning? Was there any evidence of foul play?

Damages:
>   If all of the above elements can be proven, what are the damages? What are the values of the boys' lives? Are they the same for each? How do we establish a financial measure of the worth of each boy's life? Prove what their lives are worth?

What damages did the parents suffer? Are there other family members who have suffered? Do they have a right of recovery?

The questions require both legal and factual research. By preparing such a list of questions, you are able to focus on the legal elements of negligence. Conduct some research (start with your state digest) to determine what general duty a hotel has to its clientele. As always, check with your supervising attorney for guidance. There might be other theories of relief available (for example, infliction of emotional distress). Keep possibilities in mind as the investigation proceeds.

After the initial interview you determined the scope of the investigation and developed an investigation plan, shown in Exhibit 7.2.

The investigation plan establishes how you investigate the case. The plan incorporates all facets of the investigation: the issues, witnesses, documents, site visit, and expert witnesses. For example, once you have prepared your questions, contemplate the persons to whom you might direct the questions—Manager? Employees? Guests? Independent contractors (for example, pool or linen service)? After you review your investigation strategy with your supervising attorney, you will make a trip to the site of the injury, talking with people, looking for answers to the questions listed above. Make notations of your conversations and visual observations at the scene; don't wait until you leave because memories fade fast. The use of photography to preserve the scene is discussed in Chapter 6.

Getting answers to some or even all of your questions does not end the inquiry. Assume, for example, your preliminary investigation reveals that there are state regulations that require the posting of warning signs at designated spots around the pool and that in talking to the maintenance supervisor, you learned that the signs were not up on the day of the drowning because the pool area was being repainted. During your visit to the site you also notice the absence of signs. Now you have additional questions to answer: Who removed the signs? Were any temporary signs installed?

Using the theory chart (see Exhibit 7.3), you can begin to fill in some of the blanks.

Your preliminary investigation uncovers facts to support the elements of duty and breach; the element of injury/damages is met by the boys' deaths. Once this information is in place on the chart, it is organized in a format for easy reference. Using this format or some similar organizational tool will help you stay organized. Otherwise you will be forever leafing through your notes looking for bits and pieces of information.

The last and most difficult element is causation: Was the hotel's failure to have signs warning of the dangers of the pool posted near the pool the direct and proximate cause of the boys' deaths? The hotel would argue that since the boys didn't speak or read English, signs would not have made a difference. This argument brings us back to one of the original questions regarding the regulations: Is there any requirement that they be pictorial in addition to written? If so, the boys' parents would argue that

Investigation Plan

Traveling Family

1) Interview clients
2) Issues:
    1) negligence of hotel
    2) liability of hotel to guest
    3) infliction of emotional distress
    4) respondeat superior
3) Develop theory charts
4) List of witnesses
5) Prepare area of questioning for each witness
6) Interview witnesses
    1) hotel employees
    2) pool manager
    3) lifeguards
    4) maintenance personnel
    5) ambulance crew
    6) attending physician
    7) police officers
    8) coroner
    9) independent contractors (for example, pool or linen service)
7) Field work/visit site
8) Obtain documents
    1) status of hotel (Corporation? Partnership?)
    2) hotel regulations
    3) state regulations for hotels
    4) state regulations for swimming pools
    5) registration information
    6) ambulance reports
    7) police reports
    8) hospital reports
    9) coroner reports
9) Possible experts:
    1) Psychiatrist/psychologist/therapist
    2) hotel management
    3) hotel safety
    4) actuarial

Exhibit 7.2 **Investigation Plan—Traveling Family**

Theory of Relief: Negligence
Client: Traveling Family
Date of Preparation: Today's Date
Preparer: Terry Hendren, Investigator

ELEMENT	SOURCE OF PROOF	INFORMAL FACT INVESTIGATION	FORMAL (DISCOVERY)
1) DUTY	1) Hotel regulation states signs warning about the hazards of swimming w/o lifeguard must be posted; 2) George Winden (hotel maintenance supervisor)	1) TH visited pool area on 2/12/yr & found no signs posted. (field notes; pictures/video) 2) told TH that signs had been removed for painting & maintenance on 8/31/yr; no temp. signs were installed; pool was not locked. (oral/ GW willing to sign statement)	
2) BREACH	1) George Winden	no signs posted (oral/statement/ pictures/video)	
3) CAUSATION			
4) INJURY (DAMAGES)	Mary Lance, M.D., (Coroner)	Cause of death was drowning. (report)	

Exhibit 7.3 **Theory Chart**

the failure of the hotel to post pictures as required fulfills the element of causation. Even if there is no law requiring pictures be posted, parents would argue that the boys would have understood "NO" as in "NO SWIM-MING" or "NO LIFEGUARD."

The final theory chart might look like Exhibit 7.4.

The theory chart is one of the easiest ways to maintain and organize information while you are investigating a case. It also allows you to anticipate the opposition's claims and defenses and identify potential evidence.

It is important to remember that there is not always a remedy for a tragedy, no matter how awful. Not every injury is a tort.

Theory of Relief: Negligence
Client: Traveling Family
Date of Preparation: Today's Date
Preparer: Terry Hendren, Investigator

ELEMENT	SOURCE OF PROOF	INFORMAL FACT INVESTIGATION	FORMAL (DISCOVERY)
1) DUTY	1) Hotel regulation states signs warning about the hazards of swimming w/o lifeguard must be posted; 2) George Winden (hotel maintenance supervisor)	1) TH visited pool area on 2/12/yr & found no signs posted. (field notes; pictures/video) 2) told TH that signs had been removed for painting & maintenance on 8/31/yr; no temp. signs were installed; pool was not locked. (oral/ GW willing to sign statement)	
2) BREACH	George Winden	no signs posted (oral/statement/ pictures/video)	
3) CAUSATION	no posted signs = no warning re swimming	no signs (oral statement/ pictures)	
4) INJURY (DAMAGES)	Mary Lance, M.D., (Coroner)	Cause of death was drowning. (report)	

Exhibit 7.4 **Final Theory Chart**

G. Supporting Statements

If possible, obtain a written statement to support every fact and element on the theory chart. Written statements preserve the information obtained from the witnesses while the incident is still fresh and memories clear. There must be proof for every fact stated on the chart. For the chart above, you would have a statement by George Winden, preferably signed, which included the following information:

1) that he has been the hotel maintenance supervisor since (date) and is responsible for the pool maintenance;

2) that the signs had been removed on (a certain date) for painting;
3) that no temporary signs or other measures were installed after the signs were removed.

Because George Winden is the hotel's employee, he might refuse to speak to you, or he might speak to you but refuse to sign anything. If he speaks to you but refuses to sign a statement, you will at least have your own notes as to what he said. If he refuses to speak to you, he will have to be deposed; there is little you can do about it. In the event he gives you an oral statement at the hotel, but testifies differently at his deposition, you might be able to impeach him at trial.

It is a popular misconception that statements that are either unsigned or not reduced to writing are inadmissible in evidence at trial. Often witnesses or parties to an action will tell an investigator, "I'm not signing anything," but will continue to talk to the investigator about what happened or what they know or saw. A good investigator does not stop talking or asking questions simply because a witness is reluctant or refuses to make or sign a written statement. Under these circumstances the investigator should press forward, pay very close attention to what was said, and commit the exchange to writing as soon as possible after it ends. It may even be possible to take limited notes that will enhance the accuracy of the investigator's memory of the conversation. At trial the investigator could testify about the conversation. Preservation of statements is covered in Chapter 6.

The extent of the formal discovery is dependent on the amount and quality of the information obtained through the investigation process. Once the complaint has been filed, the pretrial discovery process begins.

Assuming for purposes of illustration that the hotel is the defendant, discovery in the Traveling Family case would include at least the following:

1) Interrogatories (hotel)
2) Request for Production of Documents (hotel)
3) Depositions (owners, employees, guests, others)
4) Request for Admissions

Defining the scope of the investigation and developing a plan helps ensure a thorough, efficient investigation. You can see where you have been and where you need to go.

H.   Special Topics

Case investigation can be confined to one distinct substantive area of law, such as a real estate transaction between two individuals. But frequently more than one substantive area of law is involved in an investigation. Certain substantive legal areas that are commonly investigated require a

rather specialized knowledge of the subject matter, or at least an understanding of the vocabulary and process, to conduct an efficient and accurate
investigation. Several of these substantive areas, like real property, family,
estate planning, and business, recur in many types of investigations. For
example, the purpose of an investigation of real property or a business
might be to identify potential defendants who might be liable, to identify
assets available to pay damages, or to understand assets available for
distribution in a divorce or bankruptcy case. Using three of these areas as
examples, this section introduces the information you need to understand
to accomplish a good investigation.

1. Real Property

Investigation in cases involving real property requires familiarity with
legally complicated records and terms. A good investigator must know
the process of establishing and keeping property records, their location,
and the systems by which they are organized and cross-referenced, in
order to conduct an accurate and meaningful investigation. Words like
"fee simple absolute," "tenancy in common," and "life estate" all have
specific legal meanings and are important for the investigator to know.
Until one becomes familiar with the terminology, investigations will be
slow. Considering that the language of property is nearly a thousand years
old helps one understand why the vocabulary remains unusual.

During investigation it is often necessary to search real property
records for information. Generally you want to know who owns the property, how the property is held, and whether the property has a mortgage
or other lien on it.

You might want to know who to sue, by whom your client is being
sued, or whether a landowner has assets, in this case equity, that might
be used to satisfy a judgment.

Property can be owned by an individual or individuals, by a trust,
a business, or government. How the owners hold the property also varies.
Property interests are classified as a sole tenancy, tenancy in common, joint
tenancy, and tenancy by the entirety. It is always important to note whether
a person with a property interest is married, since the spouse may have
an interest as well. This section is not intended as a substitute for a course
on real property, but rather as an overview of some of the terms pertinent
to a "modern" investigation. The word "tenant," as it appears here does
not describe a mere renter but an owner of real property.

a. Sole Tenancy

In this tenancy, a single person or unit (for example, a corporation
or partnership) owns or "holds" the property alone. The deed might say
"Kristen Larwitz, an unmarried woman." The sole tenant has the right to
sell the property or use it as collateral to secure a loan, which latter use
is also referred to as encumbering. If your firm represents a client who

has an outstanding judgment against him or her, the judgment creditor could place a lien on the property, or in some instances, force a sale of the property.

b. Tenancy in Common

A tenancy in common has at least two, but perhaps more, unmarried owners, known as co-owners. Each tenant has a separate and distinct interest in the property but all cotenants have the right of possession. A distinguishing characteristic of this tenancy is that when a cotenant dies her interest passes to her heirs—*not* to the other cotenant(s). The deed will say "Margaret Fox and Jennifer Streeter as tenants in common."

Because the tenants' interests are separate and distinct, any tenant's interest in the property can be encumbered. If you represent the remaining tenant who wants your firm to handle the sale of the property, you might have difficulty until the lien is removed.

c. Joint Tenancy

In this form of ownership, two or more individuals own or hold the property as "joint tenants." Unlike tenants in common, when a joint tenant dies, his interest passes to the other joint tenant. This is called "right of survivorship." The deed will indicate the status as "Harold King and Maxwell Liman, joint tenants with right of survivorship."

d. Tenancy by the Entirety

Because a common law husband and wife were treated as one legal person, this form of ownership was devised for the married couple. Under this tenancy, each spouse owns all the property and neither spouse can sell or encumber the property without permission of the other. This tenancy is generally safe from creditors unless both spouses agree to the lien.

e. Community Property

"Community property" is a new term—relative to the Norman Conquest. In community property states, most real property acquired during the marriage is held equally by husband and wife or other owners. Community property states include California, Arizona, Washington, Idaho, Louisiana, Nevada, New Mexico, and Texas.

If your client in a divorce action is the spouse with the fewer assets and has the opportunity to choose the jurisdiction in which to file, he or she will chose a community property state where the property is divided equally.

f. Fee Simple Absolute

Land held in "fee simple absolute" reflects the maximum legal ownership, that is, complete, unqualified ownership with the absolute right to devise or give the property to one's heirs.

g. Life Estate

A life estate gives a person the right to benefit from the property, whether by occupancy or collecting rent, for her or his lifetime. Upon that person's death, the property devises to someone else, as predetermined by the person who granted the life estate.

h. Grantor/Grantee Indices

The Recorder of Deeds (sometimes known by other names, such as Registry of Deeds) is an office that lists the seller (grantor) of the property and the buyer (grantee) in separate indices. By knowing one or the other, you can trace the legal and equitable interests in the property.

i. Homestead Exemption

This exemption protects an owner's equity from the claims of creditors and forced sale for as long as the person holding the exemption occupies the property. Although initially used for the elderly or the disabled, in many jurisdictions this exemption is now available to any individual.

j. Title Search

A title search is a review of all records concerning a specific piece of property in order to determine whether or not the person holding title has "clear" title. In addition to learning the names of every owner of the property, you will learn both the legal and the street address of the property and whether the property is encumbered by a mortgage or other lien. For example, if the owner failed to pay for the new roof, there might be a mechanic's lien on the property. The roofing company filed this lien after the owner failed to pay. The property cannot be sold without satisfying the lien.

Title searches and other transactions at the Recorder of Deeds can be a daunting task, sometimes exacerbated by an unhelpful employee. If you handle real estate matters frequently, get to know the helpful people in the office and rely on them for guidance. There is always at least one person who loves to be asked for help. Be certain to review all records and take notice of the chronological filing order of the instruments to avoid missing one. Because recording and filing takes time, instruments recorded right before yours might not be available. Be sure to ask for them. In researching property, keep in mind that if you are unable to locate a record, try a variation of the name. For example, "2000 Morgan-Warwick Family Realty Trust" could be listed under "Morgan-Warwick Family Realty Trust 2000," "Two Thousand Morgan-Warwick Family Realty Trust," or "Warwick Family Realty Trust 2000 Morgan." Finally, write everything down so you do not have to repeat any steps if you have to continue at a later time.

> **PRACTICE TIP:** In many jurisdictions, real property information can be obtained through a computer hookup to the Recorder of Deeds.

It is wise to use a list or chart to be certain you obtain all necessary information. A sample chart is shown in Exhibit 7.5.

```
CLIENT: _____
DATE: _____
STREET ADDRESS OF PROPERTY: _____
_____
LEGAL DESCRIPTION: _____
_____
GRANTOR INDEX: _____
_____
GRANTEE INDEX: _____
_____
OWNER(S): _____
_____
PREVIOUS OWNERS:
   1) _____
   2) _____
   3) _____

TENANCY: _____
_____
ENCUMBRANCES:
   1) _____
   2) _____

MECHANIC'S LIEN:
   1) _____
   2) _____

PERSONS W/ INTEREST:
_____
OTHER DOCUMENTS (e.g., Homestead Exemption):
   1) _____
   2) _____
```

Exhibit 7.5 **Informational Chart**

One of the tasks in estate planning is to review the real property documents for information. Assume Phillip and Mary Lou Williams (Third Scenario, Chapter 1) wanted to give their vacation home to their daughter Miriam. One of your tasks might be to go (by foot or modem) to the county where the property is located and do a title search. A title search might show an encumbrance on the property—perhaps a tax lien for nonpayment of property taxes—which must be satisfied before the property can be transferred.

2. Business Organizations

Investigations pertaining to business entities involve uncovering records on file with federal, state, and local governments. The different kinds of business entities have already been covered under "D. Legal Identities," above. Every business entity—corporation, nonprofit corporation, partnership, limited liability company, or individual—is required to comply with filing and disclosure laws in its jurisdiction. The following information might be useful to anyone conducting an investigation involving a business. Sources and locations of records required to be filed by businesses are covered in Chapter 8.

a. Licenses

Businesses must be licensed to operate. Licenses might be required by the state, county, city or town—or all of them.

b. Annual Reports

Corporations must file annual reports with the office of the secretary of state or other similar office. The reports are available to the public.

c. Articles of Incorporation

In order to become incorporated, an organization must file Articles of Incorporation with the appropriate state agency, usually the Secretary of State. The Articles state the purpose of the organization, the names of the incorporators, the names of the directors, and the address of the corporation. Frequently a corporation is required to name a resident agent to accept service of process if the corporation is sued. Again, these records are available to the public.

Our client, Maggie Winchon, is interested in obtaining information about a specific builder before she approaches him with her development idea for the Hall tract of land. He may be incorporated as a business, and records relating to the ownership and length of time in business may be obtained from the Secretary of State. As a builder, he might have to be registered with or licensed by the state. Your investigation would uncover any complaints made against him on file with the state agency and whether or not his license is current. If his license is current, in most jurisdictions, he is bonded and insured. In many jurisdictions there are consumer information services or agencies such as the Attorney General's office or other regulatory bodies that regulate, oversee, or maintain data on such businesses. Your investigation should include contact with any such source of relevant information.

3.   Family

The intricacies of family law pervade many legal transactions. Because much of the legal terminology is assigned popular definitions by clients, cases involving family matters must be investigated thoroughly. Before relying on a client's representations for use in another transaction or forum, investigate the legal accuracy of the representation. For example, a client might use the term "legally separated" to mean that she is married, but living apart from her spouse, and that it is legal to do so. The term "legal separation" means at the most, that the parties have been awarded a legal separation by a court of competent jurisdiction or, at the least, that the parties have properly executed a separation agreement defining their rights and responsibilities. Terms you should know include "marriage," "divorce," "separation," and "custody."

a.   Marriage

A marriage is a contract between two people guaranteeing privileges and imposing responsibilities, usually formalized by a person licensed by the state to perform the marriage ceremony. A few jurisdictions still recognize common-law marriages, and under the Full Faith and Credit Clause of the United States Constitution, a marriage entered into in a state that recognizes common-law marriages is valid in all states. Occasionally a client will have the erroneous impression that a move to a different state nullifies the marriage; it does not.

b.   Divorce

A divorce is the legal termination of a marriage. Individuals who were married under the common-law provisions of the state are always surprised to learn that they must divorce through the court system as though they had been married by a licensed person. Words meaning "divorce" include dissolution of marriage, absolute divorce, and a divorce *a vinculo matrimonii.*

c.   Separation

A legal separation is a determination by a court that the parties can live apart without divorcing. A legal separation is also called a divorce *a mensa et thoro* (divorce from bed and board), a limited divorce, and a judicial separation. The term divorce used as a designation for a legal separation is unfortunate because it promotes confusion between a separation and a divorce.

Our client, Hannah West, has been living apart from her husband since last year. It would not be uncharacteristic for her as a client to describe their arrangement as a "legal separation," since they are separated and it is legal. Your awareness of the legal meaning of commonly used words is important to your ability to investigate the case successfully.

d. Custody

Custody of children is either agreed to by the parties who have properly executed a document stating the same or ordered by the court. The person who is in possession of the children without a document or court order does not have legal custody.

Family law terminology varies from state to state. A investigator must become knowledgeable with the terms of his or her state and be alert to the differences.

H. Paralegal as Witness

1. Circumstances

Under some circumstances you might become a witness in the case and be called to testify at trial. This usually occurs when you have interviewed a witness whose testimony at trial differs from the statement given to you. Under these circumstances, you might be called as a witness to testify to impeach or discredit his testimony. For example, using the case where the boys drown, let us assume that George Winden, the maintenance supervisor, told you when you interviewed him that the warning signs were removed for painting and that no temporary signs were installed. George would not sign a statement. Nevertheless, after the interview, you wrote a memo to the file to which you attached your notes showing George's actual words, "Nope, we didn't post any temporary signs." No deposition was taken. At trial George changes his story to say that temporary signs were posted. You might be called to impeach his testimony.

If you have no knowledge of the events other than what George told you, your testimony will likely be limited to the fact that you talked with him and he told you a story that differs from the one he told at trial. If you also observed the absence of signs, however, you might be asked to impeach him with your observations as well as with his prior inconsistent statements.

2. Procedure

There might be little time to prepare for your testimony. In the event it does happen, however, the attorney would simply ask you if you remembered talking with Mr. Winden and what if anything he said about temporary signs. You have your memory and your notes to support your testimony. Remember your notes have some of Mr. Winden's precise words, which add credibility to your testimony.

In some jurisdictions, there are rules that provide for the sequestration of trial witnesses. This means that if an attorney intends to call a witness, that witness cannot be present to hear the testimony of other witnesses. The rule ensures that one witness is not influenced by the testimony of another. The rule is not applied rigidly by all judges, especially where the impeaching witness (you) is assisting the attorney at trial and the attorney had no reason to believe you would testify until George Winden testified contrary to his prior statement.

I. The Power of Observation

Nothing can substitute for careful observation. For example, if you are investigating a Workers' Compensation insurance claim from a man who claims he injured his left hand on the job, how do you find out whether it is true? And if it is true, the extent of his injury? Your supervisor has provided you with the man's name and address. With that basic information, you can determine whether he has a driver's license and if a car is registered to him. The license will provide a physical description. Using a street map, you would find his house and make simple observations. Does he appear to be right-handed or left-handed? Is he mowing the lawn? Trimming the trees? Driving the car? Opening the car door with his left hand? Carrying objects with his left hand? Is there a boat in the driveway? Might he use the left hand water-skiing? Granted, it might take multiple trips past the house and perhaps to other places over a period of time to get the information, but your trips are a small investment for an insurance company to make if they suspect fraud and are paying lifetime benefits.

SUMMARY

Organization is the key to a thorough, efficient investigation. Utilizing theory charts helps you focus on the information needed to prove the case. Defining the scope of the investigation and drafting an investigation plan guarantees a thorough investigation. Understanding the legal identity of the parties—individual, corporation, or other—is essential to your investigation of the matter. A clear writing of your discoveries is a permanent record of your work and should be maintained in the file. In the event a witness you interviewed testifies differently at trial, your testimony can be used to impeach him or her. Learn the language of the substantive areas in which you investigate and use your powers of observation to complement the investigative process.

Key Terms

Articles of incorporation	Legal identity
Closed corporation	Life estate
Collateral	Limited liability company
Community property	Mechanic's lien
Corporation	Nonprofit corporation
Fee simple absolute	Partnership
Grantee	Sole tenancy
Grantor	Tenancy by the entirety
Homestead	Tenancy in common
Investigation plan	Title search
Joint tenancy	

REVIEW QUESTIONS

1. What are the differences between formal and informal investigation?

2. How can you be certain you receive good instructions from your supervisor?

3. Why are governments (city, state, and federal) immune from suit? Under what circumstances can you sue them?

5. Under what circumstances might you as an investigator be called to testify?

6. What limitations might affect your investigation of a case?

7. What are some legal identities? What does the term mean?

8. How is the scope of the investigation defined?

9. What is the purpose of an investigation plan? How is it designed?

10. Under what circumstances might you be called to testify at trial?

CHAPTER EXERCISES

Exercise 7-1:   Assume your firm has been contacted by a woman whose baby was born without eyes. She stated that approximately six months before her son's birth, she was drenched with a chemical while she was taking one of her daily health walks in a tomato and strawberry field. Your supervising attorney has asked you to do some preliminary investigation in order to help him decide whether to take the case. Define the scope of investigation and draft an investigation plan.

Exercise 7-2:   Assume your firm represents Amanda Solstice, who was injured when she was involved in a accident with another car at the intersection at Fifth and Main Streets in Boylston, Kansas, on June 21, (year). As Amanda was driving into the intersection, a manhole cover flipped up. When she swerved to miss it, she collided with another car. Your investigation shows that the city might be liable. Your supervising attorney has asked you to draft a letter to the city to satisfy the notice requirement. Research your state law to find the applicable statute or use the sample statute in the Appendix. Prepare the letter.

Exercise 7-3:   Complete a theory chart for the incident. What is the cause of action? What are the elements? What facts support the elements? What additional facts do you need to know?

Exercise 7-4:   You have been assigned to investigate a Workers' Compensation case where the worker alleges her back was injured at work. Make a list of the steps you would take to investigate the claim.

Exercise 7-5:   Alone or with another student, go to a public place—a mall, street corner, park. Choose a person and silently jot down your observations about that person. Compare with your partner the different things observed.

Exercise 7-6:   Draft a list of terms used in an area of law of your choice. Define each term.

Exercise 7-7:   You have been assigned to investigate each of the following factual situations. Prepare an investigation plan for each.

1. A one-story house with historical value in your town has caught fire for the second time in two years, presumably due to a painter's carelessness with a torch in removing paint. Timber damage the first time was slight and contained to the attic; smoke damage was pervasive. The second time, the roof and the contents of the attic were completely destroyed. The fire was spotted by the same person who called the fire department the first time. The owners of the property were away on vacation. After the first fire, the house was restored to its prefire condition except for the exterior painting. After the second fire, the family added a second story to the house.

2. Cliff Ahmed, a steelworker with a construction company, was injured in a fall from a bridge when his safety harness broke and he fell 40 feet to the river below. He was rescued by two fellow workers who jumped in after him and pulled him to shore. Ahmed was taken to the hospital where he was treated for a broken collar bone and a compound fracture of his left leg. State safety inspectors have been called in to investigate.

8

Investigating Skills

CHAPTER OBJECTIVES

This chapter provides insights into

- finding public and private information;
- obtaining authorizations;
- understanding sources of information.

A. Introduction

Retrieving documents, locating information, and finding individuals were, at one time, labor-intensive tasks. With the advent of the computer services, especially the Internet and other on-line services, a wealth of public information, such as corporate and property records, is available quickly and often free. Huge national and international databases offer an extraordinary amount of information. National computerized telephone books help to find the person you seek in a fraction of the time. But whether you search with a modem or with your feet, you have to identify what information you seek to determine, whether it is available publicly or only with proper authorization. Two federal acts, the Privacy Act of 1974 and the Freedom of Information Act, are among the most important laws controlling access to records. Other laws, such as open meeting laws, guarantee public access to information.

B. Federal and State Laws

1. The Privacy Act

Under the Privacy Act, 5 U.S.C. §552a, federal agencies may not disclose any record containing information about any individual to any other individual or to another agency except where necessary for law enforcement, gathering of statistical data, or internal government operations, such as performed by the Government Accounting Office. The term "record" includes information about a person's education, financial transactions, medical history, and criminal or employment history. In the event an agency makes an unlawful disclosure, the Privacy Act contains a private right of action that allows any individual to bring a civil action against the disclosing agency in federal district court. If the individual is successful, reasonable attorney's fees and costs will be assessed against the United States. If any agency employee discloses prohibited information, he or she shall be found guilty of a misdemeanor and fined up to $5,000.

Any individual may request to review and copy any records containing information about him or her kept by an agency.

Regardless of whom you represent, the Privacy Act protects the confidential nature of their records. The financial records depicting the net worth of our client, Dr. Wizzen, are confidential under the Privacy Act.

> **PRACTICE TIP:** Disclosures of certain kinds of information (for example, records concerning drug and alcohol treatment) are governed by state or federal law and require specific language in an authorization. *See, for example,* 42 C.F.R. §2.13.

---

2. The Freedom of Information Act

The Freedom of Information Act (FOIA), 5 U.S.C. §552, mandates agencies to make available information that is not protected by the Privacy Act; it does not apply to documents kept secret in the interest of national defense or foreign policy, trade secrets, certain agency memoranda, or geological and geophysical information concerning wells. Under FOIA, an individual may request agency opinions, rulings, and orders; statements of policy and interpretations of policy statements; and administrative staff manuals. The Act limits charges for searching and duplication to a reasonable amount, and advance fees are not required unless the fee will exceed $250. If an agency withholds information unreasonably, the Act provides a private right of action in federal district court. As with the Privacy Act, a successful plaintiff will be awarded costs and attorney's fees.

The agency must respond to a written request within ten days; however, the response is generally limited to a form letter advising the individual of the nature and extent of the backlog.

Our client, Maggie Winchon, the real estate developer, could request Environmental Protection Agency memoranda on the three-toed striped frog with a FOIA letter. Sample FOIA letters are in the Appendix.

3. Open Meeting Laws

Open meeting laws (sunshine laws) require federal, state, and local governing bodies to hold their meetings publicly—"in the sunshine" where the citizens can view the decision making process. Not all parts of the meeting are public. For example, an executive session discussing the firing of an employee is closed to the public.

Notice of the meetings is posted or published and provides an agenda of the topics to be considered. It is often the paralegal's job to review the agenda for an upcoming meeting. If a topic of importance to the firm appears on the agenda, the paralegal will attend the meeting (in person or by cable TV), write a summary of the discussion, and record any votes taken.

To provide competent legal representation to Maggie Winchon, the firm must keep abreast of changes in local laws, including zoning, building, and conservation.

C. Documents

In light of the requirements and restrictions of the Privacy Act and FOIA, documents pertaining to an investigation can be classified as public or private.

1. Public

Public documents are all documents available for inspection by the general public with or without a charge. They include documents from police reports to birth certificates to corporate filings and property records. Permission is not required. A verbal or written request is made, in some instances a fee may be charged, and voila!, the record is yours. A list of sources of public records is in the second half of this chapter.

The information contained in public records is often seemingly "private" to the person, or the family of the person, whose name appears in the document. Death certificates tell how and where people die; divorce records disclose an abundance of personal and financial information. Nonetheless, information contained in these records is public and available to all who are interested.

2. Private

Private documents are not available to the general public because they contain confidential information. Medical, employment, and income tax records are common examples of private documents that, because they are protected by law, will not be released without authorization. Public agencies such as the Social Security Administration, the Internal Revenue Service, and the Federal Bureau of Investigation maintain private records. Nevertheless, they are classified as confidential documents, subject to federal disclosure laws.

3. Authorizations

a. Scope of Authorization

In order to obtain a person's confidential records, the requestor of the records must furnish an authorization to the keeper of the records. An authorization is a document, signed by the person who is the subject of the records permitting the release of the records to a third person, usually the person's attorney. A properly executed authorization protects the provider from liability for an otherwise actionable breach of privacy. Often during an investigation, one needs to obtain confidential information. For example, let's suppose your client, Gladys Winston, was sexually assaulted by the police officers when they arrested her for burglary of the apartment. She has made a claim against the officers and the city. As a result of the assault, Ms. Winston was treated for severe depression by a psychiatrist, Dr. Meyers. In the course of your investigation, you need to obtain and review the records Dr. Meyers prepared as a result of the treatment. The records, however, are confidential and can only be released with Ms. Winston's authorization. An authorization enables you to gather, with Ms. Winston's consent, information otherwise considered confidential.

An authorization must be notarized. Notarization of a document is designed to prevent fraud and forgery. A notary public is a person authorized by the state to guarantee the authenticity of the identity of the person who appears before him or her. The notary examines various forms of identification, such as a driver's license, offered by the person to prove identity and if the identification is acceptable, the notary signs and seals the document. A notary public attests to the legal validity of a variety of documents, including affidavits, court documents, contracts, real property documents (deeds, mortgages, releases, liens), powers of attorney, and corporate documents. A notary keeps a record of each document notarized. Public information does not require an authorization.

b. Obtaining an Authorization

If your case involves any document that is not a public record or any document that is protected by law, you must have an authorization in order to obtain the record. Generally authorizations are obtained from the client at the initial interview. The authorization should be specific as to the records requested and include information that easily identifies the person authorizing the request. Under ideal circumstances, a separate authorization should be written for each request. It is possible, however, to have a variety of pre-printed forms on which you can fill in pertinent information available at the first meeting and have the client's signature notarized. This method saves time for you and time and money for your client. For example, if your office does a fair amount of plaintiff medical malpractice, you would have authorization forms for the hospital(s), doctors and employer.

A cover letter explaining the purpose of the request should be sent along with the notarized authorization. If your jurisdiction requires the document to be certified, for, as an example, later introduction into evidence as a self-authenticating document, include the certification language in your cover letter with specific instructions. If you know the record you are requesting is a single page, include a stamped self-addressed envelope to speed delivery. If the records are voluminous, offer to pay (the responding party will usually send a bill anyway) or offer to copy them yourself. Understand the cost per page before you agree to the charge.

PRACTICE TIP: Medical records, such as discharge summaries and progress notes (not bills), are not readily available in every state. Indeed in nearly half the states, people have no right to review or copy their own medical records. Check your state statutes and regulations or the department of health to determine whether your state has an access law.

If time permits, take the authorization to the office and request the records in person. You can then see the complete file, including the cover, first hand. You might be able to copy the records then and there making certain to get good clear copies. This method eliminates the problem of dealing with illegible copies, which often arrive from record providers. If you cannot copy the records, you will at least have had a first hand look at them and see the size of the file. It is a good idea to count the pages, front and back, and to make notes about the file so that when it arrives, you are reasonably certain you have the complete set.

The authorization form and cover letter should be brief and contain only the information necessary to allow the person to locate the records requested. Include the client's full name, date of birth, and Social Security number to avoid errors. Do not discuss theory or divulge other case information in the letter. It may be that the person to whom you direct your request will testify for your adversary. Apply to become a notary public in the state where you intend to work. Having notaries public on staff is important to most firms. A sample cover letter and authorization are shown in Exhibits 8.1 and 8.2.

Hall & Rinaldi

ATTORNEYS & COUNSELORS AT LAW

1000 Sixteenth Street, N.W.
Washington, D.C. 20005
(202) 784-1990
Fax (202) 784-1999

November 22, (year)

Personnel Administrator
Mercy Hospital
400 Elizabeth Street
Washington, D.C. 20001

Re: Marilyn Kaminski Morneau
     D.O.B. 1/16/1979
     S.S.N. 607-90-3948

Dear Madam/Sir:

Our office represents Ms. Morneau for personal injuries she sustained in an auto accident on August 5, (year). We understand that as a result of her injuries she missed several months of work in her job as a dialysis technician.

Would you kindly provide copies of her attendance records from August 5, (year), through November 1, (year), within the next two weeks?

A copy of Ms. Morneau's authorization is enclosed. I appreciate your cooperation in this matter. If you have any questions, please call.

Very truly yours,

Marsha Kemper
Paralegal

enclosure

Exhibit 8.1 **Sample Cover Letter**

Hall & Rinaldi

ATTORNEYS & COUNSELORS AT LAW

1000 Sixteenth Street, N.W.
Washington, D.C. 20005
(202) 784-1990
Fax (202) 784-1999

November 22, (year)

AUTHORIZATION

To: Personnel Administrator

I hereby authorize you to release a copy of my employment records showing my attendance between August 5, (year), and November 1, (year), to Marsha Kemper of Hall and Rinaldi, or her representative. This authorization is effective immediately and remains in effect until I revoke it in writing.

_____
Marilyn Kaminski Morneau
D.O.B. 1/16/1979
S.S.N. 607-90-3948

Subscribed and sworn to before me this ____ day of November, (year).

_____
Jane Morin, Notary Public

My commission expires on December 31, (year).

[seal]

Exhibit 8.2 **Sample Authorization**

If the records are protected by statute, cite to the statute in the request and be specific about the information you want. (*See* Exhibit 8.3.)

[letterhead]

CONSENT TO RELEASE CONFIDENTIAL INFORMATION

I, _____, born _____, S.S.N. _____, do hereby consent to and authorize _____ to disclose to _____
_____ Medical history/physical examination
_____ Psychiatric assessment/prognosis
_____ Social Service assessment
_____ Alcohol/drug history
_____ Treatment Plan (including discharge summary/after care)
_____ AIDS diagnosis/treatment plan
_____ Other
This information is needed for the following purposes:
_____
_____

I understand that the above information is protected by 42 C.F.R., Part 2, "Confidentiality of Alcohol and Drug Abuse Patient Records" and cannot be disclosed without my written consent unless otherwise provided for in the regulations. I understand that I need not consent to the release of information in order to obtain treatment services. I choose to do so willingly and voluntarily for the purposes specified above. The duration of this authorization is not longer than one year unless I specify a date, event, or condition on which it will expire sooner.

_____   _____
Signature of Client   Date

_____   _____
Signature of Witness   Date

Exhibit 8.3 **Consent to Release Confidential Information**

4.   Organization

Whether the information is public or private, it should be organized so that you can keep track of what you have and what you need. Exhibit 8.4 shows a form to help you keep track of the documents. It lists kinds of documents, possible use, whether an authorization is necessary, and if so, whether it has been received from the client, when the documents were requested, and when they were received.

DOCUMENT	FOR (if not applicable, use N/A):	AUTHORIZATIONS		DATE REQUEST	DATE RECV'D
		NECESSARY	REC'D		
POLICE REPORT					
DOCTOR REPORT					
HOSPITAL REP'T					
AMBULANCE REP'T					
WITNESS #1 Stmt.					
WITNESS #2 Stmt.					
COURT RECORDS					
CORPORATE/BUS.					
PROPERTY					
STATE					
LOCAL					
EXPERT/SCIENTIFIC					
PERMITS					

Investigation Checklist for Documents

Client: _____
Investigator: _____

Exhibit 8.4 **Investigation Checklist for Documents**

D. Finding People

Finding a person is an interesting and challenging part of investigation. Sometimes a person is easy to find, for example, when he or she works with your client. Other times a search is not so easy, for example, a witness to an accident who is not on the police report. Answer the question, "Who do you want to find and why do you want to find them?" The answer to this question might be specific: "I want to find Jeff Jones because I want to serve him with process." Or, the answer may be general: "I want to find anyone who witnessed the accident on May 3 at the intersection of Maple Street and Main Street because they might have information that will help prove our client's negligence claim against defendant (or help prove our client was not negligent)."

If you are looking for witnesses, finding them quickly is important because the sooner you find them the better will be their ability to recall events. If their recall is favorable for your client, the chances that the case will settle early and favorably for your client increase.

Depending on whether the process is specific (that is, you are looking for a named person or persons) or general (that is, you are looking for any person who might have information you need), the process varies. If specific, you will focus on depositories of information, such as, the Department of Motor Vehicles, tax rolls, telephone books, registry of vital statistics, and cross-reference directories. A listing of sources is in the last part of this chapter.

When looking for someone, be persistent and be creative. A record may be listed with misspellings or data entry mistakes, missing periods, additional commas, and so on. Jane A. Jones may be listed as Jayne A. Jones, Janie A. Jones, J. A. Jones, Jones, Jane A., or any combination of the names. Some computer programs are case sensitive, so it is important to type the request in the proper format. Problems can arise when you rely on another person to input the information, but are unable to observe them doing so. Occasionally the information was originally input incorrectly, for example, Janie AJones. Only persistence will locate a misfiled or erroneously filed record. As you try the various spellings, note each attempt to ensure an efficient, comprehensive search.

If research is general, you will cast a wider net by advertising, checking the police/ambulance reports for witnesses, visiting local merchants to see if any has information about the incident, standing on the corner at same general time the accident happened and holding a sign that asks passers-by if they have any information about the accident, or by checking local businesses for video cameras that may have recorded the event or the witnesses near it. Occasionally witnesses or potential plaintiffs are located by publishing a notice in the newspaper. This method is used in class actions to identify potential class members; the ad must be approved by the court before publication.

If your efforts to find someone are unsuccessful, consider hiring a licensed private investigator.

E. Finding Information

Be polite and be persistent. Chances are if you can't find the information you haven't looked in the right place. The most difficult part about locating information is figuring out where it is and how to access it. Imagine a 50-story building full of information. You must first find the entrance, then the floor, the suite, the room, the file cabinet, the drawer, and finally, the file. What steps do you need to take to find the information?

First you must know what it is you're looking for. What is the specific piece of information you want to learn? Then consider the possible sources. Remember when you are looking for information that "all they can say is "No."

Although considerable public and private information has been entered into databases for easy retrieval, not every city, town, or county in every state has computerized files.

1. Sources

It is impossible in this book to print a compete list of sources of information.The following is a partial list of sources and the kind of information you might gather from them. Keep in mind that fees are required for many of the records, but that an enormous variety of documents is available at no charge from the United States government.

> **PRACTICE TIP:** Collect forms from various agencies to discover the kind of information they keep.

a. *Department of Motor Vehicles*

A state department of motor vehicles (DMV) can provide you with information regarding drivers' licenses—those currently valid and those no longer valid. You should supply the person's name, address, date of birth, and Social Security number. In some jurisdictions, a person's Social Security number is the same as the driver's license number. You need not have all the above information to obtain what you seek; however, it is helpful especially when the name is a common one. If you want to know exactly what information the DMV requires of one applying for a license, call them, stop by the local office, or write and ask for an application.

Although access is restricted in some states, state departments of motor vehicles have information regarding traffic violations, including accidents and parking. Further information would include the person's eye and hair color, height, weight, date of birth, and driving restrictions. Some of this information might be less than accurate for various reasons.

Light may make gray eyes look green; the applicant might not wish to reveal his or her true height and weight, adding an inch or two and shedding 10 to 15 pounds. If a woman changes her surname when she marries, and you do not know her married name, you will not be able to find it under her married name, but the DMV keeps old records with previous surnames. If the surname is two names hyphenated, as is common in some cultures, look under each of the two names.

As people move from state to state, new licenses are issued and old ones are relinquished to the issuing state. The issuing state in turn notifies the person's former state of the change in status. If you do not have much information about a person, request the record anyway based on what you have. Sometimes you will be provided information you did not expect. If the DMV is not the proper depository for the report requested—for example, an accident report—they will most likely provide you with the name and address of the proper depository.

You can also request information from the DMV concerning vehicle registrations and sales. Frequently this request will provide you with more current address information since vehicle registrations are renewed every one to two years compared to driver's licenses, which are renewed a minimum of every four years. Be aware that some states are considering lifetime vehicle registrations and lifetime licenses for drivers.

b.   Courthouse

Every state and the federal government has a court system with two major components: courts of general jurisdiction and courts of specific jurisdiction. Courts of general jurisdiction hear all cases except those that by statute must be heard by a court of specific jurisdiction, such as bankruptcy, probate, landlord/tenant, and family.

Each state has its own court structure and court names. A court of general jurisdiction or trial court might be called Court of Common Pleas (Ohio), Superior Court (District of Columbia), Circuit Court (Illinois), or Supreme Court (New York). The highest court in a state may be called the Court of Appeals (District of Columbia and New York) or the Supreme Court (Ohio).

Some states have a two-tier appellate court system. In a two-tier system, the intermediate court might be called the Court of Appeals, and the highest court the Supreme Court (Massachusetts Court of Appeals and the Massachusetts Supreme Judicial Court), or the intermediate court might be the Court of Special Appeals and the highest court the Court of Appeals (Maryland Court of Special Appeals and the Maryland Court of Appeals).

Every jurisdiction has a depository of records of all cases filed, regardless of disposition. Some are computerized; some are on microfilm; some are paper files. Every county has a court; some cities have their own courts, called municipal courts. Each court has its own divisions with their own names. Names of divisions can vary from state to state. For example, in some states the probate court deals only with wills, trusts, and related fiduciary matters. In other states probate has a broader meaning and includes family cases. Ask how you might go about finding a particular type of case, especially when you research in an unfamiliar jurisdiction. Establish a good relationship with the file clerks; it will make your task easier.

i. Plaintiff and Defendant Tables

Every case filed is catalogued under the plaintiff's name and the defendant's name. If a case has more than one plaintiff or defendant, it might be that only the first party's name is recorded. By looking in the Defendant Table or Plaintiff Table, you will find the number and letter, if any, assigned to the case. This information is necessary to request the file, either in writing or orally, from the clerk. Once you have the correct title of the case, including the names of all parties and the number, record it so that in the event you or someone else in your office needs to retrieve the file, the initial step can be skipped. Old cases are frequently stored elsewhere in the building, the city, or even out of town. It might take days to process your request. Even if the case is in the building, it might take an hour to retrieve. If a judge has the file in chambers or it is out for microfilming, it might not be available to you that day. Always attempt to locate and read the case long before it is necessary and always bring something else to do—a case to read or something to draft in the event you have to wait.

ii. Criminal Records

Records concerning arrest or conviction of a party are available in the criminal court or division. Both misdemeanor and felony cases are covered although more than one court might be involved. You must have the defendant's name and preferably other information like a date of birth and Social Security number to be certain you obtain information on the right person. The available information will include date and nature of the arrest and the outcome of the case, whether there was a trial, or the case was dismissed.

iii. Sealed Records

Juvenile, adoption, and other miscellaneous records that the court has sealed are generally not available to the public. This is not true for juveniles tried as adults.

iv. Divorce Records

Divorce records are available from the court that granted the divorce. The records can provide a wealth of information, including the parties' full names, addresses, date and place of marriage and separation, occupations, and assets, including bank and stock accounts, real property, and any other property in which one of the parties holds an interest. Also included are the names, dates, and places of birth of any children. In some cases, where the parties have executed a separation agreement settling all the rights and obligations of the marriage, information available will be limited because the parties have chosen to keep the details of the agreement private.

v. Probate

The probate court indices catalog actions by the name of the petitioner, name of the deceased, or name of the estate. If a complaint regarding the estate has been filed, this will be noted on the court jacket. Information about beneficiaries, minors, and incompetence is also in such files.

c. Registry of Deeds

The Registry of Deeds contains information on every piece of real estate in the county. It includes the names of the grantor (seller) and grantee (buyer) under the Grantor/Grantee Index. Many jurisdictions have computerized land records or are in the process of computerizing them. Searching land records can be a tedious and daunting task for the inexperienced; ask for help to find what you need and to be certain you have made a thorough search. Information obtainable includes owners of property from the beginning of recordkeeping to the present, the mortgage or note holder(s) on the property, any liens on the property, and the legal description of the property.

d. Registry of Vital Statistics

Every time someone is born, married, divorced, or dies, the event is recorded on an official state form and retained in the county, city, or state vital statistics office. The forms are available in various state offices and provided in blank. The information contained on the forms is as accurate as the source of the information (the "informant"). For a birth certificate, the source is the mother; for a marriage certificate, the applicants; for a death certificate, the spouse, parent, daughter or son, or other relative.

The states are not uniform in their record keeping. The Consumer Education Research Center (1980 Springfield Avenue, Maplewood, New Jersey 07040), however, has produced a book, Where to Write World Wide For Vital Records, which lists the telephone number and address of each state's archives. The cost of the records is included, as well as sample forms in the event particular language is required. The book also includes addresses for requesting international records.

i. Birth

Information appearing on birth records is generally obtained from the mother after the child is born and before discharge from the hospital. The hospital forwards the information to the vital statistics office and, thereafter, a party may obtain a copy of the record for a fee by written request. The "Certificate of Live Birth" is numbered and contains the child's name, sex, hospital and city of birth, the names and ages and addresses of the mother and father, and the mother's birth name or former name. It might contain the parents' occupations and Social Security numbers. The informant listed on the certificate is usually the mother; therefore the information is whatever she provided. Social Security numbers are not given to children at birth, but must be applied for after the child's birth and before the child turns two.

To request a birth record, provide the following facts:

1) Full name
2) Sex
3) Father's name
4) Mother's birth name
5) Day, month, and year of birth
6) Name of hospital
7) City, county, and state
8) Purpose of request
9) Relationship of requestor

Birth records of alien children adopted by U.S. citizens can be obtained from the Immigration and Naturalization Service (INS).

ii.   Death

A certificate of death provides the deceased's name, address, date and place of birth, Social Security number, marital status, race, education, occupation, parents' names, date, time, place, and cause of death, and attending physician. It also states whether the case was referred to the coroner, whether an autopsy was performed, and the method and place of disposition of the body. Note that some older death certificates allow limited information concerning the cause of death. The stated cause might be the immediate cause; evidence of illness that lead to the immediate cause might not be noted. For example, a diabetic who lapsed into a coma and died might have had the cause of death listed as cardiac arrest; yet the diabetes actually caused the condition that led to the death. Newer death certificates require the physician to enter the immediate cause as well as underlying causes (the disease or injury that initiated the events resulting in death). The manner of death is also listed as natural, accidental, suicide, homicide, pending investigation, or unable to be determined.

Finally, listed on the death certificate is whether the decedent was ever in the armed forces. If so, benefits might be available to a survivor.

To request a death record, provide the same information as with the birth record, substituting "death" for "birth."

Death records for persons dying in a foreign country are available if the death is reported to the nearest U.S. consular office, along with proof of U.S. citizenship and a death certificate. Write to Passport Services, Correspondence Branch, U.S. Department of State, Washington, D.C. 20522-1705.

For military personnel who were in the military at the time of death, request records from National Personnel Records Center, Military Personnel Records, 9700 Page Avenue, St. Louis, MO 63132-5100.

iii. Marriage

A certificate of marriage contains the applicants' names, addresses, dates and places of birth, ages, witnesses, signatures, and, if there was a previous marriage, how it was terminated. After the ceremony is performed by a person licensed by the state, that person lists the date and place of the marriage (the "return") and sends it to the registry. In many jurisdictions the application and return are on the same paper.

To request a marriage record, provide:

1) Full names of bride and groom
2) Day, month and year of marriage
3) City, county, and state of marriage
4) Purpose of request
5) Relationship of requestor

iv. Divorce

Although some factual information about a divorce can be obtained from the Registry of Vital Statistics, more information can usually be obtained from the court documents. *See* section b. Courthouse, iv. Divorce Records, above.

PRACTICE TIP: It can take weeks to obtain results from a written request for documents. Do not wait until the last minute to request documents. You might not get them. If you are pressed for time, the sender might agree to fax you the record immediately with a hard copy to follow.

---

e. Real Property Tax Rolls

Each jurisdiction keeps a list of all real properties. It includes the property's legal owner, the size of the property, the assessed value of the property, and the taxes. There is also a delinquent tax list identifying all properties on which taxes are overdue and the amount of the tax due.

f. Voter Lists

If a person has registered to vote in a jurisdiction, there is a record of it. Voter lists contain the names and addresses of all persons who registered to vote whether or not they voted. These lists contain both primary and general election information. A qualified individual need not vote in the primary in order to vote in the general election.

g. Census

Every town, city, or county is required to take a census of the number of people living in their community, their addresses, occupations, ages, and pets. Schools generally rely on census lists to contact prospective students and to estimate future needs.

h.   Religious Records/Cemetery Records

Religious records contain information on baptisms, marriages and funerals. The information is provided by an official or the family.

Cemetery records contain the dates and places of death for each person interred.

i.   Military/Department of Defense Records

Military records of active duty members or DOD employees are available through different offices depending on the branch of service: air force, army, marines, navy, coast guard or the Department of Defense. Your local telephone book always has a number for a recruiting station which will provide you with an address. Records for inactive military and Department of Defense personnel are stored at the National Personnel Records Center (NPRC). The address is listed in section d. Registry of Vital Statistics, ii. Death, above.

j.   VFW and Veterans Organizations

The Veterans Administration has records for anyone who has ever served in the military. Local Veterans of Foreign Wars (VFW) chapters might be able to provide information about your subject.

k.   United States Postal Service

Formerly, the postal service provided permanent change of address information of individuals to anyone who had the individual's former address. As of December 1994 this service is no longer available except to process servers. For $3.00, one may still request a change of address of a business or private institution that has moved within the past 18 months. Exhibit 8.5 below summarizes the current policy.

l.   State Offices

The Secretary of State's office contains a variety of business records, including sole proprietorship, partnership, and corporate documents. The State Office of Consumer Affairs and Business Regulations grants licenses to individuals in many different occupations. A partial listing is shown in Exhibit 8.6.

Generally the state will provide you with the person's address, the date the license was granted and whether any complaints have been filed against that person. States participate in CLEAR (Clearinghouse on Licensure, Enforcement, and Regulation), a national disciplinary network, by reporting all disciplinary actions taken in the state to the national clearinghouse. The information is compiled quarterly and sent to the member states.

REQUESTED BY:	WILL THE SERVICE DISCLOSE BUSINESS COA OR BUSINESS BOXHOLDER?	WILL THE SERVICE DISCLOSE INDIVIDUAL/ FAMILY BOXHOLDER?	WILL THE SERVICE DISCLOSE INDIVIDUAL/ FAMILY COA OR BOXHOLDER INFORMATION OF PERSONS PROTECTED BY COURT ORDER?
GENERAL PUBLIC	Yes	No	No
PROCESS SERVER	Yes	w/ written request including a warning and certification and other specific information.	No
COURT ORDER	Yes	if field counsel agrees.	if field counsel agrees.
CRIMINAL LAW ENFORCEMENT	Yes	w/ written signed request stating information is necessary for performance of official duties; or orally after the inspection service confirms information is needed for criminal investigation.	w/ written signed request stating information is necessary for performance of official duties; or orally after the inspection service confirms information is needed for criminal investigation.
GOVERNMENT AGENCY	Yes	w/ written signed request on letterhead for official purposes.	w/ written signed request on letterhead for official purposes.

Exhibit 8.5 **Disclosure of Change of Address Information**

m. Other Records

i. Pet Licenses

Domestic pets, especially dogs, must be licensed yearly. Some jurisdictions now require that cats also be licensed because of outbreaks of rabies. The owner's name and address is on file.

accountants	notaries public	barbers	landscape architects
chiropractors	dentists	mental health professionals	doctors
plumbers	engineers	real estate brokers	social workers
veterinarians	opticians	architects	nurses
nursing home operators	appraisers	funeral services	speech pathologists
security system installers	surveyors	electrologists	physician assistants

Exhibit 8.6 **Representative Boards of State Registration**

ii.   Sporting Licenses

All states require adults to purchase licenses for the privilege of hunting or fishing in state. To determine hunting and fishing seasons, write or call the state's Department of Natural Resources, the Bureau of Wildlife or the town clerk for information.

iii.   Town Permits

Many local government units keep records of purchasers of beach stickers, dump permits, and parking permits.

n.   Martindale-Hubbell Law Directory and Bar Associations

Martindale-Hubbell Directory lists attorneys individually and by firm. You can find out where an attorney went to school, dates of admission to state bars, type of legal work the firm practices, and other miscellaneous information.

Each state has a board that licenses and oversees attorneys who practice in the state. Membership in attorney associations is not a prerequisite for practicing in the state. These associations focus instead on lobbying to protect and promote attorneys' interests, and continuing training for attorneys through seminars and publications.

In Massachusetts, the agency that licenses and oversees attorneys (and to which an attorney must pay yearly dues) is called the Board of Bar Overseers. The nonmandatory association of attorneys is called the Massachusetts Bar Association. Most state bar associations publish a comprehensive legal directory that is nearly indispensable to a legal practice.

These directories commonly contain listings of federal and state legislators, courts, and agencies, as well as taxes, fee schedules, insurance companies, maps to all courthouses, and vital statistics offices for all jurisdictions. A Table of Contents appears in the Appendix.

o. Newspapers

Newspapers provide a vast amount of information about people, places, and things. Your public library has the major newspapers on microfilm or disk. For example, if you wanted to search the papers to see whether there were any other cases where children were born without eyes after *in utero* exposure to chemicals, your search would alert you to an article in the Wall Street Journal, June 10, 1996 ("Benlate Case Won by Parents . . .").

p. Libraries

The resources of the library are too numerous to list here. You can, however, find information on all types of organizations, incorporated or unincorporated, profit or nonprofit, national or foreign. You can find medical and scientific information. Many libraries have information that duplicates the local government information, such as property records, including assessments. Most libraries now have computer hookups to other libraries and resources, giving you an enormous amount of information. Be a digital investigator. Use the library to educate yourself about the issue. For example, if you need to learn about Social Security, there is a Social Security Handbook, published by the Government Printing Office; it is available in most libraries.

If you cannot find the information, ask the resource librarian for some general help; it is unethical, unwise, and unnecessary to tell him or her about your case. Since most of the information you seek from the library is factual, confidentiality is an unlikely issue.

There are 1,400 federal depository libraries throughout the United States, at least one in every congressional district. All of these libraries contain a wide variety of free government information, both print and electronic. Staff is available to help. To find the library closest to you, go to the following cite and enter your state abbreviation:

http://www.access.gpo.gov/su_docs/dpos/adpos/adpos003.html

q. Federal Government/FOIA

In addition to military records mentioned above, the federal government maintains records in various agencies and organizations. The Internal Revenue Service, for example, keeps copies of all tax returns filed. You can obtain copies of tax returns of a third party, usually a client, by having him or her complete, sign, and file IRS release form 4506. File a Freedom of Information Act (FOIA) 5 U.S.C. §552 request to obtain an agency's final opinions, policy statements, administrative staff manuals, or your client's FBI file. The Act is discussed in the first part of the chapter. A sample request appears in the Appendix.

r. Cross-Reference Directory

The International Association of Cross-Reference Directories publishes criss-cross directories. A COLE Directory is an example of a criss-cross directory. It lists residences and businesses by street name and house or business number. It also lists telephone numbers numerically. Using the criss-cross directory, you can find an address even if you have only a telephone number but no name; you can find a telephone number if you have only an address but no name. Criss-cross directories are available for every metropolitan area and most smaller communities, including rural areas. Libraries always have a criss-cross directory for their service area.

s. Medical Records

Although patients are ethically entitled to the information in their medical records, only about half the states now actually have laws that guarantee a patient's right to view the records. The records belong to the doctor or the hospital, not to the patient. If the records have not been archived, the easiest method of retrieval is to visit the doctor's office or the hospital with a signed authorization from your client and request the records.

t. Coroner

The county coroner's office keeps death records that reflect the name or a description of the deceased, date of the inquest (if any), property found on the deceased at the time of death, disposition of the body and the property and cause of death. *See* Exhibit 8.7 for a summary of common sources.

IF SEARCHING FOR:	SOURCES INCLUDE:

INFORMATION ON INDIVIDUALS	• Dep't of Motor Vehicles
	• Court records (for courts of general jurisdiction)
	   —Criminal (misdemeanors and felonies)
	   —Civil (small claims, probate, domestic/family)
	• Land records
	• Vital statistics records (birth, marriage, and death)
	• Voter lists
	• Census
	• Religious
	• Military/VFW
	• Post office
	• Pet and sporting licenses

INFORMATION ON BUSINESSES	• Secretary of State (wherever they are incorporated or doing business) • County, city or town business records • Land records

Exhibit 8.7 **Suggested Sources for Finding People and Documents**

2.   Computer Assisted

Today, computer literacy is a requirement for the delivery of good legal services. Investigation and research through technology changes so rapidly that information listed one day is obsolete the next. Caution must be exercised since the quality of the material available, especially on the Internet, varies greatly. There is, however, an enormous amount of excellent information available.

What follows is a brief overview of terminology, systems, and available materials. Most of the sources listed above are available via computer or CD-ROM.

a.   Internet

Simply put, the Internet is a system of computers hooked together as a network to share information, worldwide. A computer with a modem is connected to another computer with a modem through a telephone line. The World Wide Web, created by the European Laboratory for Particle Physics, consists of thousands of sites including government agencies, private groups, professional organizations, and educational institutions. You can access thousands of services, including state and federal agencies, the United States Senate and House of Representatives, the Library of Congress, the Government Printing Office, educational institutions—including law libraries—and commercial groups.

If you are just learning, The Lawyer's Guide to the Internet, by G. Burgess Allison, provides, in an enjoyable manner, the basics you need to understand how the Internet works. Allison lists hundreds of addresses and explains how to use e-mail, the Web, and gopher. If you do not have access to the Internet at work or at home, your public library or local coffee bar will. Be cautious not to jeopardize client confidentiality.

i.   Access and Terminology

To access the Internet, you need an Internet Service Provider (ISP) and a Web Browser, such as Netscape Navigator or Microsoft Internet Explorer, which allows you to browse or interface with Internet sites. The browsers allow access to Protocols, which are the initial part of all Internet addresses or locations. The locations are referred to as Uniform Resource Locators or URLs. Different protocols include:

- Hypertext Transport Protocol (http://) for access to the Internet sites through the World Wide Web. The Web has advanced audio, video, and graphic capabilities;
- File Transfer Protocol (ftp://) for transfer or downloading of files or data such as documents, magazines, and graphics between computers;

- Telnet (telnet://) for connecting between two remote computers for purposes of interactive communication;
- Gopher (gopher://) for access to site information without audio, video, or graphic capabilities found on the Web;
- Usenet (usenet) for access to current news sources.

The domain is the part of the address that identifies the type of group: business (com); nonprofit (org); educational institution (edu); military (mil); network operations (net); or government (gov). A path might follow the domain extension and denotes certain material provided by that domain.

A complete address is:

protocol//server.domain name/path

Examples of the protocols listed above are:

- http://www.law.cornell.edu.supct/supct.table.html (World Wide Web URL)
- ftp://ftp.cwru.edu.hermes (FTP URL)
- telnet://www@www.lawcornell.edu (Telnet URL)
- gopher://gopher.law.cornell.edu (Gopher URL)
- new:rec.humor.funny (Usenet URL)

If you know the correct site address, type it in and the site's home page will appear. If you do not know the site or want to perform a general search, use a general Internet search engine or search directory. A search engine searches all protocols by key words and advanced search methods; engines provide much irrelevant material. A search directory searches only World Wide Web sites by subject and key word. Use the advanced search methods to focus your search.

Search engines include:

Alta Vista (http://altavista.digital.com)
Open Text (http://www.opentext.com)

Search directories include:

Yahoo (http://www.yahoo.com)
Magellan (http://magellan.mckinley.com)
Galaxy (http://galaxy.einet.net/galaxy.html)

Two search engine and search directory combinations include:

Infoseek (http://guide.infoseek.com)
Excite (http://www.excite.com)

ii. General Sites

There are thousands of web sites, many of which provide services useful to legal professionals. Some general sites providing links or connections to other sites include:

- Thomas (http://Thomas.loc.gov) publishes full texts of all House and Senate bills, the Congressional Record, and recent committee reports. Search by bill number or key word.
- United States House of Representatives Internet Law Library (http://law.house.gov) publishes primary legal materials including treaties, statutes (federal, state, and international), codes, and regulations. The site also provides links or connections to other legal sites.
- Law (http://www.findlaw.com) includes an index that allows you to connect to a wide variety of other sites including the full text of various law reviews and Supreme Court cases since 1906.
- Cornell Law School Legal Information Institute (http://fatty.law.cornell.edu) publishes core legal materials as well as an impressive index to other legal materials on the Internet.
- American Association for Paralegal Education (AAfPE) (http://www.chattanooga.net/clscc/aafpe/research.htm) provides links to legal areas, federal law, and other legal resource sites.
- United States Government Printing Office (http://www.access.gpo.gov/su_docs) provides information from the agencies, including the General Accounting Office Reports.

See Exhibit 8.8 for a partial listing of federal internet sites.

iii. Individuals and Businesses

If you are looking for the name, address, and telephone number of an individual or business, try a national telephone directory such as Switchboard and Phone Search, U.S.A. They can supply you with a telephone number and address for most people and businesses. Four11 lets you search by street address; BigBook specializes in businesses. Yahoo! Maps and Street Atlas, U.S.A. display street maps for local addresses in the United States. AT&T has a web site of toll free numbers (http://att.net/dir800/). The Consumer Education Research Center provides free public information. *See* Exhibit 8.9, Consumer Education Research Center.

iv. Medical

States have started to put doctor profiles on the Web. Although the profiles are not uniform state to state, they contain information such as malpractice suits, disciplinary actions, and criminal records. Because medical malpractice cases occasionally involve doctors who move from one state to another after disciplinary actions or multiple lawsuits, computer access to the database is an efficient way to perform a preliminary records check.

Medical information for personal injury instruction is located at the following sites:

- http://www.nlm.nih.gov (National Library of Medicine)
- http://www.pobox.com/~subhas/health.html (medical links for the lay person)

Find Government Information on *GPO Access* and Other Federal Internet Sites

Find Out More About These Tools

Search a Catalog of U.S. Government Publications (MOCAT)
Search and Order From Sales Product Catalog (SPC)
Search the Government Information Locator Service (GILS)
List of Federal Agency Internet Sites
Browse Government Internet Sites by Topic
Browse Electronic Government Information Products by Title
Search for Government Information on Selected Internet Sites (Pathway Indexer)
Core Documents of U.S. Democracy
Find a Depository Library in Your Area
New/Noteworthy from GPO
Obtain Information on Demand from U.S. Fax Watch
Federal Web Sites Hosted by *GPO Access*

Questions or comments regarding this service? Contact the *GPO Access* **User Support Team**
by Internet e-mail at gpoacess@gpo.gov;
by telephone at **1-202-512-1530** or **toll free at 1-888-293-6498**;
by fax at **1-202-512-1262**.

Back GPO Home GPO INETservices

Exhibit 8.8 **Federal Internet Sites**

- *Using Public Records to Find and Investigate Anyone*
  Locate People Without Leaving Your Home

- *Where To Write For Vital Records*
  Finding Birth Certificates, Marriage & Divorce Records and more

  http://www.planet.net/cerc/index.html

Exhibit 8.9 **Consumer Education Research Centers**

v. Corporate

Business and corporate information available on the Internet is extensive and generally reliable. Once again the Cornell University site is the most complete, providing information and links concerning securities law, state incorporation statutes and banking regulations. The address is:

http://www.law.cornell.edu/topics/corporations.html

Actual SEC filings by businesses can be reviewed at:

- http://www.sec.gov/edgarhtp.htm
- http://edgar.stern.nyu.edu/

Corporate information can be found at

- http://www.bigbook.com

vi. Miscellaneous

Federal Express will let you track your packages.

- http://www.fedex/cp,/cgi-gin/track_it

American Bar Association provides information on law, law office management, and law office technology.

- http://www.abanet.org

b. LEXIS

A joint effort between the Ohio State Bar Association and the Data Corporation developed OBAR (Ohio Bar Automated Research), a full-text computer-assisted legal research system. After Data Corporation was purchased by Mead Data Central, they devised LEXIS, a successor to OBAR. LEXIS contains state and federal statutes and court opinions, the Federal Register, and databases for foreign countries. NEXIS is the other half of the package and contains news and business information.

c. Westlaw

The product of West Publishing Company, Westlaw provides on-line access to legal materials as well as newspapers, public records, and filings. It's great to use as a research tool, but be careful about downloading too much material to print since it is very expensive and costs are charged to the client.

The "Industrial Defense Journal" on Westlaw is operated by Industrial

Defense Library (IDL) of the Industrial Database Management (IDM). The information is submitted by subscribers and contains thousands of products-liability expert-witness deposition transcripts on line.

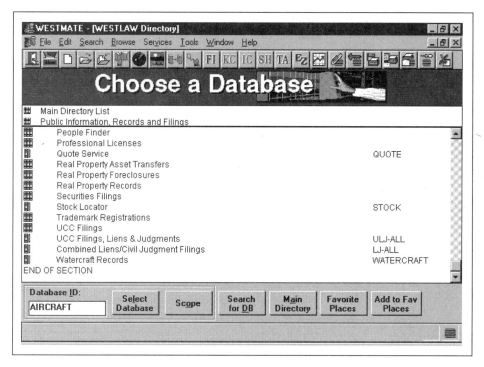

Exhibit 8.10 **Westlaw Directory—Public Information, Records, and Filings (Partial Listing)**

d. Other Databases

Various databases serve law firms, government agencies, and businesses in the United States by providing electronic access to public records twenty-four hours a day, seven days a week, every day of the year. In addition to public records, companies will investigate people, businesses, and locate assets. There are research and delivery charges.

A listing of major companies, databases, and some of the services provided can be found in Exhibit 8.11.

3. Obtaining Copies

a. Certified

A certified copy is one that may be treated as the original. Generally you should obtain a certified copy of any document that your supervising attorney intends to use at trial. A certified copy is self-authenticating; it does not have to be validated through testimony of its custodian at trial.

COMPANY/DATABASE	SERVICE
INFORMATION AMERICA	• Uncover assets • Locate people/businesses • Background checks • Public records • Retrieve official documents
WESTLAW	• Public records; Legal research
INDUSTRIAL DATABASE MANAGEMENT AND INDUSTRIAL DEFENSE LIBRARY	• Transcripts of products-liability expert witnesses
LEXIS-NEXIS	• Public records; Legal research
INTERNET/WORLD WIDE WEB	• Public records; Variety of law-related materials
EDGAR	• Electronic database of the Securities and Exchange Commission • Public filings
ACCESS	• Government Printing Office database
DIALOG	• Patents • Corporate acquisitions and mergers • Indices and abstracts in medicine, social sciences, and engineering
BUREAU OF NATIONAL AFFAIRS	• Reports re: antitrust, taxes, patents, trademark and copyrights, pensions, and energy

Exhibit 8.11 **Listing of Major Companies/Databases and Some of the Services Provided**

A certified copy can be a simple photocopy of the original with the signature of the custodian of the record and a raised seal or an attached certificate. The seal or certificate indicates that the copy has been compared by the official custodian of the record to the original and is a "true and accurate" copy. Sometimes a certified copy is backed with blue or yellow paper. Certified copies can be expensive, ranging from $2.00 to over $30.00. FED. R. CIV. P. 44(a) and FED. R. EVID. 902 and various state statutes and rules control the certification and authentication of public records.

b. Noncertified

Noncertified copies, if accurate, will provide the same information without the cost. If time permits, review the noncertified copy first to determine whether the document contains evidence that will be useful at trial. Clients will often provide you with noncertified copies of documents.

> **PRACTICE TIP:** If your client is willing and able to obtain a certified copy (for example, of a marriage license) and there is time, let him do it. Many clients like to be involved in their cases and the client will understand the costs involved.

F. Ethical Considerations

Throughout the investigation process, you must be cognizant of your ethical duties. You may not reveal your client's name or relate so many facts to others that the client's name is obvious. You should not discuss the case with a friend who happens to be a paralegal in the firm across town. You may be unwittingly providing confidential information.

SUMMARY

State and federal laws protect the privacy of personal records and guarantee access to public records and information. Confidential records may be obtained with proper authorization from the subject of the records. Some agencies require specific language in the authorization before releasing confidential records. Finding people and information has been made easier and faster with computers; not all data, however, have been entered into a system for retrieval. Document every search made and record retrieved.

Key Terms

Authorization	Privacy Act
Certification	Protocol
Cross-reference directory	Search directory
Domain	Search engine
Freedom of Information Act	Self-authenticating
Links	Server
Martindale-Hubbell Directory	Uniform resource locator
Open meeting laws	

REVIEW QUESTIONS

1. What is the function of the Privacy Act? How is the Act important to an investigator?
2. What are "sunshine laws"?
3. What kinds of information might you obtain under the Freedom of Information Act?
4. What types of records are sealed by the court? Why?
5. What are plaintiff-defendant tables?
6. What restricts you from revealing your client's name to your best friend?
7. What is an "authorization" and how does it work? Who does it protect?
8. What particular things do corporations have to do to remain in good standing?

CHAPTER EXERCISES

Exercise 8-1:   Assume your firm represents Lizzie Williard in a personal injury case. Lizzie has told you that she lost four weeks from her job as a fourth grade teacher following treatment by her doctor with a drug she did not know was experimental. Draft an authorization and a letter to obtain the records. You may invent whatever information you require.

Exercise 8-2:   What records would you want to review in the following cases:

1) Harriet Fisher's child was born at Hopewell Hospital with significant brain damage, possibly from a lack of oxygen during labor. Her doctor, Melissa Jordan, has blamed the damage on Ms. Fisher's refusal to quit smoking during pregnancy. Your firm has been retained to represent Ms. Fisher and her child against Hopewell and Jordan.
2) Georgina Gibbs holds a patent on a new type of plastic tubing for water and sewer usage. A large manufacturing firm has begun to manufacture the tubing without her permission. She has retained your firm to represent her against the manufacturer.

Exercise 8-3:   Select one or more of the following tasks to do. Share the results with your class:

1) Go to your DMV and ask to see any information that has been compiled on you. (Make sure you do not have any outstanding tickets.)
2) Make a chart of your state court system, listing every court, its location, and the kinds of cases it handles.
3) Do the same for the federal courts in your state.
4) Choose a piece of real property in your area, go to the registry of deeds, and determine who the last three owners were.
5) Request your birth record.
6) Request the marriage record of your parents, grandparents, or siblings.
7) Request a death certificate for a relative.
8) Choose a piece of real property in your area. Obtain the assessed value of the property and the taxes. Obtain the tax rate and ask to see the list of "delinquent properties."
9) Ask to see the local voters' list. How is it organized? What is a precinct? How are they designed?
10) Request to see census information. What can you learn from it? How many school-aged children are in your area? How many dogs?
11) Write to your Secretary of State and request information about the documents they compile. What statutes require they maintain this information? Where did you find the address?
12) Make a trip to your local post office. How do they trace a letter? If a return address is a box number, what information can the postal service supply? What information will they not divulge?

Exercise 8-4: Take the name of a classmate or relative (with permission) or local political or other public figure. Find out everything you can about her/him. Compare results.

Exercise 8-5: Using a legal dictionary, define the following terms: mortgage, mortgagor, mortgagee, debtor, creditor, equity, promissory note, discharge.

Exercise 8-6: Select a piece of real estate in your city, town, or county. Using public documents, find out who first owned the property. Then find the municipal map that relates to the property.

Exercise 8-7: Select a corporation operating in your state. Write to the Secretary of State or other appropriate agency for the annual report.

Exercise 8-8: Determine the agency in your state responsible for licensing. Which occupations need to be registered? How did you find the information?

Appendices

Appendix A Case Investigation File of Hannah West
Appendix B Sample Client Letters
Appendix C Intake Sheet
Appendix D Privacy Act of 1974
Appendix E Freedom of Information Act
Appendix F Sample Letters (FOIA)
Appendix G Federal Rules of Civil Procedure (Selected Rules)
Appendix H Federal Rules of Evidence (Selected Rules)
Appendix I California Notice Statute
Appendix J Massachusetts Lawyers Diary and Manual

Appendix A

Case Investigation File of Hannah West

Fourth Scenario

Hannah West called your firm this morning after the father of their three children, Jeffrey West, failed to return them to her after the weekend. She was referred by another attorney, Brian Schubert, who does not practice family law. Ms. West is panicked. She does not know where the children are and is concerned that the father has removed them from the country. Because this case may require immediate action by your supervising attorney who is in court this morning on another matter, you have been asked to gather some initial factual information about the case.

Case File

1) Intake Sheet
2) Portions of Interview
3) Interview Summary
4) Investigation Plan
5) Theory Chart
6) Interoffice Memorandum

Interview of Hannah West

(The interview begins with usual pleasantries; basic information is written on Intake Sheet. Ms. West begins talking about her marriage of 13 years to Jeffrey West and their three children, Jessica, age 11, Leah, age 8, and Oliver, age 4.)

Para: Why don't you tell me what happened this weekend?
West: Well, that's why I called Ms. Morrison this morning, because Jeff— that's my husband—did not bring the kids back last night. I don't

Intake Sheet

NAME Hannah Elizabeth West

ADDRESS 4297 Southbrook Drive

Plain City, PA 00010

MAILING ADDRESS as above

PHONE: HOME (423) 910-2938

WORK (423) 987-4892

HOW TO CONTACT home or work

WHEN TO CONTACT evenings after 6:00 best time

SPECIAL INSTRUCTIONS/RESTRICTIONS ON CONTACT no

restrictions

REFERRED BY Brian Schubert, Esquire

DATE OF FIRST CONTACT January 2, (year)

DATE OF FIRST INTERVIEW January 3, (year)

BILLING RATE $200/hr. att.; $100/hr. plgl.

RESPONSIBLE ATTORNEY Martha Morrison

COURT DATE/FILING DATE n/a

NAME OF ADVERSE PARTY Jeffrey West

OTHER INFORMATION

know where they are. I was worried he took them to Germany; he used to be stationed there when he was in the service and he's always threatened to take them there. His mother is originally from there. When will Ms. Morrison be back from court?

Para: I'm not certain; she had one matter on the court calendar. That's why she asked me to get some information from you instead of delaying your appointment until this afternoon.

West: Well, I'm grateful that you could see me on such short notice.

Para: Sure. As to your children, at this point you do not know where they are?

West: That's right. Can he do that, can he take them away like that?

Para: Well, Ms. West, that's one of the things we need to investigate.

West: Please call me Hannah.

Para: [nodding assent]

West: I thought after we separated—we're legally separated— that this wouldn't happen.

Para: I want you to tell me more about the legal separation, but first I need some additional information so we can find the children. You said you were concerned that your husband would take the children to Germany. Do your children have passports?

West: Not that I know of. We always talked about traveling, but never did. I think they'd mention it, I mean if they had passports. They seem to tell me everything they do when they're with their father. But can't he just put them on his?

Para: We will have to determine that. Did they ever mention having their pictures taken?

West: No. What if he did all this and told them to keep it a secret?

Para: That's possible. Do you have copies of their birth certificates?

West: No, I'm embarrassed to say so. We had them—you can't register children for school without them (well, except for Oliver, he's only four)—but since we moved here two years ago, I haven't been able to find them. I keep meaning to write to the records office to get copies, but I just haven't had the time.

Para: Does your husband have a passport?

West: He did when we first married, right after he got out of the service, twelve years ago.

Para: As far as you know, did he ever have it renewed?

West: He never mentioned it.

Para: Has he ever kept in contact with friends in Germany?

West: A few cards the first couple years; nothing that I recall since then. Once the kids were born there seemed to be little time for that kind of thing. What do you think?

Para: Hannah, I can tell you that in order to obtain a passport, you must fill out an application form, submit two identical photos, proof of United States citizenship, and a fee—I think it's $40 for children—and then wait three to four weeks while the application is processed. Applications can be expedited within a few days if the application is complete. So far, you've told me that—as far as you know—your children have never had passports, do not currently have passports, have not had their pictures taken; you have not seen their birth certificates since you moved here; your husband has never renewed his passport, nor has he been in contact for the past ten years with the people he used to know in Germany. Although it is not impossible for your husband to have taken the children out of the country, based on what you have told me I believe it is unlikely. Rest assured, however, that we will investigate the matter completely as soon as possible.

Right now, I want to go back to something you said earlier, that you're legally separated, correct?

West: Yes, last year.

Para: Did you and your husband sign an agreement?

West: No, we just decided to legally separate—not to be responsible for each other's credit card bills and so forth.

Para: Did you write anything down?

West: No. I guess we should have.

Para: Did you go to court at any time?

West: No. But now I want a divorce. I'm sick and tired of trying to be reasonable just for the kids.

Para: I understand. Let's go back to the children for a minute. Let me ask you this, if your husband did not leave the country with the children, where do you think he might have taken them?

West: Well, there's his mother's house in Ridgeville and his brother's apartment in Longmeade. I never did get along with them. Or his new girlfriend's place—she's over in Huntville.

Para: What about his house? Have you called?

West: Well, sure, but the phone just rings and rings. Maybe he unplugged it.

Para: Have you been to his house?

West: Yes, early this morning. No one was there.

Para: Do you have the addresses and telephone numbers for his mother, brother, and girlfriend?

West: Not with me, but I could get them to you. What's your e-mail address?

Para: Hannah, we don't use electronic mail because it's not completely secure. Could you call me as soon as you find the numbers?

West: Sure. I guess I wasn't thinking. I should have brought them with me.

Para: That's okay; this is very stressful. Could you tell me what the arrangements between you and your husband have been since you separated last year?

West: Yes. They stay with me during the week except for Wednesdays when they go to his house. Then every other Friday he picks them up from school or daycare and keeps them until Sunday night. He's supposed to bring them back by 7:00, but he's always late.

Para: So you expected him last night and he didn't arrive. Has this ever happened before?

West: Once during the summer when he took them to the state fair. He said it was too late to drive back and so they stayed overnight. I was really angry but I didn't show it. The kids had a great time at the fair.

Para: Did you call the school this morning?

West: They don't have school today. It's some sort of professional day. My neighbor was going to watch them for me until noon; I was going to work a half day. I just can't believe this.

Para: Hannah, you said you had this arrangement since you separated last year, correct?

West: Yes.

Para: Has it been consistent for the year?

West: Pretty much so. He's always late bringing them back, though.

Para: But other than bring them back late, have there been any occasions when the schedule was changed?

West: Not that I can remember.

Para: What about holidays?

West: We agreed that the kids should spend some of each holiday period with each of us and that's what we've done.

Para: Do you keep track of the kids' schedules?

West: Oh, yeah. I have a calendar program for the computer and I print out the schedules every month. It's the only way I can stay organized.

Para: Have you saved these calendars, either in your computer or hard copy?

West: Well, I'm sure they're in the computer; maybe I archived them; I'm pretty sure I did not delete them. The paper calendars, I'm not sure; sometimes I give them to the kids to keep. I could check. I just need to have something written down about the kids. I want custody, complete custody; he can pay me support.

Para: When you get home, would you please check to see whether you have the calendars?

West: Oh, sure. What about the custody—how soon can I get it?

Para: Hannah, custody here in Michigan is controlled by a special custody law. This law lists criteria to help a judge decide who should get custody. I can tell you some of the factors the judge considers, but as a paralegal, I cannot give you legal advice as to whether or not you will be able to win custody of your children.

West: I don't think it will be too hard; Jeff just lost his job, so he can't support them. They wouldn't give him custody since he can be with them, would they? I work all the time; seems we just get one big contract after another. This is going to cost me a fortune, isn't it?

The paralegal elicits from Hannah that she holds a degree in engineering from Cal Tech; Jeff has a degree in business from UCLA. The parties moved to Michigan, where Jeff is from and where his family still lives, from California several years ago to accommodate Hannah's promotion with a major engineering firm. Jeff was employed within three months after arrival but recently lost his job when the company restructured; he seems depressed about the loss of his job. He is looking, but Hannah is not sure how hard. His family owns a small grocery store in the area, but Jeff does not want to work in the family business; he and his brother had a falling out some years ago. He is spending more time with the kids, but doesn't want to give up the sitter because he might get a job interview. Money is becoming a problem and Hannah wants to let the sitter go. Jeff is opposed, and said, "I'm not your daycare," during a fight they had over money.

Hannah believes a good education is critical for the children and wants them in private school as soon as Jeff finds a new job. Jeff opposes private schools and wants to keep the two older children in the public school where they have been since their move to Michigan. Hannah and Jeff were both raised in very religious households. Hannah no longer considers herself part of any church; she just does not believe in it anymore. She does not want the children to attend services every week. Jeff takes them on the Sundays when they are with him; his mother and brother go, too. Hannah has asked him not to take them, but he refuses. She occasionally takes them to the local nondenominational church.

Hannah told the paralegal she does the grocery shopping every Saturday morning, with or without the children. She takes them to their doctors' appointments and to the mall for clothes. When the children were born, the parties shared responsibilities, depending on the nature of their jobs. Hannah's jobs are usually fairly high stress and consume 50 to 60 hours per week. She drops the kids off at school/daycare; picks them up from after-school care between 5:00 and 6:00. She cooks dinner, helps with homework, puts them to bed, and then usually works until midnight. If one of the children is sick, she can work from home via computer.

Since Jeff left the home last year, Hannah and the children have stayed in the house. Jeff's apartment is not far away; Jeff's girlfriend has a large house and the children spend time there, never overnight as far as Hannah knows.

Neither Hannah nor Jeff has ever been arrested/convicted of a crime. They own the home where Hannah and the children reside, and their home in California, which they now rent. They have considerable money in their retirement accounts. He and his family don't always agree and he wants nothing to do with the business.

Hannah saw a therapist last year before Jeff left; she could not convince him to go with her. She's afraid he will characterize her as unbalanced and use her sessions with the therapist against her.

Hannah provided the paralegal with names of the children's teachers, daycare provider, and a neighbor.

Summary of Interview of Hannah West

Date of Interview: (date)
Interviewer: Paralegal
Length of Interview: 1½ hours
Statement of Problem:

Ms. West and her husband, Jeffrey West, are living apart. They are the parents of three children: Jessica (11), Leah (8) and Oliver (4). Mr. West had the children last weekend, but failed to return them to Ms. West on Sunday night.

Client's Description of Problem

I interviewed Ms. West at approximately 11:00 A.M., on (date). The immediate problem is that she is fearful that her husband may have taken the children out of the country. She and her husband separated last year; the three children live with her during the week, except for

Wednesdays when they go to Mr. West's house. They also stay with him every other weekend from Friday after school or daycare, until Sunday evening at 7:00. Ms. West states that he seldom returns the children on time on Sunday.

Her passport has expired, and to her knowledge, her husband's passport has expired as well. The children have never had passports. None of the children has mentioned having pictures taken. Ms. West has not seen their birth certificates since they moved here two years ago. She believes they are still packed. Mr. West was stationed in Germany when he was in the service approximately 14 years ago. He has had no contact with friends in Germany for the past 10-11 years. Every time they have an argument, he threatens to take the kids out of the country.

Ms. West told me that she and Mr. West are legally separated. However, she said that there was no written agreement and that they had never been to court. She said she's "sick and tired of trying to be reasonable just for the kids." She wants a divorce and custody of the children.

Ms. West stated that on one other occasion, Mr. West did not bring the children back to her house on the day scheduled. He had taken them to the state fair, it got very late, and so they stayed overnight. He did not telephone her on that occasion.

Impressions

Ms. West seemed sincere, very concerned about the well-being of her children.

I made clear to her that in my role as a paralegal assisting Ms. Morrison, I could not give her legal advice. I did inform her of the relevant steps to obtain a passport and told her I thought it was unlikely Mr. West could accomplish passport applications for himself and three children without her knowledge of pictures, birth certificates, and so forth. I told her the factors a judge must consider before awarding custody; she feels certain she will win.

NB: Addendum to Interview

Hannah called at approximately 3:00 P.M. The children were returned to her home just before her call. Apparently they stayed overnight because they could not cross the bridge from the Upper Peninsula because of fog. She is still very angry at her husband for not calling and wants to proceed with legal action to clarify their relationship and prevent this from happening again. After her call, I telephoned Ms. West at home to verify that the call came from her and that the information was as reported. She was very appreciative of the callback.

Sample Investigation Plan
Family Case

1) Interview Client
   Issues:
   1) Date of separation
   2) Custody of 3 children (4, 8, 11 years)
   3) Real property (residence)
   4) Real property (rental)
   5) Value of family business
2) Interview Witnesses:
   Issue 1) Carol Mayer (personal knowledge of date of separation);
   Issue 2) Naomi Windner (daycare provider for 4-year-old)
       Frances Gomez (school teacher for 8-year-old)
       Nicholas Green (school teacher for 11-year-old)
       Heidi O'Leary (neighbor)
       therapist
3) Obtain Documents:
   Issue 1) Marriage license
   Issue 2) Birth certificates; school records
   Issue 3) Deed and mortgage information
   Issue 4) Deed and mortgage information
   Issue 5) Business records
4) Interview Possible Experts:
   Issue 1) N/A
   Issue 2) Psychiatrist, psychologist, therapist.
   Issue 3) Appraiser
   Issue 4) Appraiser
   Issue 5) Accountant; actuarial
5) Follow-up Interview with Client
6) Other Follow-up
   Interview:
       Mayer
       Windner
       Gomez
       Green
       O'Leary
7) Obtain documents:
       Marriage license
       Birth certificates
       School records
       Deeds, tax assessm't
8) Follow-up with client
9) Interview:
       new witnesses

Joan Quilan, M.D.
Maynard Wilson, appraiser
Sam Derman, C.P.A.
Margaret Smith, actuarial
10)   Other documents
11)   Follow-up with client

Child Custody Theory Chart

Client: Hannah West
Date of Interview: month, day, year
Children: Jessica (11); Leah (8); Oliver (4)

ELEMENT	SOURCE OF FACT	EVIDENCE
emotional ties	client, witnesses, children	
capacity of parent to love, guide, educate, including religion	client, witnesses, expert	cl. holds PhD in engineering—views a good education as critical; disciplines through "time-out" and denial of privileges; each child has household "job"; raised Catholic, no longer active in church; takes children to services occasionally.
ability to provide food, clothing, medical care	client, witnesses	cl. shops for all food, clothes for children; takes children to all routine M.D. appts.
length of time children lived in stable environment; should it be maintained	client, witnesses	children have been in home; father left over one year ago
permanence of custodial home	client, witnesses	in house last six years
moral fitness of parent	client, witnesses	no arrest/conviction
mental/physical health of parent	client, witnesses	doctor/psychiatrist?

ELEMENT	SOURCE OF FACT	EVIDENCE
home, school, community of children	client, witnesses (teachers, sitters, daycare providers)	children in same home; friends in neighborhood; same school since k'garten
children's preference	children, where age appropriate	11-year-old may be permitted to say; 4- and 8-year-old prob. not
willingness/ability of parents to foster relationship with other parent	client, witnesses who know of relationship	determine problems in past (e.g., scheduling, social, educational, medical, religious preference)
other factors		

Interoffice Memorandum

To: Ms. Morrison
From: Paralegal
Date: Today's Date
Re: Hannah West

I interviewed Hannah West on (date). A copy of the Intake Sheet and Interview Summary are attached. This memo addresses the issue of child custody under Mich. Comp. Laws Ann. §722.23 (West 1996), a copy of which is attached to this memo.

Legal Analysis

Hannah West and Jeffrey West have three children: Jessica (11), Leah (8), and Oliver (4). They separated last year after 14 years of marriage. The arrangement since the separation is as follows: The three children live with Ms. West during the week, except for Wednesdays when they go to Mr. West's house. They stay with him until Thursday morning when he drops them off at school and daycare. They also stay with him every other weekend from Friday after school or daycare until Sunday evening at 7:00. Ms. West states that he seldom returns the children on time on Sunday.

The statute lists 11 factors a judge must consider in making an award of custody; findings of fact must be made as to each of the factors:

a) The love, affection, and other emotional ties existing between the parties and the child.

b) The capacity and disposition of the parties involved to give the child love, affection, and guidance and continuation of the education and raising of the child in his or her religion or creed, if any.

c) The capacity and disposition of the parties involved to provide the child with food, clothing, medical care, or other remedial care recognized and permitted under the laws of this state in place of medical care, and other material needs.

d) The length of time the child has lived in a stable and satisfactory environment, and the desirability of maintaining continuity.

e) The permanence, as a family unit, of the existing or proposed custodial home.

f) The moral fitness of the parties.

g) The mental and physical health of the parties.

h) The home, school, and community record of the child.

i) The reasonable preference of the child, if the court deems the child to be of sufficient age to express preference.

j) The willingness and ability of each of the parents to facilitate and encourage a close and continuing parent-child relationship between the child and the other parent.

k) Any other factor considered by the court to be relevant to a particular child custody dispute.

a) Emotional Ties

Both parties seem to have strong emotional ties to the children. Currently, they are with Hannah more of the time, since Mr. West has them on every Wednesday evening and every other weekend.

b) Love, Guide, and Educate, Including Religion

Hannah takes her parenting role very seriously. Each of the children, even the four-year-old, has a job in the house (for example, taking out the garbage, feeding the hamster, and keeping his or her room straight). Hannah disciplines through "time-out," a system in which children are removed from the rest of the family for a certain period of time. She does not believe in corporal punishment. She said Jeff occasionally spanks the children (that is how he grew up), but without her approval.

The children's education is of paramount concern to Hannah. She wants the children to attend private school because she does not believe that they are working to their full potential. She herself is very educated, holding a PhD in engineering from Cal Tech.

She is not active in an organized church although she occasionally takes the children to the Unitarian Church. Jeff takes the children to the Catholic Church when they are with him.

c) Ability to Provide

Hannah can provide for the children. She shops for groceries and for the children's clothing. She states that Jeff does not approve of the amount of money she spends on the children's clothes, but she says they can afford it and does not want them to wear hand-me-downs like she had to.

d), (e) Stability of Environment/Permanence of Home

Hannah and the children have always lived together; they have lived in the same house since their move from California. She stated that the neighborhood is nice and stable. Without a compelling reason, the children should not be moved.

f) Moral Fitness of Parent

Hannah stated that she and Jeff drink "socially." Neither takes drugs, nor has either been arrested/convicted of a crime.

g) Mental/Physical Health

Hannah is concerned that Jeff will use her visits to the therapist before the separation against her. Visits were to help her deal with the problems in the marriage. She and Jeff are both in excellent physical condition, although neither exercises enough. Neither smokes.

h) Home/School/Community

Children have been in same home and school since their move here. The sitter comes to their house when necessary. They are involved in activities after school—soccer and gymnastics.

i) Children's Preference

None of the children is old enough for this to be a deciding factor, except perhaps the 11-year-old, Jessica. A judge might consider her preference if she is mature enough.

j) Parent-Parent Relationship

Hannah states she is willing to work with Jeff; she does not criticize him to the children and does not believe he criticizes her to them.

Nonlegal Concerns

Client is very concerned that she may lose the custody fight to Jeff, especially since he is not now working and is able to spend more time with the children. She is also concerned about the costs.

Follow-Up

1) Write for copy of marriage record.
2) Interview witnesses listed on Investigation Plan.
3) Obtain financial statement from client.
4) Have client provide tax returns for past three years and real property records.
5) Consider temporary restraining order to prevent Jeff from removing children from state.
6) Evaluate case to determine whether case is appropriate for mediation or other form of ADR.

Attachments

Interview Summary
Theory Chart
Intake Sheet
Statute

Michigan Compiled Laws Annotated
Chapter 722. Children
Child Custody Act of 1970

§722.23. Best interests of the child, definition

Sec. 3. As used in this act, "best interests of the child" means the sum total of the following factors to be considered, evaluated, and determined by the court:

(a) The love, affection, and other emotional ties existing between the parties involved and the child.

(b) The capacity and disposition of the parties involved to give the child love, affection, and guidance and to continue the education and raising of the child in his or her religion or creed, if any.

(c) The capacity and disposition of the parites involved to provide the child with food, clothing, medical care or other remedial care recognized and permitted under the laws of this state in place of medical care, and other material needs.

(d) The length of time the child has lived in a stable, satisfactory environment, and the desirability of maintaining continuity.

(e) The permanence, as a family unit, of the existing or proposed custodial home or homes.

(f) The moral fitness of the parties involved.

(g) The mental and physical health of the parties involved.

(h) The home, school, and community record of the child.

(i) The reasonable preference of the child, if the court considers the child to be of sufficient age to express preference.

(j) The willingness and ability of each of the parties to facilitate and encourage a close and continuing parent-child relationship between the child and the other parent or the child and the parents.

(k) Domestic violence, regardless of whether the violence was directed against or witnessed by the child.

(l) Any other factor considered by the court to be relevant to a particular child custody dispute.

Appendix B
Sample Client Letters

Letter Confirming Appointment and Requesting Documents

Law Firm Name
Address
Phone
Fax

PRIVILEGED AND CONFIDENTIAL

Client name
Address
City, state zip

Month, day, year

Re: Scheduled appointment

Dear client:

   This letter confirms our interview scheduled for Thursday, May 15, (date), at 2:00 P.M., at our offices.
   Please bring with you the following documents:

1) Your current will
2) Deed to your house
3) Life insurance policies
I look forward to meeting with you.

Sincerely,

   s/

Paralegal

Follow-Up Letter Requesting Documents

Law Firm Name
Address
Phone
Fax

PRIVILEGED AND CONFIDENTIAL

Client name
Address
City, state zip

Month, day, year

Re: Financial statement and tax returns

Dear client:

I enjoyed meeting with you today and look forward to working with you on this matter. As we discussed at the meeting, I need copies of your most recent financial statement and your tax returns from the last three years. Please drop them off at my office or mail copies of them to me at your earliest convenience.

Please call me if you have any questions.

Sincerely,

s/

Paralegal

Follow-up Letter Confirming Information

Law Firm Name
Address
Phone
Fax

PRIVILEGED AND CONFIDENTIAL

Client name
Address
City, state zip

Month, day, year

Re: Will

Dear client:

I enjoyed meeting with you today and look forward to working with you on your new will. My notes from the interview show that you wish to leave 1) to your son, Michael, your house and the land it is on; 2) to your daughter, Mary, your vacation home and your personal papers; 3) to your granddaughter, Rita, your jewelry; and 4) to your granddaughter, Sarah, your automobile.

Based on this information, I will begin to draft your new will for your review. If any information is incorrect, please contact me at once.

Sincerely,

s/

Paralegal

Follow-Up Letter with Enclosure

Law Firm Name
Address
Phone
Fax

PRIVILEGED AND CONFIDENTIAL

Client name
Address
City, state zip

Month, day, year

Re: Client v. Defendants

Dear client:

Enclosed is a copy of the complaint filed recently on your behalf in the Superior Court.

The defendants have 20 days from the day they receive the complaint to file a response. When we receive their response, we will forward a copy to you.

As we discussed at the interview, a case of this type proceeds slowly through the court system. We will probably not be given a trial date until next year.

We will keep you informed about the case as we proceed.

Sincerely,

s/

Paralegal

enclosure

Appendix C
Intake Sheet

Intake Sheet

NAME: _____

ADDRESS: _____

_____

MAILING ADDRESS: _____

PHONE: HOME: _____

WORK: _____

HOW TO CONTACT: _____

WHEN TO CONTACT: _____

SPECIAL INSTRUCTIONS/RESTRICTIONS ON CONTACT: _____

_____

REFERRED BY: _____

DATE OF FIRST CONTACT: _____

DATE OF FIRST INTERVIEW: _____

BILLING RATE: _____

RESPONSIBLE ATTORNEY: _____

COURT DATE/FILING DATE: _____

NAME OF ADVERSE PARTY: _____

OTHER INFORMATION: _____

_____

_____

_____

Appendix D

Privacy Act of 1974

§552a. Records maintained on individuals

(a) **Definitions.**—For purposes of this section—

(1) the term "agency" means agency as defined in section 552(e) of this title;

(2) the term "individual" means a citizen of the United States or an alien lawfully admitted for permanent residence;

(3) the term "maintain" includes maintain, collect, use, or disseminate;

(4) the term "record" means any item, collection, or grouping of information about an individual that is maintained by an agency, including, but not limited to, his education, financial transactions, medical history, and criminal or employment history and that contains his name, or the identifying number, symbol, or other identifying particular assigned to the individual, such as a finger or voice print or a photograph;

(5) the term "system of records" means a group of any records under the control of any agency from which information is retrieved by the name of the individual or by some identifying number, symbol, or other identifying particular assigned to the individual;

(6) the term "statistical record" means a record in a system of records maintained for statistical research or reporting purposes only and not used in whole or in part in making any determination about an identifiable individual, except as provided by section 8 of title 13;

(7) the term "routine use" means, with respect to the disclosure of a record, the use of such record for a purpose which is compatible with the purpose for which it was collected;

(8) the term "matching program"—

(A) means any computerized comparison of—

(i) two or more automated systems of records or a system of records with non-Federal records for the purpose of—

(I) establishing or verifying the eligibility of, or continuing compliance with statutory and regulatory requirements by, applicants for, recipients or beneficiaries of, participants in, or providers of services with respect to, cash or in-kind assistance or payments under Federal benefit programs, or

(II) recouping payments or delinquent debts under such Federal benefit programs, or

(ii) two or more automated Federal personnel or payroll systems of records or a system of Federal personnel or payroll records with non-Federal records,

(B) but does not include—

(i) matches performed to produce aggregate statistical data without any personal identifiers;

(ii) matches performed to support any research or statistical project, the specific data of which may not be used to make decisions concerning the rights, benefits, or privileges of specific individuals;

(iii) matches performed, by an agency (or component thereof) which performs as its principal function any activity pertaining to the enforcement of criminal laws, subsequent to the initiation of a specific criminal or civil law enforcement investigation of a named person or persons for the purpose of gathering evidence against such person or persons;

(iv) matches of tax information (I) pursuant to section 6103(d) of the Internal Revenue Code of 1986, (II) for purposes of tax administration as defined in section 6103(b)(4) of such Code, (III) for the purpose of intercepting a tax refund due an individual under authority granted by section 464 or 1137 of the Social Security Act; or (IV) for the purpose of intercepting a tax refund due an individual under any other tax refund intercept program authorized by statute which has been determined by the Director of the Office of Management and Budget to contain verification, notice, and hearing requirements that are substantially similar to the procedures in section 1137 of the Social Security Act;

(v) matches—

(I) using records predominantly relating to Federal personnel, that are performed for routine administrative purposes (subject to guidance provided by the Director of the Office of Management and Budget pursuant to subsection (v)); or

(II) conducted by an agency using only records from systems of records maintained by that agency;

if the purpose of the match is not to take any adverse financial, personnel, disciplinary, or other adverse action against Federal personnel

(vi) matches performed for foreign counterintelligence purposes or to produce background checks for, security clearances of Federal personnel or Federal contractor personnel; or

(vii) matches performed pursuant to section 6103(l)(12) of the Internal Revenue Code of 1986 and section 1144 of the Social Security Act;

(9) the term "recipient agency" means any agency, or contractor thereof, receiving records contained in a system of records from a source agency for use in a matching program;

(10) the term "non-Federal agency" means any State or local government, or agency thereof, which receives records contained in a system of records from a source agency for use in a matching program;

(11) the term "source agency" means any agency which discloses

records contained in a system of records to be used in a matching program, or any State or local government, or agency thereof, which discloses records to be used in a matching program;

(12) the term "Federal benefit program" means any program administered or funded by the Federal Government, or by any agent or State on behalf of the Federal Government, providing cash or in-kind assistance in the form of payments, grants, loans, or loan guarantees to individuals; and

(13) the term "Federal personnel" means officers and employees of the Government of the United States, members of the uniformed services (including members of the Reserve Components), individuals entitled to receive immediate or deferred retirement benefits under any retirement program of the Government of the United States (including survivor benefits).

(b) Conditions of disclosure.—No agency shall disclose any record which is contained in a system of records by any means of communication to any person, or to another agency, except pursuant to a written request by, or with the prior written consent of, the individual to whom the record pertains, unless disclosure of the record would be—

(1) to those officers and employees of the agency which maintains the record who have a need for the record in the performance of their duties;

(2) required under section 552 of this title;

(3) for a routine use as defined in subsection (a)(7) of this section and described under subsection (e)(4)(D) of this section;

(4) to the Bureau of the Census for purposes of planning or carrying out a census or survey or related activity pursuant to the provisions of title 13;

(5) to a recipient who has provided the agency with advance adequate written assurance that the record will be used solely as a statistical research or reporting record, and the record is to be transferred in a form that is not individually identifiable;

(6) to the National Archives and Records Administration as a record which has sufficient historical or other value to warrant its continued preservation by the United States Government, or for evaluation by the Archivist of the United States or the designee of the Archivist to determine whether the record has such value;

(7) to another agency or to an instrumentality of any governmental jurisdiction within or under the control of the United States for a civil or criminal law enforcement activity if the activity is authorized by law, and if the head of the agency or instrumentality has made a written request to the agency which maintains the record specifying the particular portion desired and the law enforcement activity for which the record is sought;

(8) to a person pursuant to a showing of compelling circumstances affecting the health or safety of an individual if upon such disclosure notification is transmitted to the last known address of such individual;

(9) to either House of Congress, or, to the extent of matter within

its jurisdiction, any committee or subcommittee thereof, any joint committee of Congress or subcommittee of any such joint committee;

(10) to the Comptroller General, or any of his authorized representatives, in the course of the performance of the duties of the General Accounting Office;

(11) pursuant to the order of a court of competent jurisdiction; or

(12) to a consumer reporting agency in accordance with section 3711(f) of title 31.

(c) **Accounting of certain disclosures.**—Each agency, with respect to each system of records under its control, shall—

(1) except for disclosures made under subsections (b)(1) or (b)(2) of this section; keep an accurate accounting of—

(A) the date, nature, and purpose of each disclosure of a record to any person or to another agency made under subsection (b) of this section; and

(B) the name and address of the person or agency to whom the disclosure is made;

(2) retain the accounting made under paragraph (1) of this subsection for at least five years or the life of the record, whichever is longer, after the disclosure for which the accounting is made;

(3) except for disclosures made under subsection (b)(7) of this section, make the accounting made under paragraph (1) of this subsection available to the individual named in the record at his request; and

(4) inform any person or other agency about any correction or notation of dispute made by the agency in accordance with subsection (d) of this section of any record that has been disclosed to the person or agency if an accounting of the disclosure was made.

(d) **Access to records.**—Each agency that maintains a system of records shall—

(1) upon request by any individual to gain access to his record or to any information pertaining to him which is contained in the system, permit him and upon his request, a person of his own choosing to accompany him, to review the record and have a copy made of all or any portion thereof in a form comprehensible to him, except that the agency may require the individual to furnish a written statement authorizing discussion of that individual's record in the accompanying person's presence;

(2) permit the individual to request amendment of a record pertaining to him and—

(A) not later than 10 days (excluding Saturdays, Sundays, and legal public holidays) after the date of receipt of such request, acknowledge in writing such receipt; and

(B) promptly, either—

(i) make any correction of any portion thereof which the individual believes is not accurate, relevant, timely, or complete; or

(ii) inform the individual of its refusal to amend the record in accordance with his request, the reason for the refusal, the procedures established by the agency for the individual to request a review of that refusal by the head of the agency or an officer designated by the head of the agency, and the name and business address of that official;

(3) permit the individual who disagrees with the refusal of the agency to amend his record to request a review of such refusal, and not later than 30 days (excluding Saturdays, Sundays, and legal public holidays) from the date on which the individual requests such review, complete such review and make a final determination unless, for good cause shown, the head of the agency extends such 30-day period; and if, after his review, the reviewing official also refuses to amend the record in accordance with the request, permit the individual to file with the agency a concise statement setting forth the reasons for his disagreement with the refusal of the agency, and notify the individual of the provisions for judicial review of the reviewing official's determination under subsection (g)(1)(A) of this section;

(4) in any disclosure, containing information about which the individual has filed a statement of disagreement, occurring after the filing of the statement under paragraph (3) of this subsection, clearly note any portion of the record which is disputed and provide copies of the statement and, if the agency deems it appropriate, copies of a concise statement of the reasons of the agency for not making the amendments requested, to persons or other agencies to whom the disputed record has been disclosed; and

(5) nothing in this section shall allow an individual access to any information compiled in reasonable anticipation of a civil action or proceeding.

(e) Agency requirements.—Each agency that maintains a system of records shall—

(1) maintain in its records only such information about an individual as is relevant and necessary to accomplish a purpose of the agency required to be accomplished by statute or by executive order of the President;

(2) collect information to the greatest extent practicable directly from the subject individual when the information may result in adverse determinations about an individual's rights, benefits, and privileges under Federal programs;

(3) inform each individual whom it asks to supply information, on the form which it uses to collect the information or on a separate form that can be retained by the individual—

(A) the authority (whether granted by statute, or by executive order of the President) which authorizes the solicitation of the information and whether disclosure of such information is mandatory or voluntary;

(B) the principal purpose or purposes for which the information is intended to be used;

(C) the routine uses which may be made of the information, as published pursuant to paragraph (4)(D) of this subsection; and

(D) the effects on him, if any, of not providing all or any part of the requested information;

(4) subject to the provisions of paragraph (11) of this subsection, publish in the Federal Register upon establishment or revision a notice of the existence and character of the system of records, which notice shall include—

(A) the name and location of the system;

(B) the categories of individuals on whom records are maintained in the system;

(C) the categories of records maintained in the system;

(D) each routine use of the records contained in the system, including the categories of users and the purpose of such use;

(E) the policies and practices of the agency regarding storage, retrievability, access controls, retention, and disposal of the records;

(F) the title and business address of the agency official who is responsible for the system of records;

(G) the agency procedures whereby an individual can be notified at his request if the system of records contains a record pertaining to him;

(H) the agency procedures whereby an individual can be notified at his request how he can gain access to any record pertaining to him contained in the system of records, and how he can contest its content; and

(I) the categories of sources of records in the system;

(5) maintain all records which are used by the agency in making any determination about any individual with such accuracy, relevance, timeliness, and completeness as is reasonably necessary to assure fairness to the individual in the determination;

(6) prior to disseminating any record about an individual to any person other than an agency, unless the dissemination is made pursuant to subsection (b)(2) of this section, make reasonable efforts to assure that such records are accurate, complete, timely, and relevant for agency purposes;

(7) maintain no record describing how any individual exercises rights guaranteed by the First Amendment unless expressly authorized by statute or by the individual about whom the record is maintained or unless pertinent to and within the scope of an authorized law enforcement activity;

(8) make reasonable efforts to serve notice on an individual when any record on such individual is made available to any person under compulsory legal process when such process becomes a matter of public record;

(9) establish rules of conduct for persons involved in the design, development, operation, or maintenance of any system of records, or in maintaining any record, and instruct each such person with respect to such rules and the requirements of this section, including any other rules and procedures adopted pursuant to this section and the penalties for noncompliance;

(10) establish appropriate administrative, technical, and physical safeguards to insure the security and confidentiality of records and to protect against any anticipated threats or hazards to their security or

integrity which could result in substantial harm, embarrassment, inconvenience, or unfairness to any individual on whom information is maintained;

(11) at least 30 days prior to publication of information under paragraph (4)(D) of this subsection, publish in the Federal Register notice of any new use or intended use of the information in the system, and provide an opportunity for interested persons to submit written data, views, or arguments to the agency; and

(12) if such agency is a recipient agency or a source agency in a matching program with a non-Federal agency, with respect to any establishment or revision of a matching program, at least 30 days prior to conducting such program, publish in the Federal Register notice of such establishment or revision.

(f) Agency rules.—In order to carry out the provisions of this section, each agency that maintains a system of records shall promulgate rules, in accordance with the requirements (including general notice) of section 553 of this title, which shall—

(1) establish procedures whereby an individual can be notified in response to his request if any system of records named by the individual contains a record pertaining to him;

(2) define reasonable times, places, and requirements for identifying an individual who requests his record or information pertaining to him before the agency shall make the record or information available to the individual;

(3) establish procedures for the disclosure to an individual upon his request of his record or information pertaining to him, including special procedure, if deemed necessary, for the disclosure to an individual of medical records, including psychological records, pertaining to him;

(4) establish procedures for reviewing a request from an individual concerning the amendment of any record or information pertaining to the individual, for making a determination on the request, for an appeal within the agency of an initial adverse agency determination, and for whatever additional means may be necessary for each individual to be able to exercise fully his rights under this section; and

(5) establish fees to be charged, if any, to any individual for making copies of his record, excluding the cost of any search for and review of the record.

The Office of the Federal Register shall biennially compile and publish the rules promulgated under this subsection and agency notices published under subsection (e)(4) of this section in a form available to the public at low cost.

(g)(1) Civil remedies.—Whenever any agency

(A) makes a determination under subsection (d)(3) of this section not to amend an individual's record in accordance with his request, or fails to make such review in conformity with that subsection;

(B) refuses to comply with an individual request under subsection (d)(1) of this section;

(C) fails to maintain any record concerning any individual with such accuracy, relevance, timeliness, and completeness as is necessary to assure fairness in any determination relating to the qualifications, character, rights, or opportunities of, or benefits to the individual that may be made on the basis of such record, and consequently a determination is made which is adverse to the individual; or

(D) fails to comply with any other provision of this section, or any rule promulgated thereunder, in such a way as to have an adverse effect on an individual,

the individual may bring a civil action against the agency, and the district courts of the United States shall have jurisdiction in the matters under the provisions of this subsection.

(2)(A) In any suit brought under the provisions of subsection (g)(1)(A) of this section, the court may order the agency to amend the individual's record in accordance with his request or in such other way as the court may direct. In such a case the court shall determine the matter de novo.

(B) The court may assess against the United States reasonable attorney fees and other litigation costs reasonably incurred in any case under this paragraph in which the complainant has substantially prevailed.

(3)(A) In any suit brought under the provisions of subsection (g)(1)(B) of this section, the court may enjoin the agency from withholding the records and order the production to the complainant of any agency records improperly withheld from him. In such a case the court shall determine the matter de novo, and may examine the contents of any agency records in camera to determine whether the records or any portion thereof may be withheld under any of the exemptions set forth in subsection (k) of this section, and the burden is on the agency to sustain its action.

(B) The court may assess against the United States reasonable attorney fees and other litigation costs reasonably incurred in any case under this paragraph in which the complainant has substantially prevailed.

(4) In any suit brought under the provisions of subsection (g)(1)(C) or (D) of this section in which the court determines that the agency acted in a manner which was intentional or willful, the United States shall be liable to the individual in an amount equal to the sum of—

(A) actual damages sustained by the individual as a result of the refusal or failure, but in no case shall a person entitled to recovery receive less than the sum of $1,000; and

(B) the costs of the action together with reasonable attorney fees as determined by the court.

(5) An action to enforce any liability created under this section may be brought in the district court of the United States in the district in which the complainant resides, or has his principal place of business, or in which the agency records are situated, or in the District of Columbia, without regard to the amount in controversy, within two years from the

date on which the cause of action arises, except that where an agency has materially and willfully misrepresented any information required under this section to be disclosed to an individual and the information so misrepresented is material to establishment of the liability of the agency to the individual under this section, the action may be brought at any time within two years after discovery by the individual of the misrepresentation. Nothing in this section shall be construed to authorize any civil action by reason of any injury sustained as the result of a disclosure of a record prior to September 27, 1975.

(h) **Rights of legal guardians.**—For the purposes of this section, the parent of any minor, or the legal guardian of any individual who has been declared to be incompetent due to physical or mental incapacity or age by a court of competent jurisdiction, may act on behalf of the individual.

(i)(1) **Criminal penalties.**—Any officer or employee of an agency, who by virtue of his employment or official position, has possession of, or access to, agency records which contain individually identifiable information the disclosure of which is prohibited by this section or by rules or regulations established thereunder, and who knowing that disclosure of the specific material is so prohibited, willfully discloses the material in any manner to any person or agency not entitled to receive it, shall be guilty of a misdemeanor and fined not more than $5,000.

(2) Any officer or employee of any agency who willfully maintains a system of records without meeting the notice requirements of subsection (e)(4) of this section shall be guilty of a misdemeanor and fined not more than $5,000.

(3) Any person who knowingly and willfully requests or obtains any record concerning an individual from an agency under false pretenses shall be guilty of a misdemeanor and fined not more than $5,000.

(j) **General exemptions.**—The head of any agency may promulgate rules, in accordance with the requirements (including general notice) of sections 553(b)(1), (2), and (3), (c), and (e) of this title, to exempt any system of records within the agency from any part of this section except subsections (b), (c)(1) and (2), (e)(4)(A) through (F), (e)(6), (7), (9), (10), and (11), and (i) if the system of records is—

(1) maintained by the Central Intelligence Agency; or

(2) maintained by an agency or component thereof which performs as its principal function any activity pertaining to the enforcement of criminal laws, including police efforts to prevent, control, or reduce crime or to apprehend criminals, and the activities of prosecutors, courts, correctional, probation, pardon, or parole authorities, and which consists of (A) information compiled for the purpose of identifying individual criminal offenders and alleged offenders and consisting only of identifying data and notations of arrests, the nature and disposition of criminal charges, sentencing, confinement, release, and parole and probation status; (B) information compiled for the purpose of a criminal investigation, including reports of informants and investigators, and associated with an identifiable individual; or (C) reports identifiable to an individ-

ual compiled at any stage of the process of enforcement of the criminal laws from arrest or indictment through release from supervision.

At the time rules are adopted under this subsection, the agency shall include in the statement required under section 553(c) of this title, the reasons why the system of records is to be exempted from a provision of this section.

(k) **Specific exemptions.**—The head of any agency may promulgate rules, in accordance with the requirements (including general notice) of sections 553(b)(1), (2), and (3), (c), and (e) of this title, to exempt any system of records within the agency from subsections (c)(3), (d), (e)(1), (e)(4)(G), (H), and (I) and (f) of this section if the system of records is—

(1) subject to the provisions of section 552(b)(1) of this title;

(2) investigatory material compiled for law enforcement purposes, other than material within the scope of subsection (j)(2) of this section: *Provided, however,* That if any individual is denied any right, privilege, or benefit that he would otherwise be entitled by Federal law, or for which he would otherwise be eligible, as a result of the maintenance of such material, such material shall be provided to such individual, except to the extent that the disclosure of such material would reveal the identity of a source who furnished information to the Government under an express promise that the identity of the source would be held in confidence, or, prior to the effective date of this section, under an implied promise that the identity of the source would be held in confidence;

(3) maintained in connection with providing protective services to the President of the United States or other individuals pursuant to section 3056 of title 18;

(4) required by statute to be maintained and used solely as statistical records;

(5) investigatory material compiled solely for the purpose of determining suitability, eligibility, or qualifications for Federal civilian employment, military service, Federal contracts, or access to classified information, but only to the extent that the disclosure of such material would reveal the identity of a source who furnished information to the Government under an express promise that the identity of the source would be held in confidence, or, prior to the effective date of this section, under an implied promise that the identity of the source would be held in confidence;

(6) testing or examination material used solely to determine individual qualifications for appointment or promotion in the Federal service the disclosure of which would compromise the objectivity or fairness of the testing or examination process; or

(7) evaluation material used to determine potential for promotion in the armed services, but only to the extent that the disclosure of such material would reveal the identity of a source who furnished information to the Government under an express promise that the identity of the source would be held in confidence, or, prior to the effective date of

this section, under an implied promise that the identity of the source would be held in confidence.

At the time rules are adopted under this subsection, the agency shall include in the statement required under section 553(c) of this title, the reasons why the system of records is to be exempted from a provision of this section.

(*l*)(1) **Archival records.**—Each agency record which is accepted by the Archivist of the United States for storage, processing, and servicing in accordance with section 3103 of title 44 shall, for the purposes of this section, be considered to be maintained by the agency which deposited the record and shall be subject to the provisions of this section. The Archivist of the United States shall not disclose the record except to the agency which maintains the record, or under rules established by that agency which are not inconsistent with the provisions of this section.

(2) Each agency record pertaining to an identifiable individual which was transferred to the National Archives of the United States as a record which has sufficient historical or other value to warrant its continued preservation by the United States Government, prior to the effective date of this section, shall, for the purposes of this section, be considered to be maintained by the National Archives and shall not be subject to the provisions of this section, except that a statement generally describing such records (modeled after the requirements relating to records subject to subsections (e)(4)(A) through (G) of this section) shall be published in the Federal Register.

(3) Each agency record pertaining to an identifiable individual which is transferred to the National Archives of the United States as a record which has sufficient historical or other value to warrant its continued preservation by the United States Government, on or after the effective date of this section, shall, for the purposes of this section, be considered to be maintained by the National Archives and shall be exempt from the requirements of this section except subsections (e)(4)(A) through (G) and (e)(9) of this section.

(m)(1) **Government contractors.**—When an agency provides by a contract for the operation by or on behalf of the agency of a system of records to accomplish an agency function, the agency shall, consistent with its authority, cause the requirements of this section to be applied to such a system. For purposes of subsection (i) of this section any such contractor and any employee of such contractor, if such contract is agreed to on or after the effective date of this section, shall be considered to be an employee of an agency.

(2) A consumer reporting agency to which a record is disclosed under section 3711(f) of title 31 shall not be considered a contractor for the purposes of this section.

(n) **Mailing lists.**—An individual's name and address may not be sold or rented by an agency unless such action is specifically authorized by law. This provision shall not be construed to require the withholding of names and addresses otherwise permitted to be made public.

(*o*) **Matching agreements.**—(1) No record which is contained in a system of records may be disclosed to a recipient agency or non-Federal agency for use in a computer matching program except pursuant to a written agreement between the source agency and the recipient agency or non-Federal agency specifying—

(A) the purpose and legal authority for conducting the program;

(B) the justification for the program and the anticipated results, including a specific estimate of any savings;

(C) a description of the records that will be matched, including each data element that will be used, the approximate number of records that will be matched, and the projected starting and completion dates of the matching program;

(D) procedures for providing individualized notice at the time of application, and notice periodically thereafter as directed by the Data Integrity Board of such agency (subject to guidance provided by the Director of the Office of Management and Budget pursuant to subsection (v)), to—

(i) applicants for and recipients of financial assistance or payments under Federal benefit programs, and

(ii) applicants for and holders of positions as Federal personnel,

that any information provided by such applicants, recipients, holders, and individuals may be subject to verification through matching programs;

(E) procedures for verifying information produced in such matching program as required by subsection (p);

(F) procedures for the retention and timely destruction of identifiable records created by a recipient agency or non-Federal agency in such matching program;

(G) procedures for ensuring the administrative, technical, and physical security of the records matched and the results of such programs;

(H) prohibitions on duplication and redisclosure of records provided by the source agency within or outside the recipient agency or the non-Federal agency, except where required by law or essential to the conduct of the matching program;

(I) procedures governing the use by a recipient agency or non-Federal agency of records provided in a matching program by a source agency, including procedures governing return of the records to the source agency or destruction of records used in such program;

(J) information on assessments that have been made on the accuracy of the records that will be used in such matching program; and

(K) that the Comptroller General may have access to all records of a recipient agency or a non-Federal agency that the Comptroller General deems necessary in order to monitor or verify compliance with the agreement.

(2)(A) A copy of each agreement entered into pursuant to paragraph (1) shall—

(i) be transmitted to the Committee on Governmental Affairs of the Senate and the Committee on Government Operations of the House of Representatives; and

(ii) be available upon request to the public.

(B) No such agreement shall be effective until 30 days after the date on which such a copy is transmitted pursuant to subparagraph (A)(i).

(C) Such an agreement shall remain in effect only for such period, to exceed 18 months, as the Data Integrity Board of the agency determines is appropriate in light of the purposes, and length of time necessary for the conduct, of the matching program.

(D) Within 3 months prior to the expiration of such an agreement pursuant to subparagraph (C), the Data Integrity Board of the agency may, without additional review, renew the matching agreement for a current, ongoing matching program for not more than one additional year if—

(i) such program will be conducted without any change; and

(ii) each party to the agreement certifies to the Board in writing that the program has been conducted in compliance with the agreement.

(p) **Verification and opportunity to contest findings.**—(1) In order to protect any individual whose records are used in a matching program, no recipient agency, non-Federal agency, or source agency may suspend, terminate, reduce, or make a final denial of any financial assistance or payment under a Federal benefit program to such individual, or take other adverse action against such individual, as a result of information produced by such matching program, until—

(A)(i) the agency has independently verified the information; or

(ii) the Data Integrity Board of the agency, or in the case of a non-Federal agency the Data Integrity Board of the source agency, determines in accordance with guidance issued by the Director of the Office of Management and Budget that—

(I) the information is limited to identification and amount of benefits paid by the source agency under a Federal benefit program; and

(II) there is a high degree of confidence that the information provided to the recipient agency is accurate;

(B) the individual receives a notice from the agency containing a statement of its findings and informing the individual of the opportunity to contest such findings; and

(C)(i) the expiration of any time period established for the program by statute or regulation for the individual to respond to that notice; or

(ii) in the case of a program for which no such period is established, the end of the 30-day period beginning on the date on which notice under subparagraph (B) is mailed or otherwise provided to the individual.

(2) Independent verification referred to in paragraph (1) requires investigation and confirmation of specific information relating to an individual that is used as a basis for an adverse action against the individual, including where applicable investigation and confirmation of—

(A) the amount of any asset or income involved;

(B) whether such individual actually has or had access to such asset or income for such individual's own use; and

(C) the period or periods when the individual actually had such asset or income.

(3) Notwithstanding paragraph (1), an agency may take any appropriate action otherwise prohibited by such paragraph if the agency determines that the public health or public safety may be adversely affected or significantly threatened during any notice period required by such paragraph.

(q) **Sanctions.**—(1) Notwithstanding any other provision of law, no source agency may disclose any record which is contained in a system of records to a recipient agency or non-Federal agency for a matching program if such source agency has reason to believe that the requirements of subsection (p), or any matching agreement entered into pursuant to subsection (o), or both, are not being met by such recipient agency.

(2) No source agency may renew a matching agreement unless—

(A) the recipient agency or non-Federal agency has certified that it has complied with the provisions of that agreement; and

(B) the source agency has no reason to believe that the certification is inaccurate.

(r) **Report on new systems and matching programs.**—Each agency that proposes to establish or make a significant change in a system of records or a matching program shall provide adequate advance notice of any such proposal (in duplicate) to the Committee on Government Operations of the House of Representatives, the Committee on Governmental Affairs of the Senate, and the Office of Management and Budget in order to permit an evaluation of the probable or potential effect of such proposal on the privacy or other rights of individuals.

(s) **Biennial report.**—The President shall biennially submit to the Speaker of the House of Representatives and the President pro tempore of the Senate a report—

(1) describing the actions of the Director of the Office of Management and Budget pursuant to section 6 of the Privacy Act of 1974 during the preceding 2 years;

(2) describing the exercise of individual rights of access and amendment under this section during such years;

(3) identifying changes in or additions to systems of records;

(4) containing such other information concerning administration of this section as may be necessary or useful to the Congress in reviewing the effectiveness of this section in carrying out the purposes of the Privacy Act of 1974.

(t)(1) **Effect of other laws.**—No agency shall rely on any exemption contained in section 552 of this title to withhold from an individual any record which is otherwise accessible to such individual under the provisions of this section.

(2) No agency shall rely on any exemption in this section to withhold from an individual any record which is otherwise accessible to such individual under the provisions of section 552 of this title.

(u) **Data Integrity Boards.**—(1) Every agency conducting or participating in a matching program shall establish a Data Integrity Board to oversee and coordinate among the various components of such agency the agency's implementation of this section.

(2) Each Data Integrity Board shall consist of senior officials designated by the head of the agency, and shall include any senior official designated by the head of the agency as responsible for implementation of this section, and the inspector general of the agency, if any. The inspector general shall not serve as chairman of the Data Integrity Board.

(3) Each Data Integrity Board—

(A) shall review, approve, and maintain all written agreements for receipt or disclosure of agency records for matching programs to ensure compliance with subsection (o), and all relevant statutes, regulations, and guidelines;

(B) shall review all matching programs in which the agency has participated during the year, either as a source agency or recipient agency, determine compliance with applicable laws, regulations, guidelines, and agency agreements, and assess the costs and benefits of such programs;

(C) shall review all recurring matching programs in which the agency has participated during the year, either as a source agency or recipient agency, for continued justification for such disclosures;

(D) shall compile an annual report, which shall be submitted to the head of the agency and the Office of Management and Budget and made available to the public on request, describing the matching activities of the agency, including—

(i) matching programs in which the agency has participated as a source agency or recipient agency;

(ii) matching agreements proposed under subsection (o) that were disapproved by the Board;

(iii) any changes in membership or structure of the Board in the preceding year;

(iv) the reasons for any waiver of the requirement in paragraph (4) of this section for completion and submission of a cost-benefit analysis prior to the approval of a matching program;

(v) any violations of matching agreements that have been alleged or identified and any corrective action taken; and

(vi) any other information required by the Director of the Office of Management and Budget to be included in such report;

(E) shall serve as a clearinghouse for receiving and providing information on the accuracy, completeness, and reliability of records used in matching programs;

(F) shall provide interpretation and guidance to agency components and personnel on the requirements of this section for matching programs;

(G) shall review agency recordkeeping and disposal policies and practices for matching programs to assure compliance with this section; and

(H) may review and report on any agency matching activities that are not matching programs.

(4)(A) Except as provided in subparagraphs (B) and (C), a Data Integrity Board shall not approve any written agreement for a matching program unless the agency has completed and submitted to such Board a cost-benefit analysis of the proposed program and such analysis demonstrates that the program is likely to be cost effective.

(B) The Board may waive the requirements of subparagraph (A) of this paragraph if it determines in writing, in accordance with guidelines prescribed by the Director of the Office of Management and Budget, that a cost-benefit analysis is not required.

(C) A cost-benefit analysis shall not be required under subparagraph (A) prior to the initial approval of a written agreement for a matching program that is specifically required by statute. Any subsequent written agreement for such a program shall not be approved by the Data Integrity Board unless the agency has submitted a cost-benefit analysis of the program as conducted under the preceding approval of such agreement.

(5)(A) If a matching agreement is disapproved by a Data Integrity Board any party to such agreement may appeal the disapproval to the Director of the Office of Management and Budget. Timely notice of the filing of such an appeal shall be provided by the Director of the Office of Management and Budget to the Committee on Governmental affairs of the Senate and the Committee on Government Operations of the House of Representatives.

(B) The Director of the Office of Management and Budget may approve a matching agreement notwithstanding the disapproval of a Data Integrity Board if the Director determines that—

(i) the matching program will be consistent with all applicable legal, regulatory, and policy requirements;

(ii) there is adequate evidence that the matching agreement will be cost-effective; and

(iii) the matching program is in the public interest.

(C) The decision of the Director to approve a matching agreement shall not take effect until 30 days after it is reported to committees described in subparagraph (A).

(D) If the Data Integrity Board and the Director of the Office of Management and Budget disapprove a matching program proposed by the inspector general of an agency, the inspector general may report the disapproval to the head of the agency and to the Congress.

(6) The Director of the Office of Management and Budget shall, annually during the first 3 years after the date of enactment of this

subsection and biennially thereafter, consolidate in a report to the Congress the information contained in the reports from the various Data Integrity Boards under paragraph (3)(D). Such report shall include detailed information about costs and benefits of matching programs that are conducted during the period covered by such consolidated report, and shall identify each waiver granted by a Data Integrity Board of the requirement for completion and submission of a cost-benefit analysis and the reasons for granting the waiver.

(7) In the reports required by paragraphs (3)(D) and (6), agency matching activities that are not matching programs may be reported on an aggregate basis, if and to the extent necessary to protect ongoing law enforcement or counterintelligence investigations.

(v) **Office of Management and Budget responsibilities.**—The Director of the Office of Management and Budget shall—

(1) develop and, after notice and opportunity for public comment, prescribe guidelines and regulations for the use of agencies in implementing the provisions of this section; and

(2) provide continuing assistance to and oversight of the implementation of this section by agencies.

Appendix E

Freedom of Information Act

§552. Public information; agency rules, opinions, orders, records, and proceedings

(a) Each agency shall make available to the public information as follows:

(1) Each agency shall separately state and currently publish in the Federal Register for the guidance of the public—

(A) descriptions of its central and field organization and the established places at which, the employees (and in the case of a uniformed service, the members) from whom, and the methods whereby, the public may obtain information, make submittals or requests, or obtain decisions;

(B) statements of the general course and method by which its functions are channeled and determined, including the nature and requirements of all formal and informal procedures available;

(C) rules of procedure, descriptions of forms available or the places at which forms may be obtained, and instructions as to the scope and contents of all papers, reports, or examinations;

(D) substantive rules of general applicability adopted as authorized by law, and statements of general policy or interpretations of general applicability formulated and adopted by the agency; and

(E) each amendment, revision, or repeal of the foregoing. Except to the extent that a person has actual and timely notice of the terms thereof, a person may not in any manner be required to resort to, or be adversely affected by, a matter required to be published in the Federal Register and not so published. For the purpose of this paragraph, matter reasonably available to the class of persons affected thereby is deemed published in the Federal Register when incorporated by reference therein with the approval of the Director of the Federal Register.

(2) Each agency, in accordance with published rules, shall make available for public inspection and copying—

(A) final opinions, including concurring and dissenting opinions, as well as orders, made in the adjudication of cases;

(B) those statements of policy and interpretations which have been adopted by the agency and are not published in the Federal Register; and

(C) administrative staff manuals and instructions to staff that
affect a member of the public;
unless the materials are promptly published and copies offered for sale. To
the extent required to prevent a clearly unwarranted invasion of personal
privacy, an agency may delete identifying details when it makes available
or publishes an opinion, statement of policy, interpretation, or staff manual
or instruction. However, in each case the justification for the deletion shall
be explained fully in writing. Each agency shall also maintain and make
available for public inspection and copying current indexes providing
identifying information for the public as to any matter issued, adopted,
or promulgated after July 4, 1967, and required by this paragraph to be
made available or published. Each agency shall promptly publish, quarterly or more frequently, and distribute (by sale or otherwise) copies of
each index or supplements thereto unless it determines by order published
in the Federal Register that the publication would be unnecessary and
impracticable, in which case the agency shall nonetheless provide copies
of such index on request at a cost not to exceed the direct cost of duplication.
A final order, opinion, statement of policy, interpretation, or staff manual
or instruction that affects a member of the public may be relied on, used,
or cited as precedent by an agency against a party other than an agency
only if—

(i) it has been indexed and either made available or published
as provided by this paragraph; or

(ii) the party has actual and timely notice of the terms thereof.

(3) Except with respect to the records made available under paragraphs (1) and (2) of this subsection, each agency, upon any request for
records which (A) reasonably describes such records and (B) is made
in accordance with published rules stating the time, place, fees (if any),
and procedures to be followed, shall make the records promptly available to any person.

(4)(A)(i) In order to carry out the provisions of this section, each
agency shall promulgate regulations, pursuant to notice and receipt
of public comment, specifying the schedule of fees applicable to the
processing of requests under this section and establishing procedures
and guidelines for determining when such fees should be waived or
reduced. Such schedule shall conform to the guidelines which shall be
promulgated, pursuant to notice and receipt of public comment, by the
Director of the Office of Management and Budget and which shall
provide for a uniform schedule of fees for all agencies.

(ii) Such agency regulations shall provide that—

(I) fees shall be limited to reasonable standard charges for
document search, duplication, and review, when records are requested for commercial use;

(II) fees shall be limited to reasonable standard charges for
document duplication when records are not sought for commercial use and the request is made by an educational or noncommer-
cial scientific institution, whose purpose is scholarly or scientific
research; or a representative of the news media; and

(III) for any request not described in (I) or (II), fees shall be limited to reasonable standard charges for document search and duplication.

(iii) Documents shall be furnished without any charge or at a charge reduced below the fees established under clause (ii) if disclosure of the information is in the public interest because it is likely to contribute significantly to public understanding of the operations or activities of the government and is not primarily in the commercial interest of the requester.

(iv) Fee schedules shall provide for the recovery of only the direct costs of search, duplication, or review. Review costs shall include only the direct costs incurred during the initial examination of a document for the purposes of determining whether the documents must be disclosed under this section and for the purposes of withholding any portions exempt from disclosure under this section. Review costs may not include any costs incurred in resolving issues of law or policy that may be raised in the course of processing a request under this section. No fee may be charged by any agency under this section—

(I) if the costs of routine collection and processing of the fee are likely to equal or exceed the amount of the fee; or

(II) for any request described in clause (ii)(II) or (III) of this subparagraph for the first two hours of search time or for the first one hundred pages of duplication.

(v) No agency may require advance payment of any fee unless the requester has previously failed to pay fees in a timely fashion, or the agency has determined that the fee will exceed $250.

(vi) Nothing in this subparagraph shall supersede fees chargeable under a statute specifically providing for setting the level of fees for particular types of records.

(vii) In any action by a requester regarding the waiver of fees under this section, the court shall determine the matter de novo: *Provided,* That the court's review of the matter shall be limited to the record before the agency.

(B) On complaint, the district court of the United States in the district in which the complainant resides, or has his principal place of business, or in which the agency records are situated, or in the District of Columbia, has jurisdiction to enjoin the agency from withholding agency records and to order the production of any agency records improperly withheld from the complainant. In such a case the court shall determine the matter de novo, and may examine the contents of such agency records in camera to determine whether such records or any part thereof shall be withheld under any of the exemptions set forth in subsection (b) of this section, and the burden is on the agency to sustain its action.

(C) Notwithstanding any other provision of law, the defendant shall serve an answer or otherwise plead to any complaint made under this subsection within thirty days after service upon the defenant of the pleading in which such complaint is made, unless the court otherwise directs for good cause shown.

[(D) Repealed. Pub.L. 98-620, Title IV, §402(2), Nov. 8, 1984, 98 Stat. 3357]

(E) The court may assess against the United States reasonable attorney fees and other litigation costs reasonably incurred in any case under this section in which the complainant has substantially prevailed.

(F) Whenever the court orders the production of any agency records improperly withheld from the complainant and assesses against the United States reasonable attorney fees and other litigation costs, and the court additionally issues a written finding that the circumstances surrounding the withholding raise questions whether agency personnel acted arbitrarily or capriciously with respect to the withholding, the Special Counsel shall promptly initiate a proceeding to determine whether disciplinary action is warranted against the officer or employee who was primarily responsible for the withholding. The Special Counsel, after investigation and consideration of the evidence submitted, shall submit his findings and recommendations to the administrative authority of the agency concerned and shall send copies of the findings and recommendations to the office or employee or his representative. The administrative authority shall take the corrective action that the Special Counsel recommends.

(G) In the event of noncompliance with the order of the court, the district court may punish for contempt the responsible employee, and in the case of a uniformed service, the responsible member.

(5) Each agency having more than one member shall maintain and make available for public inspection a record of the final votes of each member in every agency proceeding.

(6)(A) Each agency, upon any request for records made under paragraph (1), (2), or (3) of this subsection, shall—

(i) determine within ten days (excepting Saturdays, Sundays, and legal public holidays) after the receipt of any such request whether to comply with such request and shall immediately notify the person making such request of such determination and the reasons therefor, and of the right of such person to appeal to the head of the agency any adverse determination; and

(ii) make a determination with respect to any appeal within twenty days (excepting Saturdays, Sundays, and legal public holidays) after the receipt of such appeal. If on appeal the denial of the request for records is in whole or in part upheld, the agency shall notify the person making such request of the provisions for judicial review of that determination under paragraph (4) of this subsection.

(B) In unusual circumstances as specified in this subparagraph the time limits prescribed in either clause (i) or clause (ii) of subparagraph (A) may be extended by written notice to the person making such request setting forth the reasons for such extension and the date on which a determination is expected to be dispatched. No such notice shall specify a date that would result in an extension for more than ten working days. As used in this subparagraph, "unusual circumstances" means, but only to the extent reasonably necessary to the proper processing of the particular request—

(i) the need to search for and collect the requested records from field facilities or other establishments that are separate from the office processing the request;

(ii) the need to search for, collect, and appropriately examine a voluminous amount of separate and distinct records which are demanded in a single request; or

(iii) the need for consultation, which shall be conducted with all practicable speed, with another agency having a substantial interest in the determination of the request or among two or more components of the agency having substantial subject-matter interest therein.

(C) Any person making a request to any agency for records under paragraph (1), (2), or (3) of this subsection shall be deemed to have exhausted his administrative remedies with respect to such request if the agency fails to comply with the applicable time limit provisions of this paragraph. If the Government can show exceptional circumstances exist and that the agency is exercising due diligence in responding to the request, the court may retain jurisdiction and allow the agency additional time to complete its review of the records. Upon any determination by an agency to comply with a request for records, the records shall be made promptly available to such person making such request. Any notification of denial of any request for records under this subsection shall set forth the names and titles or positions of each person responsible for the denial of such request.

(b) This section does not apply to matters that are—

(1)(A) specifically authorized under criteria established by an Executive order to be kept secret in the interest of national defense or foreign policy and (B) are in fact properly classified pursuant to such Executive order;

(2) related solely to the internal personnel rules and practices of an agency;

(3) specifically exempted from disclosure by statute (other than section 552b of this title), provided that such statute (A) requires that the matters be withheld from the public in such a manner as to leave no discretion on the issue, or (B) establishes particular criteria for withholding or refers to particular types of matters to be withheld;

(4) trade secrets and commercial or financial information obtained from a person and privileged or confidential;

(5) inter-agency or intra-agency memorandums or letters which would not be available by law to a party other than an agency in litigation with the agency;

(6) personnel and medical files and similar files the disclosure of which would constitute a clearly unwarranted invasion of personal privacy;

(7) records or information compiled for law enforcement purposes, but only to the extent that the production of such law enforcement records or information (A) could reasonably be expected to interfere with enforcement proceedings, (B) would deprive a person of a right to a fair trial or an impartial adjudication, (C) could reasonably be expected to constitute an unwarranted invasion of personal privacy, (D) could reasonably be expected to disclose the identity of a confidential source, including a State, local, or foreign agency or authority or any private institution which furnished information on a confidential basis, and, in the case of a record or information compiled by criminal law enforcement authority in the course of a criminal investigation or by an agency conducting a lawful national security intelligence investigation, information furnished by a confidential source, (E) would disclose techniques and procedures for law enforcement investigations or prosecutions, or would disclose guidelines for law enforcement investigations or prosecutions if such disclosure could reasonably be expected to risk circumvention of the law, or (F) could reasonably be expected to endanger the life or physical safety of any individual;

(8) contained in or related to examination, operating, or condition reports prepared by, on behalf of, or for the use of an agency responsible for the regulation or supervision of financial institutions; or

(9) geological and geophysical information and data, including maps, concerning wells.
Any reasonably segregable portion of a record shall be provided to any person requesting such record after deletion of the portions which are exempt under this subsection.

(c)(1) Whenever a request is made which involves access to records described in subsection (b)(7)(A) and—

(A) the investigation or proceeding involves a possible violation of criminal law; and

(B) there is reason to believe that (i) the subject of the investigation or proceeding is not aware of its pendency, and (ii) disclosure of the existence of the records could reasonably be expected to interfere with enforcement proceedings,
the agency may, during only such time as that circumstance continues, treat the records as not subject to the requirements of this section.

(2) Whenever informant records maintained by a criminal law enforcement agency under an informant's name or personal identifier are requested by a third party according to the informant's name or personal identifier, the agency may treat the records as not subject to the requirements of this section unless the informant's status as an informant has been officially confirmed.

(3) Whenever a request is made which involves access to records maintained by the Federal Bureau of Investigation pertaining to foreign intelligence or counterintelligence, or international terrorism, and the

existence of the records is classified information as provided in subsection (b)(1), the Bureau may, as long as the existence of the records remains classified information, treat the records as not subject to the requirements of this section.

(d) This section does not authorize withholding of information or limit the availability of records to the public, except as specifically stated in this section. This section is not authority to withhold information from Congress.

(e) On or before March 1 of each calendar year, each agency shall submit a report covering the preceding calendar year to the Speaker of the House of Representatives and President of the Senate for referral to the appropriate committees of the Congress. The report shall include—

(1) the number of determinations made by such agency not to comply with requests for records made to such agency under subsection (a) and the reasons for each such determination;

(2) the number of appeals made by persons under subsection (a)(6), the result of such appeals, and the reason for the action upon each appeal that results in a denial of information;

(3) the names and titles or positions of each person responsible for the denial of records requested under this section, and the number of instances of participation for each;

(4) the results of each proceeding conducted pursuant to subsection (a)(4)(F), including a report of the disciplinary action taken against the officer or employee who was primarily responsible for improperly withholding records or an explanation of why disciplinary action was not taken;

(5) a copy of every rule made by such agency regarding this section;

(6) a copy of the fee schedule and the total amount of fees collected by the agency for making records available under this section; and

(7) such other information as indicates efforts to administer fully this section.

The Attorney General shall submit an annual report on or before March 1 of each calendar year which shall include for the prior calendar year a listing of the number of cases arising under this section, the exemption involved in each case, the disposition of such case, and the cost, fees, and penalties assessed under subsections (a)(4)(E), (F), and (G). Such report shall also include a description of the efforts undertaken by the Department of Justice to encourage agency compliance with this section.

(f) For purposes of this section, the term "agency" as defined in section 551(1) of this title includes any executive department, military department, Government corporation, Government controlled corporation, or other establishment in the executive branch of the Government (including the Executive Office of the President), or any independent regulatory agency.

Appendix F

Sample Letters (FOIA)

**Freedom of Information Act Sample Letter
for Personal Records (FOIA)**

(Return Address)

(Date)

Freedom of Information Act Request
Office of the Secretary
Federal Bureau of Investigation
Washington, D.C. 20009

Re: FOIA request

Dear Secretary:

In accordance with 5 U.S.C. §552, the Freedom of Information Act, I hereby request copies of all records relating to me retained by your agency, or by any other custodian, at your agency's direction.

I agree to pay reasonable standard charges for document research and duplication.

Please respond within ten working days from the receipt of this letter as is required by law.

Sincerely,

Signature

Freedom of Information Act Sample Letter
for Agency Records (FOIA)

(Return Address)

(Date)

Freedom of Information Act Request
Office of the Secretary
Department of Agriculture
Washington, D.C. 20009

Re: FOIA request

Dear Secretary:

  In accordance with 5 U.S.C. §552, the Freedom of Information
Act, I hereby request copies of all records and materials including
policy statements concerning the domestic milk production.
  I agree to pay reasonable standard charges for document research
and duplication.
  Please respond within ten working days from the receipt of this
letter as is required by law.

Sincerely,

Paralegal

Appendix G

Federal Rules of Civil Procedure (Selected Rules)

Rule 7. Pleadings Allowed; Form of Motions

(a) Pleadings. There shall be a complaint and an answer; a reply to a counterclaim denominated as such; an answer to a cross-claim, if the answer contains a cross-elaim; a third-party complaint, if a person who was not an original party is summoned under the provisions of Rule 14; and a third-party answer, if a third-party complaint is served. No other pleading shall be allowed, except that the court may order a reply to an answer or a third-party answer.

Rule 11. Signing of Pleadings, Motions, and Other Papers; Representations to Court; Sanctions

(a) Signature. Every pleading, written motion, and other paper shall be signed by at least one attorney of record in the attorney's individual name, or, if the party is not represented by an attorney, shall be signed by the party. Each paper shall state the signer's address and telephone number, if any. Except when otherwise specifically provided by rule or statute, pleadings need not be verified or accompanied by affidavit. An unsigned paper shall be stricken unless omission of the signature is corrected promptly after being called to the attention of the attorney or party.

(b) Representations to Court. By presenting to the court (whether by signing, filing, submitting, or later advocating) a pleading, written motion, or other paper, an attorney or unrepresented party is certifying that to the best of the person's knowledge, information, and belief, formed after an inquiry reasonable under the circumstances,—

    (1) it is not being presented for any improper purpose, such as to harass or to cause unnecessary delay or needless increase in the cost of litigation;

    (2) the claims, defenses, and other legal contentions therein are warranted by existing law or by a nonfrivolous argument for the extension, modification, or reversal of existing law or the establishment of new law;

    (3) the allegations and other factual contentions have evidentiary support or, if specifically so identified, are likely to have evidentiary support after a reasonable opportunity for further investigation or discovery; and

(4) the denials of factual contentions are warranted on the evidence or, if specifically so identified, are reasonably based on a lack of information or belief.

(c) Sanctions. If, after notice and a reasonable opportunity to respond, the court determines that subdivision (b) has been violated, the court may, subject to the conditions stated below, impose an appropriate sanction upon the attorneys, law firms, or parties that have violated subdivision (b) or are responsible for the violation. . . .

(2) Nature of Sanction; Limitations. A sanction imposed for violation of this rule shall be limited to what is sufficient to deter repetition of such conduct or comparable conduct by others similarly situated. Subject to the limitations in subparagraphs (A) and (B), the sanction may consist of, or include, directives of a nonmonetary nature, an order to pay a penalty into court, or, if imposed on motion and warranted for effective deterrence, an order directing payment to the movant of some or all of the reasonable attorneys' fees and other expenses incurred as a direct result of the violation.

(A) Monetary sanctions may not be awarded against a represented party for a violation of subdivision (b)(2).

(B) Monetary sanctions may not be awarded on the court's initiative unless the court issues its order to show cause before a voluntary dismissal or settlement of the claims made by or against the party which is, or whose attorneys are, to be sanctioned.

(3) Order. When imposing sanctions, the court shall describe the conduct determined to constitute a violation of this rule and explain the basis for the sanction imposed.

(d) Inapplicability to Discovery. Subdivisions (a) through (c) of this rule do not apply to disclosures and discovery requests, responses, objections, and motions that are subject to the provisions of Rules 26 through 37.

Rule 26. General Provisions Governing Discovery; Duty of Disclosure

(a) Required Disclosures; Methods to Discover Additional Matter.

(1) Initial Disclosures. Except to the extent otherwise stipulated or directed by order or local rule, a party shall, without awaiting a discovery request, provide to other parties:

(A) the name and, if known, the address and telephone number of each individual likely to have discoverable information relevant to disputed facts alleged with particularity in the pleadings, identifying the subjects of the information;

(B) a copy of, or a description by category and location of, all documents, data compilations, and tangible things in the possession, custody, or control of the party that are relevant to disputed facts alleged with particularity in the pleadings;

(C) a computation of any category of damages claimed by the disclosing party, making available for inspection and copying as under Rule 34 the documents or other evidentiary material, not privileged or protected from disclosure, on which such computation is based, including materials bearing on the nature and extent of injuries suffered; and

(D) for inspection and copying as under Rule 34 any insurance agreement under which any person carrying on an insurance business may be liable to satisfy part or all of a judgment which may be entered in the action or to indemnify or reimburse for payments made to satisfy the judgment.

Unless otherwise stipulated or directed by the court, these disclosures shall be made at or within 10 days after the meeting of the parties under subdivision (f). A party shall make its initial disclosures based on the information then reasonably available to it and is not excused from making its disclosures because it has not fully completed its investigation of the case or because it challenges the sufficiency of another party's disclosures or because another party has not made its disclosures.

(2) Disclosure of Expert Testimony.

(A) In addition to the disclosures required by paragraph (1), a party shall disclose to other parties the identity of any person who may be used at trial to present evidence under Rules 702, 703, or 705 of the Federal Rules of Evidence. . . .

(3) Pretrial Disclosures. In addition to the disclosures required in the preceding paragraphs, a party shall provide to other parties the following information regarding the evidence that it may present at trial other than solely for impeachment purposes:

(A) the name and, if not previously provided, the address and telephone number of each witness, separately identifying those whom the party expects to present and those whom the party may call if the need arises;

(B) the designation of those witnesses whose testimony is expected to be presented by means of a deposition and, if not taken stenographically, a transcript of the pertinent portions of the deposition testimony; and

(C) an appropriate identification of each document or other exhibit, including summaries of other evidence, separately identifying those which the party expects to offer and those which the party may offer if the need arises. . . .

(b) Discovery Scope and Limits. Unless otherwise limited by order of the court in accordance with these rules, the scope of discovery is as follows:

(1) In General. Parties may obtain discovery regarding any matter, not privileged, which is relevant to the subject matter involved in the pending action, whether it relates to the claim or defense of the party seeking discovery or to the claim or defense of any other party, including the existence, description, nature, custody, condition, and location of any books, documents, or other tangible things and the identity and location of persons having knowledge of any discoverable matter. The information sought need not be admissible at the trial if the information sought appears reasonably calculated to lead to the discovery of admissible evidence. . . .

(4) Trial Preparation: Experts.

(A) A party may depose any person who has been identified as an expert whose opinions may be presented at trial. If a report from the expert is required under subdivision (a)(2)(B), the deposition shall not be conducted until after the report is provided.

(B) A party may, through interrogatories or by deposition, discover facts known or opinions held by an expert who has been retained or specially employed by another party in anticipation of litigation or preparation for trial and who is not expected to be called as a witness at trial, only as provided in Rule 35(b) or upon a showing of exceptional circumstances under which it is impracticable for the party seeking discovery to obtain facts or opinions on the same subject by other means. . . .

(5) Claims of Privilege or Protection of Trial Preparation Materials. When a party withholds information otherwise discoverable under these rules by claiming that it is privileged or subject to protection as trial preparation material, the party shall make the claim expressly and shall describe the nature of the documents, communications, or things not produced or disclosed in a manner that, without revealing information itself privileged or protected, will enable other parties to assess the applicability of the privilege or protection. . . .

(e) Supplementation of Disclosures and Responses. A party who has made a disclosure under subdivision (a) or responded to a request for discovery with a disclosure or response is under a duty to supplement or correct the disclosure or response to include information thereafter acquired if ordered by the court or in the following circumstances:

(1) A party is under a duty to supplement at appropriate intervals its disclosures under subdivision (a) if the party learns that in some material respect the information disclosed is incomplete or incorrect and if the additional or corrective information has not otherwise been made known to the other parties during the discovery process or in writing. With respect to testimony of an expert from whom a report is required under subdivision (a)(2)(B) the duty extends both to information contained in the report and to information provided through a deposition of the expert, and any additional or other changes to this information shall be disclosed by the time the party's disclosures under Rule 26(a)(3) are due.

(2) A party is under a duty seasonably to amend a prior response to an interrogatory, request for production, or request for admission if the party learns that the response is in some material respect incomplete or incorrect and if the additional or corrective information has not otherwise been made known to the other parties during the discovery process or in writing. . . .

Rule 30. Depositions Upon Oral Examination

(a) When Depositions May Be Taken; When Leave Required.

(1) A Party may take the testimony of any person, including a party, by deposition upon oral examination without leave of court except as provided in paragraph (2). The attendance of witnesses may be compelled by subpoena as provided in Rule 45. . . .

(b) Notice of Examination: General Requirements; Method of Recording; Production of Documents and Things; Deposition of Organization; Deposition by Telephone.

(1) A party desiring to take the deposition of any person upon oral examination shall give reasonable notice in writing to every other party to the action. The notice shall state the time and place for taking the deposition and the name and address of each person to be examined, if known, and, if the name is not known, a general description sufficient to identify the person or the particular class or group to which the person belongs. If a subpoena duces tecum is to be served on the person to be examined, the designation of the materials to be produced as set forth in the subpoena shall be attached to, or included in, the notice.

(2) The party taking the deposition shall state in the notice the method by which the testimony shall be recorded. Unless the court orders otherwise, it may be recorded by sound, sound-and-visual, or stenographic means, and the party taking the deposition shall bear the cost of the recording. Any party may arrange for a transcription to be made from the recording of a deposition taken by nonstenographic means.

(3) With prior notice to the deponent and other parties, any party may designate another method to record the deponent's testimony in addition to the method specified by the person taking the deposition. The additional record or transcript shall be made at that party's expense unless the court otherwise orders.

Rule 33.   Interrogatories to Parties

(a) Availability. Without leave of court or written stipulation, any party may serve upon any other party written interrogatories, not exceeding 25 in number including all discrete subparts, to be answered by the party served or, if the party served is a public or private corporation or a partnership or association or governmental agency, by any officer or agent, who shall furnish such information as is available to the party. Leave to serve additional interrogatories shall be granted to the extent consistent with the principles of Rule 26(b)(2). Without leave of court or written stipulation, interrogatories may not be served before the time specified in Rule 26(d). . . .

Rule 34. Production of Documents and Things and Entry Upon Land for Inspection and Other Purposes

(a) Scope. Any party may serve on any other party a request (1) to produce and permit the party making the request, or someone acting on the requestor's behalf, to inspect and copy, any designated documents (including writings, drawings, graphs, charts, photographs, phonorecords, and other data compilations from which information can be obtained, translated, if necessary, by the respondent through detection devices into reasonably usable form), or to inspect and copy, test, or sample any tangible things which constitute or contain matters within the scope of Rule 26(b) and which are in the possession, custody or control of the party upon whom the request is served; or (2) to permit entry upon designated land or other property in the possession or control of the party upon whom the request is served for the purpose of inspection and measuring, surveying, photographing, testing, or sampling the property or any designated object or operation thereon, within the scope of Rule 26(b). . . .

Rule 35. Physical and Mental Examinations of Persons

(a) Order for Examination. When the mental or physical condition (including the blood group) of a party or of a person in the custody or under the legal control of a party, is in controversy, the court in which the action is pending may order the party to submit to a physical or mental examination by a suitably licensed or certified examiner or to produce for examination the person in the party's custody or legal control. The order may be made only on motion for good cause shown and upon notice to the person to be examined and to all parties and shall specify the time, place, manner, conditions, and scope of the examination and the person or persons by whom it is to be made. . . .

Rule 36. Requests for Admission

(a) Request for Admission. A party may serve upon any other party a written request for the admission, for purposes of the pending action only, of the truth of any matters within the scope of Rule 26(b)(1) set forth in the request that relate to statements or opinions of fact or of the application of law to fact, including the genuineness of any documents described in the request. Copies of documents shall be served with the request unless they have been or are otherwise furnished or made available for inspection and copying. Without leave of court or written stipulation, requests for admission may not be served before the time specified in Rule 26(d). . . .

Appendix H

Federal Rules of Evidence
(Selected Rules)

Rule 401. Definition of "Relevant Evidence"

"Relevant evidence" means evidence having any tendency to make the existence of any fact that is of consequence to the determination of the action more probable or less probable than it would be without the evidence.

Rule 402. Relevant Evidence Generally Admissible; Irrelevant Evidence Inadmissible

All relevant evidence is admissible, except as otherwise provided by the Constitution of the United States, by Act of Congress, by these rules, or by other rules prescribed by the Supreme Court pursuant to statutory authority. Evidence which is not relevant is not admissible.

Rule 403. Exclusion of Relevant Evidence on Grounds of Prejudice, Confusion, or Waste of Time

Although relevant, evidence may be excluded if its probative value is substantially outweighed by the danger of unfair prejudice, confusion of the issues, or misleading the jury, or by considerations of undue delay, waste of time, or needless presentation of cumulative evidence.

Rule 404. Character Evidence Not Admissible To Prove Conduct; Exceptions, Other Crimes

(a) **Character evidence generally.** Evidence of a person's character or a trait of character is not admissible for the purpose of proving action in conformity therewith on a particular occasion, except:

(1) **Character of accused.** Evidence of a pertinent trait of character offered by an accused, or by the prosecution to rebut the same;

(2) **Character of victim.** Evidence of a pertinent trait of character of the victim of the crime offered by an accused, or by the prosecution to rebut the same, or evidence of a character trait of peacefulness of the victim offered by the prosecution in a homicide case to rebut evidence that the victim was the first aggressor;

(3) **Character of witness.** Evidence of the character of a witness, as provided in rules 607, 608, and 609.

(b) **Other crimes, wrongs, or acts.** Evidence of other crimes, wrongs, or acts is not admissible to prove the character of a person in order to show action in conformity therewith. It may, however, be admissible for other purposes, such as proof of motive, opportunity, intent, preparation, plan, knowledge, identity, or absence of mistake or accident, provided that upon request by the accused, the prosecution in a criminal case shall provide reasonable notice in advance of trial, or during trial if the court excuses pretrial notice on good cause shown, of the general nature of any such evidence it intends to introduce at trial.

Rule 407. Subsequent Remedial Measures

When, after an event, measures are taken which, if taken previously, would have made the event less likely to occur, evidence of the subsequent measures is not admissible to prove negligence or culpable conduct in connection with the event. This rule does not require the exclusion of evidence of subsequent measures when offered for another purpose, such as proving ownership, control, or feasibility of precautionary measures, if controverted, or impeachment.

Rule 408. Compromise and Offers to Compromise

Evidence of (1) furnishing or offering or promising to furnish, or (2) accepting or offering or promising to accept, a valuable consideration in compromising or attempting to compromise a claim which was disputed as to either validity or amount, is not admissible to prove liability for or invalidity of the claim or its amount. Evidence of conduct or statements made in compromise negotiations is likewise not admissible. This rule does not require the exclusion of any evidence otherwise discoverable merely because it is presented in the course of compromise negotiations. This rule also does not require exclusion when the evidence is offered for another purpose, such as proving bias or prejudice of a witness, negativing a contention of undue delay, or proving an effort to obstruct a criminal investigation or prosecution.

Rule 409. Payment of Medical and Similar Expenses

Evidence of furnishing or offering or promising to pay medical, hospital, or similar expenses occasioned by an injury is not admissible to prove liability for the injury.

Rule 411. Liability Insurance

Evidence that a person was or was not insured against liability is not admissible upon the issue whether the person acted negligently or otherwise wrongfully. This rule does not require the exclusion of evidence of insurance against liability when offered for another purpose, such as proof of agency, ownership, or control, or bias or prejudice of a witness.

Rule 607. Who May Impeach

The credibility of a witness may be attacked by any party, including the party calling the witness.

Rule 608. Evidence of Character and Conduct of Witness

(a) **Opinion and reputation evidence of character.** The credibility of a witness may be attacked or supported by evidence in the form of opinion or reputation, but subject to these limitations: (1) the evidence may refer only to character for truthfulness or untruthfulness, and (2) evidence of truthful character is admissible only after the character of the witness for truthfulness has been attacked by opinion or reputation evidence or otherwise.

(b) **Specific instances of conduct.** Specific instances of the conduct of a witness, for the purpose of attacking or supporting the witness' credibility, other than conviction of crime as provided in rule 609, may not be proved by extrinsic evidence. They may, however, in the discretion of the court, if probative of truthfulness or untruthfulness, be inquired into on cross-examination of the witness (1) concerning the witness' character for truthfulness or untruthfulness, or (2) concerning the character for truthfulness or untruthfulness of another witness as to which character the witness being cross-examined has testified.

The giving of testimony, whether by an accused or by any other witness, does not operate as a waiver of the accused's or the witness' privilege against self-incrimination when examined with respect to matters which relate only to credibility.

Rule 609. Impeachment by Evidence of Conviction of Crime

(a) **General rule.** For the purpose of attacking the credibility of a witness,

(1) evidence that a witness other than an accused has been convicted of a crime shall be admitted, subject to Rule 403, if the crime was punishable by death or imprisonment in excess of one year under the law under which the witness was convicted, and evidence that an accused has been convicted of such a crime shall be admitted if the court determines that the probative value of admitting this evidence outweighs its prejudicial effect to the accused; and

(2) evidence that any witness has been convicted of a crime shall be admitted if it involved dishonesty or false statement, regardless of the punishment. . . .

(d) **Juvenile adjudications.** Evidence of juvenile adjudications is generally not admissible under this rule. The court may, however, in a criminal case allow evidence of a juvenile adjudication of a witness other than the accused if conviction of the offense would be admissible to attack the credibility of an adult and the court is satisfied that admission in evidence is necessary for a fair determination of the issue of guilt or innocence. . . .

Rule 613. Prior Statements of Witnesses

(a) **Examining witness concerning prior statement.** In examining a witness concerning a prior statement made by the witness, whether written or not, the statement need not be shown nor its contents disclosed to the witness at that time, but on request the same shall be shown or disclosed to opposing counsel.

(b) **Extrinsic evidence of prior inconsistent statement of witness.** Extrinsic evidence of a prior inconsistent statement by a witness is not admissible unless the witness is afforded an opportunity to explain or deny the same and the opposite party is afforded an opportunity to interrogate the witness thereon, or the interests of justice otherwise require. This provision does not apply to admissions of a party-opponent as defined in rule 801(d)(2).

Rule 615. Exclusion of Witnesses

At the request of a party the court shall order witnesses excluded so that they cannot hear the testimony of other witnesses, and it may make the order of its own motion. This rule does not authorize exclusion of (1) a party who is a natural person, or (2) an officer or employee of a party which is not a natural person designated as its representative by its attorney, or (3) a person whose presence is shown by a party to be essential to the presentation of the party's cause.

Rule 701. Opinion Testimony by Lay Witnesses

If the witness is not testifying as an expert, the witness' testimony in the form of opinions or inferences is limited to those opinions or inferences which are (a) rationally based on the perception of the witness and (b) helpful to a clear understanding of the witness' testimony or the determination of a fact in issue.

Rule 702. Testimony by Experts

If scientific, technical, or other specialized knowledge will assist the trier of fact to understand the evidence or to determine a fact in issue, a witness qualified as an expert by knowledge, skill, experience, training, or education, may testify thereto in the form of an opinion or otherwise.

Rule 801. Definitions

The following definitions apply under this article:

(a) **Statement.** A "statement" is (1) an oral or written assertion or (2) nonverbal conduct of a person, if it is intended by the person as an assertion.

(b) **Declarant.** A "declarant" is a person who makes a statement.

(c) **Hearsay.** "Hearsay" is a statement, other than one made by the declarant while testifying at the trial or hearing, offered in evidence to prove the truth of the matter asserted.

(d) Statements which are not hearsay. A statement is not hearsay if—

(1) Prior statement by witness. The declarant testifies at the trial or hearing and is subject to cross-examination concerning the statement, and the statement is (A) inconsistent with the declarant's testimony, and was given under oath subject to the penalty of perjury at a trial, hearing, or other proceeding, or in a deposition, or (B) consistent with the declarant's testimony and is offered to rebut an express or implied charge against the declarant of recent fabrication or improper influence or motive, or (C) one of identification of a person made after perceiving the person; or

(2) Admission by party-opponent. The statement is offered against a party and is (A) the party's own statement in either an individual or a representative capacity or (B) a statement of which the party has manifested an adoption or belief in its truth, or (C) a statement by a person authorized by the party to make a statement concerning the subject, or (D) a statement by the party's agent or servant concerning a matter within the scope of the agency or employment, made during the existence of the relationship, or (E) a statement by a coconspirator of a party during the course and in furtherance of the conspiracy.

Rule 802. Hearsay Rule

Hearsay is not admissible except as provided by these rules or by other rules prescribed by the Supreme Court pursuant to statutory authority or by Act of Congress.

Rule 803. Hearsay Exceptions; Availability of Declarant Immaterial

The following are not excluded by the hearsay rule, even though the declarant is available as a witness:

(1) Present sense impression. A statement describing or explaining an event or condition made while the declarant was perceiving the event or condition, or immediately thereafter.

(2) Excited utterance. A statement relating to a startling event or condition made while the declarant was under the stress of excitement caused by the event or condition.

(3) Then existing mental, emotional, or physical condition. A statement of the declarant's then existing state of mind, emotion, sensation, or physical condition (such as intent, plan, motive, design, mental feeling, pain, and bodily health), but not including a statement of memory or belief to prove the fact remembered or believed unless it relates to the execution, revocation, identification, or terms of declarant's will.

(4) Statements for purposes of medical diagnosis or treatment. Statements made for purposes of medical diagnosis or treatment and describing medical history, or past or present symptoms, pain, or sensations, or the inception or general character of the cause or external source thereof insofar as reasonably pertinent to diagnosis or treatment.

(5) Recorded recollection. A memorandum or record concerning a matter about which a witness once had knowledge but now has insufficient recollection to enable the witness to testify fully and accurately, shown to have been made or adopted by the witness when the matter was fresh in the witness' memory and to reflect that knowledge correctly. If admitted, the memorandum or record may be read into evidence but may not itself be received as an exhibit unless offered by an adverse party.

(6) Records of regularly conducted activity. A memorandum, report, record, or data compilation, in any form, of acts, events, conditions, opinions, or diagnoses, made at or near the time by, or from information transmitted by, a person with knowledge, if kept in the course of a regularly conducted business activity, and if it was the regular practice of that business activity to make the memorandum, report, record, or data compilation, all as shown by the testimony of the custodian or other qualified witness, unless the source of information or the method or circumstances of preparation indicate lack of trustworthiness. The term "business" as used in this paragraph includes business, institution, association, profession, occupation, and calling of every kind, whether or not conducted for profit. . . .

(8) Public records and reports. Records, reports, statements, or data compilations, in any form, of public offices or agencies, setting forth (A) the activities of the office or agency, or (B) matters observed pursuant to duty imposed by law as to which matters there was a duty to report, excluding, however, in criminal cases matters observed by police officers and other law enforcement personnel, or (C) in civil actions and proceedings and against the Government in criminal cases, factual findings resulting from an investigation made pursuant to authority granted by law, unless the sources of information or other circumstances indicate lack of trustworthiness. . . .

(17) Market reports, commercial publications. Market quotations, tabulations, lists, directories, or other published compilations, generally used and relied upon by the public or by persons in particular occupations. . . .

(21) Reputation as to character. Reputation of a person's character among associates or in the community.

(22) Judgment of previous conviction. Evidence of a final judgment, entered after a trial or upon a plea of guilty (but not upon a plea of nolo contendere), adjudging a person guilty of a crime punishable by death or imprisonment in excess of one year, to prove any fact essential to sustain the judgment, but not including, when offered by the Government in a criminal prosecution for purposes other than impeachment, judgments against persons other than the accused. The pendency of an appeal may be shown but does not affect admissibility.

Rule 804. Hearsay Exceptions; Declarant Unavailable

(a) Definition of unavailability. "Unavailability as a witness" includes situations in which the declarant—

(1) is exempted by ruling of the court on the ground of privilege from testifying concerning the subject matter of the declarant's statement; or

(2) persists in refusing to testify concerning the subject matter of the declarant's statement despite an order of the court to do so; or

(3) testifies to a lack of memory of the subject matter of the declarant's statement; or

(4) is unable to be present or to testify at the hearing because of death or then existing physical or mental illness or infirmity; or

(5) is absent from the hearing and the proponent of a statement has been unable to procure the declarant's attendance (or in the case of a hearsay exception under subdivision (b)(2), (3), or (4), the declarant's attendance or testimony) by process or other reasonable means.

A declarant is not unavailable as a witness if exemption, refusal, claim of lack of memory, inability, or absence is due to the procurement or wrongdoing of the proponent of a statement for the purpose of preventing the witness from attending or testifying.

(b) Hearsay exceptions. The following are not excluded by the hearsay rule if the declarant is unavailable as a witness:

(1) Former testimony. Testimony given as a witness at another hearing of the same or a different proceeding, or in a deposition taken in compliance with law in the course of the same or another proceeding, if the party against whom the testimony is now offered, or, in a civil action or proceeding, a predecessor in interest, had an opportunity and similar motive to develop the testimony by direct, cross, or redirect examination.

(2) Statement under belief impending death. In a prosecution for homicide or in a civil action or proceeding, a statement made by a declarant while believing that the declarant's death was imminent, concerning the cause or circumstances of what the declarant believed to be impending death.

(3) Statement against interest. A statement which was at the time of its making so far contrary to the declarant's pecuniary or proprietary interest, or so far tended to subject the declarant to civil or criminal liability, or to render invalid a claim by the declarant against another, that a reasonable person in the declarant's position would not have made the statement unless believing it to be true. A statement tending to expose the declarant to criminal liability and offered to exculpate the accused is not admissible unless corroborating circumstances clearly indicate the trustworthiness of the statement.

Rule 901. Requirement of Authentication or Identification

(a) General provision. The requirement of authentication or identification as a condition precedent to admissibility is satisfied by evidence sufficient to support a finding that the matter in question is what its proponent claims.

(b) Illustrations. By way of illustration only, and not by way of limitation, the following are examples of authentication or identification conforming with the requirements of this rule:

(1) **Testimony of witness with knowledge.** Testimony that a matter is what it is claimed to be.

(2) **Nonexpert opinion on handwriting.** Nonexpert opinion as to the genuineness of handwriting, based upon familiarity not acquired for purposes of the litigation.

(3) **Comparison by trier or expert witness.** Comparison by the trier of fact or by expert witnesses with specimens which have been authenticated.

(4) **Distinctive characteristics and the like.** Appearance, contents, substance, internal patterns, or other distinctive characteristics, taken in conjunction with circumstances.

(5) **Voice identification.** Identification of a voice, whether heard firsthand or through mechanical or electronic transmission or recording, by opinion based upon hearing the voice at any time under circumstances connecting it with the alleged speaker.

(6) **Telephone conversations.** Telephone conversations, by evidence that a call was made to the number assigned at the time by the telephone company to a particular person or business, if (A) in the case of a person, circumstances, including self-identification, show the person answering to be the one called, or (B) in the case of a business, the call was made to a place of business and the conversation related to business reasonably transacted over the telephone.

(7) **Public records or reports.** Evidence that a writing authorized by law to be recorded or filed and in fact recorded or filed in a public office, or a purported public record, report, statement, or data compilation, in any form, is from the public office where items of this nature are kept.

(8) **Ancient documents or data compilation.** Evidence that a document or data compilation, in any form, (A) is in such condition as to create no suspicion concerning its authenticity, (B) was in a place where it, if authentic, would likely be, and (C) has been in existence 20 years or more at the time it is offered.

(9) **Process or system.** Evidence describing a process or system used to produce a result and showing that the process or system produces an accurate result.

(10) **Methods provided by statute or rule.** Any method of authentication or identification provided by Act of Congress or by other rules prescribed by the Supreme Court pursuant to statutory authority.

Rule 902. Self-authentication

Extrinsic evidence of authenticity as a condition precedent to admissibility is not required with respect to the following:

(1) **Domestic public documents under seal.** A document bearing a seal purporting to be that of the United States, or of any State, district,

Commonwealth, territory, or insular possession thereof, or the Panama Canal Zone, or the Trust Territory of the Pacific Islands, or of a political subdivision, department, officer, or agency thereof, and a signature purporting to be an attestation or execution.

(2) Domestic public documents not under seal. A document purporting to bear the signature in the official capacity of an officer or employee of any entity included in paragraph (1) hereof, having no seal, if a public officer having a seal and having official duties in the district or political subdivision of the officer or employee certifies under seal that the signer has the official capacity and that the signature is genuine.

(3) Foreign public documents. A document purporting to be executed or attested in an official capacity by a person authorized by the laws of a foreign country to make the execution or attestation, and accompanied by a final certification as to the genuineness of the signature and official position (A) of the executing or attesting person, or (B) of any foreign official whose certificate of genuineness of signature and official position relates to the execution or attestation or is in a chain of certificates of genuineness of signature and official position relating to the execution or attestation. A final certification may be made by a secretary of an embassy or legation, consul general, consul, vice consul, or consular agent of the United States, or a diplomatic or consular official of the foreign country assigned or accredited to the United States. If reasonable opportunity has been given to all parties to investigate the authenticity and accuracy of official documents, the court may, for good cause shown, order that they be treated as presumptively authentic without final certification or permit them to be evidenced by an attested summary with or without final certification.

(4) Certified copies of public records. A copy of an official record or report or entry therein, or of a document authorized by law to be recorded or filed and actually recorded or filed in a public office, including data compilations in any form, certified as correct by the custodian or other person authorized to make the certification, by certificate complying with paragraph (1), (2), or (3) of this rule or complying with any Act of Congress or rule prescribed by the Supreme Court pursuant to statutory authority.

(5) Official publications. Books, pamphlets, or other publications purporting to be issued by public authority.

(6) Newspapers and periodicals. Printed materials purporting to be newspapers or periodicals.

(7) Trade inscriptions and the like. Inscriptions, signs, tags, or labels purporting to have been affixed in the course of business and indicating ownership, control, or origin.

(8) Acknowledged documents. Documents accompanied by a certificate of acknowledgment executed in the manner provided by law by a notary public or other officer authorized by law to take acknowledgments.

(9) Commercial paper and related documents. Commercial paper, signatures thereon, and documents relating thereto to the extent provided by general commercial law.

(10) Presumptions under Acts of Congress. Any signature, document, or other matter declared by Act of Congress to be presumptively or prima facie genuine or authentic.

Rule 1001. Definitions

For purposes of this article the following definitions are applicable:

(1) Writings and recordings. "Writings" and "recordings" consist of letters, words, or numbers, or their equivalent, set down by handwriting, typewriting, printing, photostating, photographing, magnetic impulse, mechanical or electronic recording, or other form of data compilation.

(2) Photographs. "Photographs" include still photographs, X-ray films, video tapes, and motion pictures.

(3) Original. An "original" of a writing or recording is the writing or recording itself or any counterpart intended to have the same effect by a person executing or issuing it. An "original" of a photograph includes the negative or any print therefrom. If data are stored in a computer or similar device, any printout or other output readable by sight, shown to reflect the data accurately, is an "original."

(4) Duplicate. A "duplicate" is a counterpart produced by the same impression as the original, or from the same matrix, or by means of photography, including enlargements and miniatures, or by mechanical or electronic re-recording, or by chemical reproduction, or by other equivalent techniques which accurately reproduces the original.

Rule 1002. Requirement of Original

To prove the content of a writing, recording, or photograph, the original writing, recording, or photograph is required, except as otherwise provided in these rules or by Act of Congress.

Rule 1003. Admissibility of Duplicates

A duplicate is admissible to the same extent as an original unless (1) a genuine question is raised as to the authenticity of the original or (2) in the circumstances it would be unfair to admit the duplicate in lieu of the original.

Rule 1005. Public Records

The contents of an official record, or of a document authorized to be recorded or filed and actually recorded or filed, including data compilations in any form, if otherwise admissible, may be proved by copy, certified as correct in accordance with rule 902 or testified to be correct by a witness who has compared it with the original. If a copy which complies with the foregoing cannot be obtained by the exercise of reasonable diligence, then other evidence of the contents may be given.

Appendix I

California Notice Statute

§911.2. Time of presentation of claims; limitation

A claim relating to a cause of action for death or for injury to person or to personal property or growing crops shall be presented as provided in Article 2 (commencing with Section 915) of this chapter not later than six months after the accrual of the cause of action. A claim relating to any other cause of action shall be presented as provided in Article 2 (commencing with Section 915) of this chapter not later than one year after the accrual of the cause of action.

Appendix J

Massachusetts Lawyers Diary and Manual

1998

MASSACHUSETTS

LAWYERS DIARY

AND

MANUAL®

INCLUDING BAR DIRECTORY

Provided with the 1998 Massachusetts Courts, Maps and Judges Supplement including the legal pages®.

MASSACHUSETTS LAWYERS DIARY AND MANUAL®

240 Mulberry Street, P.O. Box 50

Newark, N.J. 07101-0050

(973) 642-1440

(800) 444-4041

FAX (973) 642-4280

E-mail: mail@lawdiary.com

Visit our web site at http://www.lawdiary.com

Reprinted with permission from the 1998 Massachusetts Lawyers Diary Manual® © 1996, Skinder-Strauss Associates.

TABLE OF CONTENTS

Index 5
Courts, Judges and Officials
  United States 17
  Massachusetts
    State Courts... 25
    County Courts and Offices 31
      including Courts, Registry Offices, Sheriffs, Deputy Sheriffs, Jails,
      District Attorneys, Law Libraries, County Commissioners, Treasurers
      and Public Administrators
Municipal Directories
  Municipal Officials.. 80
  Municipal Tax Rates 134
  Municipality/Zip Code/Area Code Chart................................... 137
Court Reporters
  Official Court Reporters... 140
Costs and Fees
  United States Courts 141
  State Courts 143
  Secretary of the Commonwealth 147
  Registry of Deeds 149
  Document Stamp Rates 150
  Sheriffs, Deputy Sheriffs and Constables.................................. 151
Legal Summaries
  Digest of Massachusetts Civil Procedure 152
  Digest of the Federal Rules of Civil Procedure............................ 161
  Marriage and Divorce Laws, All States 168
  ABC's of Massachusetts Divorce Practice.................................. 176
  Massachusetts Estate Tax.. 189
  Table of Life Expectancy and Mortality 191
  Table for Computation of Expiration Dates 192
Departments and Agencies
  State 198
  Federal
    Legislative Branch 215
    Executive Branch 215
    Independent Establishments and Government Corporations............... 224
    Quasi-Official Agencies... 233
National Directory of States
  including key state offices throughout the country 234
  Non-Military Service Affidavits 296
  Weather Records 296
  Overseas Birth and Death Records... 296
Miscellaneous Directories
  Correctional Institutions... 297
  Hospitals... 299
  Insurance Companies and Claims Managers................................ 310
  Bar Associations... 318
  Professional Associations... 325
  Alternative Dispute Resolution Providers 327
  Legal Aid and Referral Offices 332
  Pro Bono Organizations... 337
  Law Schools 341
  Map of Massachusetts 342
  U.S. Customs Service Directory 344
  Naturalization Information Field Offices 347
  Degrees of Kindred Chart 348
Holidays and Dates to Remember
  Holidays
    All States 349
    Massachusetts.. 351
  Tax Dates 352
Directory of Judges 769
Directory of the Bar
  Alphabetically (Green Pages) 779
  Boston... 1100
  By City, Outside Boston.. 1129
Miscellaneous Charts
  Lawyers Medical Charts 1181
  50 States and their Counties.. 1191
  Section of Land Showing Acreage and Distances............................ 1196
  Pro-Rating Table for Rent, Taxes and Insurance........................... 1197
  Loan Amortization Chart... 1198
Attorney Advertisement
  Expanded Information for Attorneys and Firms 1200
  Patent Attorneys 1201
  by Areas of Practice 1203

Side tabs:
Court & Governmental Information
Municipal Information
Filing Fees
Digest of Civil Procedure Rule
Probate & Family Information
Departments & Agencies
National Directory of States
Directory of Judges

Reprinted with permission from the 1998 Massachusetts Lawyers Diary Manual® © 1996, Skinder-Strauss Associates.

GLOSSARY

Active listening. A method of listening in which the listener encourages a person to talk without judging or threatening.

American Bar Association. A voluntary organization that establishes ethical standards and promotes the legal profession.

Articles of Incorporation. Documents that an organization must file with the state to become a corporation.

Attorney-client privilege. A privilege held by a client that protects the confidentiality of the relationship between the client and his or her attorney.

Authorization. Notarized document that permits the release of confidential information.

Boolean query. Method of inquiry in Computer Assisted Legal Research (CALR) using terms and connectors to search.

Breach of contract. A theory of law in which one of the parties to a contract has not done what is required under the terms of the contract.

By-laws. Laws regulating city, towns, corporations, and associations.

Case facts. Facts that tend to prove or disprove a theory of law or that form the basis of a transaction.

Case law. Court decisions.

Case management. Organizing and tracking cases on a daily basis to be certain all deadlines are met and no case is neglected.

CD-ROM. Compact disk-read-only memory; full text research tool.

Certified copy. A copy of an original document that has been sworn by the keeper of the original to be true and accurate, usually bearing an official seal.

Charter. The governing document of a city, town, or group.

Chronology. Events given in order by time.

Circumstantial evidence. Evidence that requires the finder of fact to draw a reasonable inference from other facts that have been proven.

Citator. A volume (or computer legal research program) that indicates whether certain law is still valid. A citator can lead to cases that discuss, distinguish, limit, or expand the cited law.

Civil case. A matter of a noncriminal nature involving private or public parties seeking damages or injunctive relief.

Claim. Assertion of entitlement to recovery under law.

Client facts. Facts related by the client to the interviewer that the client believes supports his or her position or claim.

Closed corporation. Corporation with fewer shareholders and fewer formalities than a regular corporation but one that provides similar legal protection.

Code. Federal or state laws and statutes organized into volumes.

Collateral. Real or personal property used to secure a loan; can be sold in the event of a default.

Common law. Judge-made law.

Community property. Property held equally by the husband and the wife.

Comparative negligence. An affirmative defense to negligence that apportions liability for injuries between the plaintiff and the defendant according to extent of each party's negligence.

Complaint. The pleading filed by the aggrieved party to begin a civil action.

Conflict of interest. Competing interests usually characterized by the representation by the same firm of two or more clients with adverse interests.

Contingency fee. A type of retainer agreement in which attorney's fees are equal to a percentage of the recovery after costs are deducted. No recovery, no fees.

Contract. An agreement between two or more people or entities enforceable by law.

Corporation. Legal entity formed by a group of individuals (or other entities) who operate a business accountable to shareholders who generally are not liable for wrongdoing of the corporation.

Correspondence file. File containing all correspondence pertinent to the case.

Corroboration. Validation, usually of a client's statement.

Court documents/Pleadings file. File containing every document filed with the court.

Credible. Believable.

Criminal action. A matter in which a state or federal government brings an action against an individual accused of violating a criminal law. The burden of proof is on the government (prosecution) and requires proof beyond reasonable doubt. In the event of conviction, a criminal case may result in a financial penalty, imprisonment, and in capital cases, death.

Damages. Money requested by the plaintiff from the defendant in a civil action.

Default. Failure of a party to answer the complaint resulting in judgment being granted to the other party.

Defendant. Person against whom the complaint (civil) or charge or indictment (criminal) is brought.

Defense. Legal reason why liability should not attach.

Demonstrative evidence. Evidence that is not the actual (real) evidence in the litigation; rather, it is evidence prepared by a party to demonstrate something to the judge or jury to help them understand a fact in the case.

Deposition. Testimony taken under oath before an authorized reporter, usually as part of pretrial discovery.

Deposition file. File containing deposition transcripts and summaries.

Digest. A collection of volumes of case notes arranged in topical order for research purposes.

Direct evidence. Evidence that does not require the finder of fact to draw an inference from any other facts.

Discoverable information. Information held by one party that must be made available to the other party. Information need not be admissible as evidence to be discoverable.

Discovery. The process in litigation in which the parties are required to trade information about their respective cases.

Documents file. The file that contains originals and copies of all relevant documents.

Encyclopedia. A resource to research legal topics by subject area.

Evidence (admissible). Written, spoken or graphic information that the court has deemed acceptable to prove or disprove any aspect of a case.

Evidence (inadmissible). Information that is not accepted by the court to prove or disprove any aspect of a case, for reasons including relevancy, privilege, and bias.

Expert witness. Witness qualified by the court to give expert opinion on a particular matter.

Federal Rules of Civil Procedure. The rules issued by the Judicial Conference of the United States that control the process of litigation.

Federal Rules of Evidence. The rules issued by the Judicial Conference of the United States to regulate evidence during litigation.

Fee simple absolute. Complete ownership of real property with unqualified right to devise.

File memorandum. Memorandum to the case file detailing some aspect of the case.

First-hand knowledge. Information a person knows because she has experienced it through one of her senses.

Fixed fee. A type of retainer agreement in which client fees are established at the outset of the case and do not change.

Floor control. A method of keeping the interview orderly and on time, usually by interrupting the speaker.

Formal investigation. Fact investigation through the regulated discovery process.

Grantee. Buyer of real property.

Grantor. Seller of real property.

Hearsay. Oral, written, or demonstrative statement made out of court and offered in court to prove the matter contained in the statement.

Homestead exemption. Protects an owner's equity in the property he occupies from creditors.

Hostile witness. A witness whose testimony is unfavorable to your case or who has a bias against your client.

Hourly fee. Client fees are determined by the number of hours worked on the case.

Impeachment. The discrediting of a witness or evidence at trial.

Informal investigation. Fact investigation conducted outside the discovery process.

Inhibitor. A reason a person is unwilling or unable to provide information.

Intake form. Initial form completed by client to provide preliminary information.

Internet. Worldwide system of computers hooked together to share information.

Interoffice memorandum. An organized recitation of facts, information obtained from the interview, application of law, and recommendations.

Interrogatories. Discovery mechanism in the form of written questions to another party.

Interview summary. A synopsis of the interview prepared from outline notes and consisting of facts, statement of problem, narrative summary, impressions of client, and follow-up.

Joint tenancy. A form of property ownership in which two or more individuals hold the property with the right of survivorship.

Jury instructions. Statements of law given by the judge to the jury to guide the jury in reaching its decision.

Kinesics. Relationship between body language and speech.

Lawsuit. *See* civil case.

Leading question. A question that suggests the answer, often presented to a witness as an assertion to which the witness either agrees or disagrees.

Legal theory. The legal principle that establishes the rights and responsibilities of a person.

LEXIS. Direct-dial commercial full-text research tool.

Life estate. An interest in real property that gives a person complete rights to the property during his or her life.

Limited liability company. Hybrid partnership/simplified corporation.

Litigation. The entire process from the filing of a complaint to the final judgment, including appeal.

Litigation chart. Chart organizing elements of law, sources of proof, and results of investigation.

Motivator. A mechanism to encourage conversation.

Natural language. Method of inquiry in Computer Assisted Legal Research (CALR) using regular language to search.

Negligence. A theory of law in which a successful plaintiff can show that the defendant failed to conform to a standard of conduct and that failure resulted in damages to the plaintiff.

Nonleading question. A question that does not suggest the answer.

Nonprofit corporation. Corporation that reinvests profits in corporation. Also called a 501(c)(3) corporation.

Ordinance. A law enacted by a city or a town.

Outline. Sketch of interview using words and phrases.

Partnership. A legal relationship involving two or more individuals participating in a business venture sharing profits and risks.

Passive listening. A method of listening in which, through eye contact and gestures, a person is encouraged to talk.

Personal jurisdiction. Personal jurisdiction is the power of a court over an individual.

Plaintiff. Person who brings the lawsuit.

Pleadings. Claims for relief, including complaints, counterclaims, and crossclaims, and responses to the claims.

Pocket part. The current update to various research materials, usually fitting in the "pocket" in the back of the volume.

Primary law. Constitutions, statutes, regulations, and court decisions.

Privilege. The ability of a person who holds the privilege to prevent testimony about a confidential communication (for example, spousal; attorney-client; doctor-patient; priest-penitent).

Procedural law. The law that controls the process of the lawsuit.

Rapport. Relationship between two people (in this case, the client and the paralegal) based on mutual trust; allows for full disclosure.

Real evidence. Generally, physical evidence directly involved in the litigation.

Regulation. A law enacted by an agency, also called an "administrative regulation" or "rule."

Relevant. "Relating to," "pertaining to," or "of some consequence to" the case.

Reporter. A collection of volumes that contains case decisions for a particular geographic area or, on the federal level, nationwide.

Request for admission. Discovery device that asks another party to admit to certain uncontested facts before trial.

Research file. File holding research addressing a legal issue.

Respondeat superior. A principle of agency law imputing the liability of an employee to the employer.

Search directory. An Internet tool that searches sites by subject and key words.

Search engine. An Internet tool that searches all protocols by key words and advanced search methods.

Self-authenticating. A document that does not have to be validated by its custodian at trial (for example, a certified copy of a record).

Shepard's. A well-known citator.

Sole tenancy. A type of ownership of real property in which a single individual or entity holds the property alone.

Statute. A federal or state law enacted by the legislature.

Statute of limitations. A law that limits the time in which a person has to bring a lawsuit.

Subject matter jurisdiction. Power of the court over the subject matter of the case (for example, a bankruptcy court has the authority to hear bankruptcy cases).

Subpoena. Document issued by court or agency mandating appearance at a deposition, trial, or other legal proceeding.

Substantive law. Law that controls the legal aspects of a case.

Summary. Précis of the interview, including statement of problem, description, analysis, other concerns, and follow-up.

Tenancy by the entirety. A form of property ownership limited to married persons in which each person owns 100 percent of the property and neither person may encumber the property without the consent of the other.

Tenancy in common. A form of property ownership in which two or more unmarried individuals hold the property with no right of survivorship.

Theory chart. Chart that organizes the elements, supporting facts, and discovery for a cause of action. Also called a litigation chart.

Tickler system. Reminder system.

Time-line. Chronological statement of events.

Title search. Review of property records in order to determine whether the owner has clear title to the property.

Topic control. Bringing the client or witness back to the discussion, usually by interruption, after the person digresses.

Tort. A civil wrong, like negligence, trespass, assault, or battery.

Tort claims act. Federal or state statute that allows a government unit to be sued.

Transaction. Nonadversarial (nonlitigation) work done for a client.

Trial. The adversarial process by which parties present evidence to a judge/jury to resolve a complaint.

Westlaw. Direct-dial commercial full-text research tool.

Witness. A person, including a party, who has first-hand information about an incident.

Witness file. File containing the name, addresses, phone numbers, testimony summaries, and subpoena information for all witnesses.

Work product. Work performed by an attorney or paralegal and not discoverable by the other party.

Bibliography

Bastress, Robert M., and Joseph D. Harbaugh, Interviewing, Counseling, and Negotiating, Little, Brown and Co., 1990.

Best, Arthur, Evidence: Examples and Explanations, Little, Brown and Co., 1994.

Binder, David A., Paul Bergman & Susan C. Price, Lawyers as Counselors: A Client-Centered Approach, West Publishing Co., 1991.

Burns, Marilyn, The Book of Think, Little, Brown and Co., 1976.

Cannon, Therese A., Ethics and Professional Responsibility for Legal Assistants, Little, Brown and Co., 1992.

Culligan, Joseph, You, Too, Can Find Anybody, Hallmark Press, 1993.

Eimermann, Thomas E., Fundamentals of Paralegalism, 3d ed., Little, Brown and Co., 1992.

Gillers, Stephen, and Roy D. Simon, Jr., Regulation of Lawyers: Statutes and Standards, Little, Brown & Co., 1995.

Jandt, Fred E., Effective Interviewing for Paralegals, Anderson Publishing Company, 1995.

Mauet, Thomas, and Marlene A. Maerowitz, Fundamentals of Litigation for Paralegals, Little, Brown and Co., 1996.

Mueller, Christopher B., and Laird C. Kirkpatrick, Evidence, Little, Brown & Co., 1995.

Pener, Michael, Discovery: Interviewing and Investigation, Pearson Publications Co., 1995.

Rogers, Carl, On Becoming A Person, Houghton Mifflin Publishers, 1961.

Tannen, Deborah, You Just Don't Understand: Women and Men in Conversation, Ballentine Books, 1990.

White, E. B., and William Strunk, Jr., Elements of Style, 3d Edition, Allyn and Bacon, 1979.

Zinsser, William, On Writing Well, Harper Perennial, 1994.

Zinsser, William, Writing to Learn, Harper Perennial, 1988.

Index

Abacus Law Plus
  calendaring, 141
  case management, 141
  conflict of interest check, 78
  preserving files, 137
ABA Model Code of Professional
    Responsibility
  payment to witness, 102
ABA Model Guidelines for Utilization of Legal
    Assistant Services, 32
ABA Model Rules of Professional Conduct
  attorney-client privilege, 15
  confidentiality, 77–78
  conflict of interest, 78–79
  discovery, 11
  paralegal responsibility, 76–77
  payment to witness, 102
  third persons, respect for rights of, 102
Agency opinions, 35
Annual reports, 164
Articles of incorporation, 164–165
Asking questions
  chronology, obtaining, 58–59
  closed questions, 51, 52
  direct questions, 51, 53
  follow-up questions, 57
  indirect questions, 51
  introduction, 50–51
  keeping it simple, 59–60
  leading questions, 53–54
  nonleading questions, 51–53
  open questions, 51, 52, 53
  silence, 57
  time-lines, 58–59
Assignment sheet, 34
Assumptions, 64
Attorney-client privilege
  ABA Mode Rules of Professional Conduct,
    rule 1.6, 15
  exceptions to, 14
  incompetent, 15
  nondiscoverable information, 12, 14–15
  third party, 14, 15
  underage person, 15
Attorney-client relationship
  children, 69
Audio recording
  preserving information, 131–132
Authoritative client, 90
Authorizations, *See* Documents

Bar Associations
  source of information, as, 189–190
Behaviorism, 95
Birth records
  source of information, as, 184–185
Boolean query, 37
Breach of contract, 42
  jury instruction, 41
Business organizations
  annual reports, 164
  articles of incorporation, 164–165
  custody, 166
  divorce, 165
  family, 165
  generally, 164
  licenses, 164
  marriage, 165
  separation, 165–166
By-laws, 35

Calendaring, 140–141
California Statute, Appendix I
Case facts, 8–9
Case investigation file
  Hannah West, Appendix A
Case law, 35
Case management, 140–141
CD-ROM
  computer-assisted legal research, 37
Cemetery records
  source of information, as, 187
Census
  source of information, as, 186–187
Change of address
  source of information, as, 187–188
Charters, 35
Child in need of assistance (CHINA), 69
Child in need of supervision (CHINS), 69
Children
  attorney-client relationship, 69
  Court Appointed Special Advocate, 69
  guardian ad litem, 69
  interviewing, 68–70
Chronology
  obtaining, 58–59
Circumstantial evidence, 18–19
Citators, 35, 37
Civil cases
  discovery, 10

Clearinghouse on Licensure, Enforcement, and
    Regulation (CLEAR)
  source of information, as, 187–188
Client, 7
  authoritative client, 90
  case facts, 8–9
  competency of client, 68
  facts, 8–9
  preparing case with, 7
  subservient client, 90
Client facts, 8–9
Client interview
  angry client, 94
  client rapport, See Client rapport
  client who lies, 93
  criminal accusation, 92
  difficult clients
    angry client, 94
    client who lies, 93
  doing the right thing, 88
  empathy, 87–88
  helping theories, See Helping theories
  inhibitors
    authoritative client, 90
    embarrassment, 90
    generally, 88–89, 91
    importance of information, unawareness
      of, 91
    inability to focus, 90–91
    jeopardy to case, 89
    subservient client, 90
    threat to self-esteem, 89
  introduction, 75–76
  motivators
    doing the right thing, 88
    empathy, 87–88
    generally, 91
    praise, 88
    winning the prize, 88
  paralegal-client relationship, See Paralegal-
      client relationship
  praise, 88
  preparing client for interview, See Preparing
      client for interview
Client rapport
  attorney-client relationship, 79
  correspondence, 86
  dress, 80
  electronic mail, 87
  establishing rapport, 80
  maintaining rapport
    correspondence, 86
    electronic mail, 87
    telephone calls, 86–87
  telephone calls, 86–87
Closed corporation
  legal identity, 149
Common law, 35
Community property, 161
Competency of client
  interviewing skills, 68
Computer-assisted legal research
  Boolean query, 37
  CD-ROM, 37

Cornell Law School Legal Information
    Institute, 38
  Government Printing Office Access System,
    38
  internet, 38–39
  internet sites (representative), 39
  Lawyers Legal Research, 38
  LEXIS, 37
  LOIS Law Library, 38
  natural language search, 37
  Westlaw, 37
Confidentiality
  attorney-client privilege, See Attorney-client
      privilege
  consent to release confidential information,
    178
  paralegal responsibility, 77–78
Conflict of interest
  check, 78
  paralegal responsibility, 78–79
Constitutions, 34
Contract action, 42–43
  organization chart, 42–43
Controlling the interview, 62
Copies
  certified, 197–198
  uncertified, 198
Cornell Law School Legal Information
    Institute, 38
Coroner
  source of information, as, 191
Corporation
  legal identity, 149
Correspondence file
  preserving, 138
Court Appointed Special Advocate
  children, 69
Court decisions, 35
Courthouse
  source of information, as, 182–183
Criminal cases
  client interview, 92
  discovery, 10
Criminal records
  source of information, as, 183
Cross-reference directory
  source of information, as, 191
Cultural differences
  dynamics of communication, 66–67
Curriculum vitae
  expert witness, 108
Custody, 166

Databases, 197, 198
Death records
  source of information, as, 185
Deeds, registry of
  source of information, as, 184
Demonstrative evidence
  preserving information, 134
Department of Defense records
  source of information, as, 187

Department of Motor Vehicles (DMV)
  source of information, as, 181–182
Deposition file
  preserving, 140
Depositions upon oral examination, 11
Direct evidence, 18
Discovery
  civil, 10
  criminal, 10
  devices, 13
  effect on interview and investigative
    process, 9
  ethical rules, 11–12
  formal discovery, 9–12
  informal discovery, 9
  pretrial discovery, 9
Divorce, 165
Divorce records
  source of information, as, 183–184, 186
Documents
  authorizations
    obtaining, 174–178
    sample authorization, 177
    sample coverletter, 176
    scope of, 174
  consent to release confidential information,
    178
  investigation checklist for documents, 179
  organization, 179
  private, 173–174
  production of documents, 11
  public, 173
Documents file
  preserving, 139
Dynamics of communication
  assumptions, 64
  cultural differences, 66–67
  gender, 67
  nonverbal communication, 65–66

Elderly
  interviewing skills, 67–68
Empathy
  client interview, 87–88
Ethics
  discovery, 11–12
  interview, 71
  investigation process, 199
  paralegal-client relationship, *See* Paralegal-
    client relationship
  paralegals, 6–7
  witness interview, *See* Witness interview
Evidence
  character, of, 19
  circumstantial evidence, 18–19
  demonstrative evidence, 134
  direct evidence, 18
  hearsay, *See* Hearsay
  insurance coverage, 20
  introduction, 17
  911 tapes, 134
  offer to compromise, 20
  offer to pay expenses, 20

pathology reports, 134
preserving information, *See* Preserving
  information
real evidence, 134
relevant evidence, 17–18
subsequent repair, 19–20
surveillance tapes, 134
television news stories, 134
Evidence of character, 19
Executive orders, 35
Expert witness
  curriculum vitae, 108
  finding experts, 108
  theirs, 108
  when used, 107
  yours, 107

Family, 165
Federal Government
  source of information, as, 190–191
Federal Reporter (F.), 35
Federal Reporter 2d (F.2d), 35
Federal Reporter 3d (F.3d), 35
Federal Rules Decisions (F.R.D.), 35
Federal Rules of Civil Procedure
  depositions upon oral examination, 11
  discovery, 11
  interrogatories to parties, 11
  physical and mental examination of persons,
    12
  production of documents, 11
  requests for admission, 12
  rule 26, 11
  rule 30, 11
  rule 33, 11
  rule 34, 11
  rule 35, 12
  rule 36, 12
  rule 45, 11
  selected rules, text, Appendix G
Federal Rules of Evidence
  admission of a party opponent, 21
  dying declaration, 22
  excited utterance, 21–22
  insurance coverage, 20
  offer to compromise, 20
  offer to pay expenses, 20
  present sense impression, 21–22
  relevant evidence, 17–18
  rule 401, 17–18
  rule 404, 19
  rule 407, 19–20
  rule 408, 20
  rule 409, 20
  rule 411, 20
  rule 802, 21
  rule 803, 21–22
  rule 804, 22
  selected rules, text, Appendix H
  subsequent repair, 19–20
Federal Supplement (F. Supp), 35
Fee simple absolute, 161
Floor control, 62

Follow-up questions, 57
Formal discovery, 9–12
Freedom of Information Act (FOIA)
    investigating, 172
    request for information, 190–191
    sample letters, Appendix F
    text, Appendix E

Gender
    dynamics of communication, 67
General laws, 35
Governmental unit
    legal identity, 150
Government Printing Office Access System, 38
Grantor/grantee indices, 162
Guardian ad litem, 69

Hearsay
    admission of party opponent, 21
    defined, 20
    dying declaration, 22
    exceptions, 23
    excited utterance, 21–22
    generally, 20–21
    present sense impression, 21–22
    records, 21
    statements against interest, 22
    state of mind, statements regarding, 22
Helping theories
    behaviorism, 95
    generally, 94
    person-centered theory, 95
    psychoanalysis, 94–95
    rational-emotive therapy, 95
    transactional analysis, 95–96
Homestead exemption, 162

Illiteracy
    client's, 68
Impeachment
    bias of witness, 24
    contradiction, 24
    defined, 22
    grounds for, 24
    interest, 24
    prior conviction, 22
    prior inconsistent statement, 24
    reputation for truthfulness, 24
Incompetent
    attorney-client privilege, 15
Individuals
    legal identity, 148
Informal discovery, 9
Insurance coverage
    evidence, exempt from, 20
Intake sheet, Appendix C
Internet
    access, 192–193
    general sites, 194
    preparing for interview, 38–39
    source of information, as

businesses, finding, 194–195
    corporate, 195–196
    finding people and documents, 192
    generally, 191–192
    individuals, finding, 194–195
    medical, 195
    miscellaneous, 196
    terminology, 192–193
Interrogatories to parties, 11
Interview
    asking questions, See Asking questions
    case facts, 8–9
    client facts, 8–9
    controlling the interview, 62
    defined, 1
    discovery, See Discovery
    model interview, 54–56
    preparing for, See Preparing for interview
    purpose, 31–32
    role of paralegal, 32
    scenarios, 1–3
    structuring the interview, 49–50
    telephone, See Telephone interview
    witness interview, See Witness interview
Interviewing skills
    asking questions, See Asking questions
    children, 68–70
    competency of client, 68
    controlling the interview, 62
    dynamics of communication, See Dynamics
        of communication
    elderly, 67–68
    ethical considerations, 71
    flexible thinking, 70
    illiteracy, client's, 68
    listening to client, See Listening to client
    structuring the interview, 49–50
Investigating skills
    documents, See Documents
    Federal and State laws
        Freedom of Information Act (FOIA), 172
        Open Meeting Laws, 173
        Privacy Act, 171–172
    finding information
        generally, 181
        sources, See Sources of information
    finding people, 180
    introduction, 171
    obtaining copies
        certified, 197–198
        noncertified, 198
Investigation
    defined, 1
    discovery, See Discovery
Investigation plan, 152–158
    final theory chart, 158
    theory chart, 153, 157
Investigation process
    business organizations, See Business
        organizations
    defining scope
        generally, 150–151
        how, 152
        what, 151

when, 152
where, 152
who, 151
why, 151
ethical considerations, 199
formal, 146
informal, 146
introduction, 145
legal identities, *See* Legal identities
observation, 167
paralegal as witness, *See* Paralegal as witness
real property, *See* Real property
supporting statements, 159–160
unexpected, 146–147

Joint tenancy, 161
Jury instruction, 41

Lawyers Legal Research, 38
Legal identities
    closed corporation, 149
    corporation, 149
    governmental unit, 150
    individuals, 148
    limited liability company (LLC), 149–150
    nonprofit corporation, 149
    partnership, 149
Legal sources
    generally, 34–35
    locations, and, 36
Legal theory, 34
LEXIS, 37
Libraries
    source of information, as, 190
Licenses, 164
Life estate, 162
Limited liability company (LLC)
    legal identity, 149–150
Listening to client
    active listening, 60–61
    effectively, 60
    passive listening, 61–62
Litigation
    formal discovery, 10
    generally, 1
    overview, 4
    process, 4
LOIS Law Library, 38

Malpractice claim
    preserving information, 113–114
Marriage, 165
Marriage, certificate of
    source of information, as, 186
Martindale-Hubbell Law Directory
    source of information, as, 189–190
Massachusetts Lawyers Diary and Manual,
        Appendix J
Medical records
    source of information, as, 191

Military records
    source of information, as, 187
Model Code of Professional Responsibility,
        ABA
    payment to witness, 102
Model Guidelines for Utilization of Legal
        Assistant Services, ABA, 32
Model Jury Instructions, 41
Model Rules of Professional Conduct, *See* ABA
        Model Rules of Professional Conduct

National Association of Legal Assistants
        (NALA), 7
National Federation of Paralegal Associations
        (NFPA), 7
Natural language search, 37
Negligence action, 40–41, 43
Newspapers
    source of information, as, 190
911 tapes
    preserving information, 134
Nondiscoverable information
    attorney-client privilege, 12, 14–15
    work product doctrine, 15–16
Nonlitigation, 5
Nonprofit corporation
    legal identity, 149
Nonverbal communication, 65–66

Offer to compromise
    evidence, exempt from, 20
Offer to pay expenses
    evidence, exempt from, 20
Open Meeting Laws, 173
Ordinances, 35
Organization chart, 41–43, 44, 45
Organizing law for interview, 39–45
    Model Jury Instructions, 41
    organization chart, 41–43, 44, 45
    theory chart, 40

Paralegal
    assignment sheet, 34
    ethics, 6–7
    role of, 6, 32
Paralegal as witness
    circumstances, 166
    procedure, 166–167
Paralegal-attorney relationship
    interview, 32–34
    investigation
        getting good instructions, 147
        understanding limitations, 147–148
Paralegal-client relationship
    ABA Model Rules of Professional Conduct,
        76–77, 78, 79
    client rapport, See Client rapport
    confidentiality, 77–78
    conflict of interest, 78–79
    ethics
        confidentiality, 77–78

conflict of interest, 78–79
  paralegal responsibility, 76–77
introduction, 76
paralegal responsibility, 76–77
Partnership
  legal identity, 149
Pathology reports
  preserving information, 134
Payment to witness, 102
Person-centered theory, 95
Person in need of supervision (PINS), 69
Pet licenses
  source of information, as, 188
Photographs
  preserving information, 132–134
Photo sheet
  preserving information, 135
Physical and mental examination of persons, 12
Plaintiff and defendant tables
  source of information, as, 183
Pleadings
  preserving, 139
Postal Service
  source of information, as, 187
Preparing client for interview
  greeting the client, 81–82
  initial contact, 81
  physical setting, 82–84
  seating configuration, 83
  setting the tone, 84–86
Preparing for interview
  citators, 35, 37
  introduction, 29
  legal sources, 34–35
  legal theory, 34
  organization chart, 41–43, 44, 45
  organizing law, *See* Organizing law for interview
  purpose, 31–32
Preserving information
  accurate record, 112
  audio recording, 131–132
  client information
    follow-up interview, 118
    Gladys Winston file, 118–127
    interoffice memorandum, 118, 125–127
    interview, 120–123
    interview summary, 124
    post-interview, 123
    pre-interview, 118
    preliminary information, 114
    sample intake form, 115
    taking notes, 116
    theory chart, 119, 125
    writing summary, 116–118
  demonstrative evidence, 134
  evidentiary considerations
    demonstrative evidence, 134–136
    photo sheet, 135
    real evidence, 134
  files
    Abacus Law Plus, 137
    correspondence file, 138

court documents file, 139
deposition file, 140
documents file, 139
generally, 136–137
miscellaneous, 140
other files, 140
paperless firm, 136
partially completed status sheet, 138
pleadings, 139
research file, 139
status/notes file, 137–138
witness file, 140
importance of
  accurate record, 112–113
  malpractice claim, 113–114
  reliance on information in another forum, 113
introduction, 111
malpractice claim, 113–114
photographs, 132–134
real evidence, 134
reliance on information in another forum, 113
video recording, 132
witness information
  decision to preserve, 127
  diagrams, 130–131
  memorandum to the file, 129–130
  written statement, 127–129
Prior conviction
  impeachment, 22
Privacy Act, 171–172
Privacy Act of 1974, Appendix D
Privileged communications
  attorney-client privilege, *See* Attorney-client privilege
  examples, 17
  generally, 16–17
Probate
  source of information, as, 184
Procedural law
  defined, 5
Psychoanalysis, 94–95

Questions, *See* Asking questions

Rapport
  client, *See* Client rapport
Rational-emotive therapy, 95
Real evidence
  preserving information, 134
Real property
  community property, 161
  fee simple absolute, 161
  generally, 160
  grantor/grantee indices, 162
  homestead exemption, 162
  joint tenancy, 161
  life estate, 162
  sole tenancy, 160–161
  tenancy by the entirety, 161

tenancy in common, 161
title search, 162–164
Real property tax rolls
    source of information, as, 186
Records
    admissibility as evidence, 21
Registry of deeds
    source of information, as, 184
Registry of vital statistics
    source of information, as, 184
Regulations, 34
Relevant evidence, 17–18
Religious records
    source of information, as, 187
Reporters, 35
Representative Boards of State Registration
    source of information, as, 189
Requests for admissions, 12
Research file
    preserving, 139
Rules, 34

Sample client letters, Appendix B
Sealed records
    source of information, as, 183
Separation, 165–166
Shepardizing, 37
Shephard's Citations, 35
Silence, 57
Sole tenancy, 160–161
Sources of information
    Bar associations, 189–190
    birth records, 184–185
    cemetery records, 187
    census, 186–187
    Clearinghouse on Licensure, Enforcement,
        and Regulation (CLEAR), 187–188
    computer assisted
        databases, 197
        generally, 191
        Industrial Defense Journal, 196–197
        internet, 191–196
        LEXIS, 196
        Westlaw, 196–197
    coroner, 191
    Courthouse, 182–183
    criminal records, 183
    cross-reference directory, 191
    death records, 185
    Department of Defense records, 187
    Department of Motor Vehicles (DMV),
        181–182
    disclosure change of address information,
        188
    divorce records, 183–184, 186
    federal government, 190
    Freedom of Information Act (FOIA) request,
        190–191
    libraries, 190
    marriage, certificate of, 186
    Martindale-Hubbell Law Directory, 189–190
    medical records, 191
    military records, 187

newspapers, 190
    pet licenses, 188
    postal service, 187
    probate, 184
    real property tax rolls, 186
    registry of deeds, 184
    registry of vital statistics, 184
    religious records, 187
    representative Boards of State registration,
        189
    sealed records, 183
    sporting licenses, 189
    state offices, 187–188
    town permits, 189
    Veterans Administration records, 187
    Veterans of Foreign Wars (VFW), 187
    voter lists, 186
Sporting licenses
    source of information, as, 189
State offices
    source of information, as, 187–188
Statute of limitations, 5
Statutes, 34, 35
Structuring the interview, 49–50
Subsequent repair
    evidence, exempt from, 19–20
Subservient client, 90
Substantive law
    defined, 5
Supporting statements
    investigation, 159–160
Surveillance tapes
    preserving information, 134

Telephone interview
    advantages, 63
    caveats, 63–64
    considerations, 64
    disadvantages, 63
    preparation, 62–63
    recording, 63–64
    speaker phone, 63
Television news stories
    preserving information, 134
Tenancy by the entirety, 161
Tenancy in common, 161
Theory chart, 40
Third party
    attorney-client privilege, 14, 15
    witness interview, 102
Tickler system, 140–141
Time-lines, 58–59
Title search, 162–164
Topic control, 62
Town permits
    source of information, as, 189
Transactional analysis, 95–96
Transaction interview
    preparing for, 43–45
Treatises, 35

Underage person
    attorney-client privilege, 15

United States Code, 35
United States Code Annotated, 35
United States Code Service, 35

Veterans Administration records
    source of information, as, 187
Veterans of Foreign Wars (VFW)
    source of information, as, 187
Video recording
    preserving information, 132
Vital statistics, registry of
    source of information, as, 184
Voter lists
    source of information, as, 186

Westlaw
    computer-assisted legal research, 37
    directory, 38
Witness
    expert witness, See Expert witness
    paralegal as, See Paralegal as witness
    payment to, 102
Witness file
    preserving, 140
Witness interview
    arranging interview, 102–103
    dress, 103

ethical considerations
    contact with unrepresented persons,
        101–102
    guidelines and rules, 101–102
    overview, 100–101
    third persons, respect for rights of, 102
    truthfulness, 101
evaluation of witness, 103
expert witness, See Expert witness
first-hand knowledge, 104–106
introduction, 99
level of interest, 100
manner, 103–104
payment to witness, 102
purpose, 100
relationship, 99–100
reluctant witness, 106
strategy
    dress, 103
    first-hand knowledge, 104–106
    manner, 103–104
    reluctant witness, 106
writing about interview, 106–107
Work product, 32
Work product doctrine
    nondiscoverable information, 15–16
World Wide Web
    internet service provider (ISP), 192
    source of information, as, 192